Literacy and Community

The Twentieth Yearbook
A Peer Reviewed Publication of
The College Reading Association
1998

Editors

Betty Sturtevant
George Mason University

JoAnn Dugan
Texas A&M University-Commerce

Patricia Linder
Texas A&M University-Commerce

Wayne M. Linek
Texas A&M University-Commerce

Editorial Assistants

Janice Winters
George Mason University

Vicky Spencer
George Mason University

Michelle Fazio
Texas A&M University-Commerce

Anupama Indukuri
Texas A&M University-Commerce

ISBN 1-883604-04-4

Printed at Texas A&M University-Commerce

Cover Design: Elizabeth G. Sturtevant

CRA Editorial Advisory Board 1997-98

TABLE OF CONTENTS

LITERACY AND COMMUNITY:
AN INTRODUCTION

The significance of creating a *literate community* was underscored by the theme of the 1997 College Reading Association conference: "It Takes a Village to Raise a Reader." In reviewing manuscripts from that conference for potential inclusion in this volume, we found the theme of "community" reflected again and again, in diverse ways. As you read, you will find authors discussing a wide variety of community influences—including those in homes, schools, workplaces, and other settings. Communities also span age groups, as shown in the cover photos. A "community" can be as simple as two young children sharing a book or a group of adults performing music on a street corner. Literate communities occur throughout the world and across generations. They inspire us to *want to participate*, and they facilitate our growth as readers, writers, and learners.

The College Reading Association is an excellent example of *community*, as members and friends are enriched through a continuing conversation across place and time. Our CRA community develops through sharing—in serious administrative meetings, intense academic discussions, informal hallway conversations, and laughter-filled evening gatherings. The organization has grown and is strengthened by "older" and newer members, who inspire one another to look both forward and backward when seeking answers. New members later become the mentors of even newer members, and the *community* grows.

As CRA *Yearbook* Editors, we also have a growing editorial community, as our team doubled in size this year with the addition of JoAnn Dugan and Patricia Linder, of Texas A&M-Commerce. We also consider the *Yearbook* Editorial Assistants, the Editorial Review Board, the CRA Board of Directors, and all of the CRA membership to be part of our team. Without this array of talented and dedicated individuals, there would be no CRA *community*, and also no *Yearbook*.

Our "thank-you's" begin again with all of the authors who submitted manuscripts, including those not included in this volume. Each year, all CRA conference presenters are encouraged to submit their work for consideration. While only a small portion can eventually be published, the *Yearbook* represents the efforts of all. The Editorial Review Board members, listed in the preceding pages, also deserve great thanks for their scholarship and dedication. While only authors and editors see the work of this group, a high quality publication is truly impossible without them. Support in the reviewer selection process and other administrative matters was expertly provided by the CRA Publications Committee, chaired by Michael McKenna of Georgia Southern University.

The editorial assistants who worked with us throughout the year also deserve accolades. Editorial assistants at both George Mason University and Texas A&M-Commerce are master's and doctoral students. While they claim to "learn a lot" about both literacy and publishing, tasks require an extreme commitment to details and organization. At George Mason University, we thank Janice Winters, who assisted with developing the Editorial Review Board and sending manuscripts for review. We also thank Vicky Spencer, who has diligently assisted with final editorial details in the last few months. At Texas A&M-Commerce, we appreciate the clerical support provided by our secretarial staff, Frances Norman and Jan Hazelip, student assistant Carol Adams, and graduate assistants, Anupama Indukuri and Michelle Fazio.

Editors also appreciate the extensive university support we have received. At George Mason University, Graduate School of Education Dean Gary Galluzzo and Associate Dean Martin Ford have recognized the importance of this project over an extended time period through their continuing encouragement and financial support. We also thank the university administration, including President Alan Merten, and the Graduate School of Education faculty and staff, for creating an academic community environment that inspires collaboration and excellence.

At Texas A&M-Commerce, we thank President Keith McFarland, Provost and Academic Vice President Donald Coker, and Dean Jerry Hutton for the financial assistance that makes the production of the *Yearbook* possible. Likewise, we are grateful for the ongoing moral support of faculty in the Department of Elementary Education. We also thank Vivian Freeman and Lyndal Burnett for their expertise in the production process.

Finally, we wish to dedicate this volume to our own literacy communities, wherever they have been or will be in the future. Our families, teachers, students, colleagues, friends—and unknown others—have created communities for our own literate development and have inspired us to create communities for others.

EGS, JRD, PEL, & WML
Fall, 1998

Presidential Address

ADOLESCENT LITERACY: ARE WE IN CONTACT?

Presidential Address

Marino C. Alvarez

Tennessee State University

Marino Alvarez is a professor of graduate and undergraduate reading classes in the Department of Teaching and Learning in the College of Education. He is a former middle and secondary school social studies teacher. He has served on national committees on editorial advisory boards, and as president of the Action Research Special Interest Group of the American Educational Research Association. his publications have appeared in edited chapters and in a variety of journals. professor Alvarez was the 1995 recipient of both the Teacher-of-the-Year and Distingsuished Researcher-of-the-Year Awards at TSU. He also directs the Explorers of the Universe, a scientific literacy project, which involves teachers and their students in various NASA earth/space projects.

Ever wonder about the role of paper clips and staples? The only thing they have in common is that they come in a box. Staples are invariant. They don't change shape, and they serve a singular function: to keep papers in place. Paper clips, on the other hand, are flexible. They can be made of metal (like the staple) or of plastic. Plastic seems preferable because it does not leave a paper clip trace on the page like metal clips. They can be independently selected and reused again and again. Paper clips are colorful and serve multiple purposes. They can keep papers in place, they can be removed from a collection of papers and the papers can again be joined by the same paper clip. They can be manipulated into different shapes and can be used as a probe. For example, I was able to bend one into a hook and use it to retrieve a screw that fell into my garbage disposal. Paper clips can also be joined together to form a chain. Staples give one a sense of permanency. When you staple papers together you sense a final product. When you use a paper clip you get a feeling that you're not really done. These papers are in a state of transition. They either need to be revised or rearranged before they can be stapled.

Paper Clips and Staples

Students are often treated by teachers and policymakers as if they are either paper clips or staples. There are those who want students to explore, imagine, exercise critical thinking, learn *from* the future, and learn from mistakes. These educators and policymakers believe that students are in transition with knowledge and that learning new knowledge helps them to grasp future knowledge. However, there are others who believe in permanency and that learning involves mastering what is known. Like a staple, this knowledge is in place. All one needs to do is learn what is known to succeed in schooling. Imagination, curiosity, and exploration are fine, as long as it takes place *after* knowing what is known. For many students, thinking about learning seldom happens. For others, it takes place after formal schooling.

Although indoctrination of facts begins at an early age of one's formal schooling, no where is it more prominent than during the adolescent years. It is during this period that students either "learn how to learn," learn "how to play school" or falter by the wayside because they have never "learned how to learn," or learned "how to play school." Literacy proficiency plays a crucial role in dividing these students. Students who have the most difficulty with literacy skills are often neglected by teachers who are not aware of strategies to use to help them comprehend texts and supplementary readings. This situation is compounded by a lack of reading specialists to aid students in their understanding of narrative and expository discourse.

Limited Funding and Lack of Research

Funding for adolescent literacy programs by the federal government under Title I's compensatory education program is only 16 percent to grades 7, 8, and 9. It is even less for grades 10, 11, and 12, at 5 percent. However, 69 percent of Title I funds are earmarked for grades 1, 2, 3, 4, 5, and 6 (U.S. Department of Education, 1994-95). These funding levels remain consistent with findings reported ten and twenty-three years ago (Davidson &

Koppenhaver, 1988). Davidson and Koppenhaver (1988) further report that in 1985 only 54 out of every 100 eligible students were being served by Chapter I funds. Clearly this discrepancy in funding exemplifies the minimal priority that adolescents needing literacy support are given.

Couple this finding with a move toward licensure by the states to minimize or abolish content literacy course requirements, the lack of funding for reading specialists at the middle and secondary levels, the use of basal readers to teach reading skills by an English teacher or a teacher assigned the task, the limited number of research articles that involve middle and high school populations appearing in our literacy research journals, and you begin to understand the problem. These situations are compounded by federal and state legislators moving toward national and state curricula, common standards, and curriculum and instruction policies and procedures that hinder meaningful learning.

Fragmented Adolescent Literacy Programs

Adolescent literacy programs are fragmented into those that follow an elementary school model of structured skills instruction, those that rely on published materials and worksheets that accompany the text for literacy instruction and learning, and pull-out programs that take the student away from a subject. There are a few literacy programs that incorporate the subject discipline with conventional and electronic readings and writings from other related content areas. However, most of these programs lack a coordinated effort among the content teachers to include strategies in their lesson planning to aid students in their literacy development.

Lost in all this milieu are the voices of adolescents and those of thoughtful teachers who strive to make school a place for learning rather than endurance. These voices are outshouted by those who hold onto what was done in the past, imposing standards that they may not have attained given the same circumstances, clinging to the notion that there is a given body of knowledge that everyone needs to know. Also included are those who have difficulty with the concept that electronic literacy and the information age is upon us. The combining of narrative with expository texts that require students to select, analyze, synthesize, recombine, and think about unrealized possibilities is needed for meaningful adolescent literacy programs to flourish.

Students are already accessing, communicating, publishing papers with interactive reference linkages to other sources, and developing their own e-mail and web pages. They are using metacognitive interactive tools (e.g., concept maps and Interactive Vee Diagrams) to plan, carry-out, and finalize their assignments and research investigations. Their electronic literacy skills surpass those measured in typical pencil and paper literacy tests. It will take several years before reading tests are constructed to reflect these types of electronic reading and reasoning abilities. The obstacles that face test-makers are formidable. Many of these students are using their imagination for enhancing their learning using electronic literacy in ways that extend those of the typical teacher and extend the parameters of closure that challenge test-makers.

Electronic Literacy

A literate person living in our society is drastically different from one who lived in 14th century England. The literacy skills of yesterday are no longer practical in today's fast-pace world of information. The printing press, invented in the 1400s, changed the way people thought and accessed information; so too, is the electronic information age changing the ways we view literacy. The societal needs of the 21st century demand that literacy definitions be revised to include this new information age. This electronic literacy requires individuals to access large quantities of information, determine their accuracy and worth, communicate with others over distances, and become involved collaboratively and interactively.

Thinkers and Tinkers

Little opportunity is given for teachers and students to be thinkers and tinkers in our schools (Alvarez, 1996a; Alvarez, 1997a). Fixed curricula, required course content, and state and national policies do little to foster thinking and tinkering. Those few teachers and students that recognize the nonsense that restrictive environments impose and are willing to trust themselves and each other are succeeding in making school a place for learning and exchanging ideas.

The English teachers and librarians in the Gallatin High School Literacy Project and the astronomy and physics teachers in the Explorers of the Universe Scientific/Literacy Interdisciplinary Project (http://coe2.tsuniv.edu/explorers) are part of these few (Alvarez, 1993; Alvarez, 1995; Alvarez, Binkley, Bivens, Highers, Poole, & Walker, 1991; Alvarez & Rodriguez, 1995). These teachers are willing to try something different. They are willing to trust their thinking about what is best for their students to learn. They use meaningful materials in problem-oriented contexts that invite students to "show what they can do." They also include their students in their curriculum by offering opportunities to involve them in reading both narrative and expository texts, writing reports and journals, and incorporating the curriculum with other subject disciplines. Students who have more knowledge about programming mathematical computations than their teachers are encouraged to write the programs. In situations where students wish to study a related topic for which a case has not been developed, they do so in conjunction with their teacher. The lessons that make up the emergent curriculum are more meaningful. Metacognitive tools such as concept maps and interactive Vee diagrams through the Internet are used by students to share ideas and information. The conversations that occur between teachers and their students are more inquiry than answer producing. Instead of being subjected to the "one best system," they are searching for the ways in which to tinker with the existing knowledge and to extend its meaning. These teachers "teach," and their students "student." Teachers don't speak of "covering" the material; instead, they demonstrate by example and facilitate the "teaching" of the material. Instead of focusing on compartmentalizing the subject discipline, they are looking for ways to incorporate music, art, literature, history, mathematics, industrial technology, and multimedia into their lessons and assignments—and so are their students.

Elizabeth Binkley, Judy Bivens, Patricia Highers, and Cynthia Poole (1991) are teachers who are both thinkers and tinkers at Gallatin High School. They were willing to try a case-based approach to teaching and learning with their students that revolved around the study of *To Kill A Mockingbird*. Students were given cases to explore that were thematically linked to the story. They were also given the opportunity to develop their own cases with the aid of the teacher. These students were asked to participate in a variety of literacy building activities. They read related sources, interviewed authors, lawyers, and ministers, and they videotaped related episodes that they wanted to incorporate into their cases. Students designed blueprints and built models, visited local and distant libraries seeking information, and used their critical thinking and imaginative processes to search out information. Five years later with over twenty cases written by the teacher and her students, a videodisc was developed. This videodisc was the first of its kind to be designed and developed by teachers for their students instead of by outside professionals.

Bill Rodriguez (astronomy and physics teacher) at the University School of Nashville, and Lee Ann Hennig (astronomy teacher) at Thomas Jefferson High School for Science and Technology, Alexandria Virginia are two teachers who are both thinkers and tinkers in the Explorers of the Universe Scientific/Literacy Project. They wrote a technical manual for the Explorers Project, *Finding Periods in Variable Star Data: Using Remote FORTRAN and Local Windows Software*. The manual is based on analyzing data that they are receiving from automatic photoelectric telescopes that reside at the Fairborn Observatory in Washington Camp, near Nogales, Arizona. These automatic telescopes are controlled over the Internet by astronomers at Tennessee State University in Nashville, Tennessee. These teachers field-tested this manual with their students. Students offered suggestions for revision of the materials, and a few also wrote several programs to analyze the data. The manual has been revised and is now on the web site for use by students affiliated with the project. The students who field-tested the manual and those who will do so in the future will make recommendations for change and, in all probability, develop different methods of evaluations. They will make changes and develop new methods because they will be encouraged to do so. This manual is one of many that will be developed and will remain open for revision.

This emergent curriculum is negotiated throughout the process. Students share their concept maps with each other and their teacher. They send e-mail messages to other teachers affiliated with our project and to our astronomers who in turn guide them to other sources or to specific areas of scientific papers. I have developed an Interactive Vee Diagram where students enter their research questions, describe how they plan to carry out their study, name the instruments they will use to collect the data, list the concepts that need to be defined, and state the theory they are testing (Gowin, 1981).

Electronically over the Internet they submit this information along with any problems or suggestions to our base of operations at Tennessee State University's Center of Excellence in Information Systems. I review their entries and reply with comments. Our astronomers do the same. These students can share their ideas with others at other affiliated schools and receive feedback electronically from them. These Vee diagrams are revisited several times as they carry out their case investigations with variable stars. Within their case they are encouraged to incorporate literature, music, art, history, and other subject disciplines into their case. Their papers are then published on the World Wide Web to be read and commented on by people throughout the world (Alvarez, 1996b; Alvarez, 1997b).

This process differs from conventional product-learning outcomes. Thinking of ways to achieve learning outcomes is different from focusing on ways that learning outcomes can be achieved. The former is a process, the latter an outcome. When teachers and administrators focus on students achieving prescribed outcomes, thought processes become product oriented. In contrast, when students learn in ways that involve them in thinking about problem-oriented tasks and assignments that actively engage them in mutual discussions with their teacher, peers, and others, the process becomes mufti-faceted, meaningful, and negotiable.

In both the Gallatin High School Interdisciplinary Project and the Explorers of the Universe Scientific/Literacy Projects, our efforts focus on ways that students can use a variety of processes to reach multiple resolutions. Our efforts are directed toward divergent rather than convergent learning outcomes. It is interesting to see the different types of paths that students pursue when resolving their inquiry. The emphasis is on melding society with the formal school curriculum by having students apply what they are learning to meaningful settings. Robert Frost may have had this notion in mind when he wrote At Woodward's Garden (Frost, 1956).

Frost's *At Woodward's Garden*

At Woodward's Garden is one of two poems Robert Frost wrote that has a moral similar to Aesop's Fables. The setting takes place in Woodward's Garden, which is a zoo. A boy wants to show off his knowledge to two monkeys who are caged. He has a magnifying glass which he uses to try to show the monkeys how the instrument can be used. He knows that words will not do the trick. First he uses the sun's rays and the glass to focus on one monkey's nose and then the other's. The monkeys are puzzled, and their eyes begin to blink. He then uses the glass and the sun's rays to sting the knuckles of the monkeys. Tired of this experiment, one of the monkey's reaches out from the cage and grabs the burning glass. The monkeys bite the glass. They hold it up to their ears and listen to it. They break the handle. But their lack of knowledge of the whys and wherefores of a magnifying glass leads to boredom and a lack of interest with the glass. This causes them to give up the weapon and place it under their bedding straw. Again the monkeys come to the bars of the cage no wiser than before as to the purpose, function, or use of the instrument. Frost concludes his poem with the parable, "It's knowing what to do with things that counts."

How many adolescents know what to do with things that count in their daily lessons of mathematics, science, literature, history, foreign language, art, music, health education, business education, and industrial technology? How often do they relate what they are learning in school to their society?

Conclusion

The degree of contact we have with adolescents and their literacy skills and development is codependent upon the amount of interplay between them and their teachers and their ability to exercise their imagination in an emergent curriculum. When students are given tasks and lessons under a fixed curriculum with defined outcomes, opportunities to pursue inquisitive paths of inquiry are diminished for both teachers and students. So too, are opportunities for students to "show what they can do."

Adolescents need opportunities to engage in meaningful learning experiences that include reading, writing, investigating, analyzing, synthesizing, and rethinking of facts and ideas. Teachers need these same opportunities to engage in meaningful learning experiences that include reading, writing, analyzing, synthesizing, and rethinking of facts and ideas. In an environment such as this both students and teachers become communities of thinkers.

Communities where ideas are shared and valued and opportunities to engage in forums of discussion are more than just cursory exercises which direct students toward reaching that final "right" answer.

How many of our students, like the monkeys in Frost's poem, are given information of which they have little or no understanding? How many of our students are given time to think about learning what to do with this new knowledge to make it count before they are told they need to move on to a different topic? Finally, to return to the analogy from which I began: How many of our students are treated like a staple or a paper clip? For those students who master what is known about a given topic the staple is in place. However, for those students who view knowledge in transition as they would the function of a paper clip—the final product is elusive.

Support for the Explorers of the Universe Project is provided, in part, by the Tennessee State University and the Center of Excellence in Information Systems—Astrophysics Component, and by NASA through the Tennessee Space Grant Consortium NGT 5-40054.

References

Alvarez, M. C. (1993). Imaginative uses of self-selected cases. *Reading Research and Instruction, 32*(2), 1-18.

Alvarez, M. C. (1995). Explorers of the universe: An action research scientific literacy project. In K. Camperell, B. L. Hayes, & R. Telfer (eds.) *Linking literacy: Past, present, and future* (pp. 55-62). American Reading Forum, Vol. 15. Logan: Utah State University.

Alvarez, M. C. (1996a). A community of thinkers: Literacy environments with interactive technology. In K. Camperell, B. L. Hayes, & R. Telfer (Eds.) *Literacy: The information highway to success* (pp. 17-29). American Reading Forum, vol. 16. Logan, UT: Utah State University.

Alvarez, M. C. (1996b). Explorers of the universe: Students using the world wide web to improve their reading and writing. In B. Neate (Ed.), *Literacy saves lives* (pp. 140-145). Winchester, England: United Kingdom Reading Association.

Alvarez, M. C. (1997a). Communities of thinkers: investigating interactive scientific literacy environments. In J. Willis, J. D. Price, S. McNeil, B. Robin, & D. A. Willis (Eds.), *Technology and Teacher Education Annual: Vol. 2* (pp. 1236-1239). Charlottesville, VA: Association for the Advancement of Computing in Education (AACE).

Alvarez, M. C. (1997b). Thinking and learning with technology: Helping students construct meaning. *NASSP Bulletin, 81,* (592), 66-72.

Alvarez, M. C., Binkley, E., Bivens, J., Highers, P., Poole, C., & Walker, P. (1991). Case-based instruction and learning: An interdisciplinary project. In T. V. Rasinski, N. D. Padak, & J. Logan (Eds.), *Reading is knowledge* (pp. 53-62). Thirteenth Yearbook of the College Reading Association. Pittsburg, KS: College Reading Association.

Alvarez, M. C., Rodriguez, W. J. (1995). Explorers of the universe: A pilot study. In W. M. Linek & B. G. Sturtevant (Eds.) *Generations of literacy* (pp. 221-236). The

Seventeenth Yearbook of the College Reading Association. Commerce, Texas: College Reading Association.

Davidson, J. & Koppenhaver, D. (1988). *Adolescent literacy: What works and why*. New York: Garland.

Frost, R. (1956). *Complete poems of Robert Frost*. New York: Holt, Rinehart and Winston.

Gowin, D. B. (1981). *Educating*. Ithaca, NY: Cornell University Press.

U.S. Department of Education. (1994-5). *Compensatory Education Programs*. Washington, DC: Author.

KEYNOTE
ADDRESSES

My Life in Reading

Keynote Address

Jeanne S. Chall

Harvard University

Jeanne S. Chall, is emeritus professor at Harvard University, Graduate School of Education where she founded and directed the graduate program in reading, language and learning disabilities. She has written widely. Among her books are Learning to Read: The Great Debate, Stages of Reading Development, The Reading Crisis: Why Poor Children Fall Behind, Creating Successful Readers, Readability Revisited and the New Dale-Chall Readability Formula, *and* Qualitative Assessment of Text Difficulty.

She is a member of the National Academy of Education and the Reading Hall of Fame and has served on the Board of Directors of the International Reading Association and the National Society for the Study of Education. She is also a member of the Orton Dyslexia Society Council of Advisors. She has received many awards, including the Edward L. Thorndike award from the American Psychological Association for distinguished psychological contributions to education and the American Educational Research Association's award for significant contributions to educational research. She has received the Samuel T. Orton Award from the Orton Dyslexia Society, as well.

I taught my first class as a student teacher in New York City's Taft High School in 1941. I had looked forward to teaching, having been an education major. I was introduced to educational research a year later at Teachers College, Columbia University. My love for educational research was unexpected and came as a complete surprise. I had no idea that one could work in education doing research. Nor do I recall that any of my instructors in education were engaged in research. If they were, I was not aware of it.

Within a few days at the Institute of Psychological Research at Teachers College I was smitten as I observed such notable researchers as Irving Lorge and Sophia M. Robinson. My role was to keep notes and to calculate means, standard deviations, and correlations—it was before computers. But it seemed that I could not find a more exciting way to spend my time and with a more exciting group of people. They were helping children and furthering knowledge in a disciplined way. I knew, then, that I wanted to do the same.

Thus, I came to my two loves in education early—my love of teaching and educational practice and my love of inquiry. Although research and practice are often seen as different pursuits, I found that, for me, they had great similarities and were intimately related to each other.

At Teachers College, the project with which I assisted sought workable solutions to one of the great pressing educational problems of that time and today—how best to educate juvenile delinquents and to prevent delinquency—whether to place delinquents in separate schools or to provide them with psychological services and an improved curriculum in regular schools. Among the findings, which are still being found today, 50 years later, were that psychological services (counseling and social services) and a curriculum that had a better match with students' achievement were effective in decreasing the number of delinquents in the regular schools—more effective than special schools. I realized early how practical research can be.

Several years later I learned a similar lesson at Ohio State University as Edger Dale's research assistant. Our task was to assist the National Tuberculosis Association by finding ways to make their pamphlets and other print media more readable for the layman. This very practical mission led to basic research on readability and vocabulary; the Dale-Chall Readability Formula was developed to help assess the difficulty of the pamphlets. It also led to the development of a manual on clear and simple writing. Research and practice were intimately related—with research leading to good practice and real problems leading to useful research.

Throughout my long career I have engaged in both practice and research, usually at the same time. Since educational practice does not leave tracks as does educational research, I should like to mention at least some of the practice I have engaged in.

I have taught students of all ages for more than a half century. Much of it was at the college and graduate level, but much, too, has been with students at all levels who needed special help with their reading.

I have also worked as an advisor and as a consultant on a variety of educational projects, including children's encyclopedias, an educational comic book, computer programs, and the Children's Television Workshop's "Sesame Street" and "The Electric Company." I have consulted with schools and school systems to help them ask and answer educational questions.

These practical assignments helped me gain perspective on the important questions being asked in education—by teachers, administrators, educational publishers, and the media—and they kept me from being too theoretical, too removed from reality. I learned to make the most out of the knowledge that existed and not to resort, unless absolutely necessary, to the use of "we need more research" as an answer to questions. I realized early that even the most theoretical studies ultimately boil down to a yes or no response. Is this or that idea more useful? Should this or that be done? If neither, what should be done?

I was a member of various investigative and policy making committees and commissions organized by professional associations, state and national departments of education, and also a member of the boards of directors of various professional groups. Thus, I had further opportunity to blend research and practice and to broaden my educational perspective.

Focus on Reading

Most of my work—research and practice—has focused on reading. From time to time I have wandered off to mathematics, or to the non-print media, but I soon came back to reading. It offers a broad panorama and great challenge—vast and almost endless issues for research and practice. At the same time, I found reading to be very basic, very much like the bread and butter of education. It is the oldest and most enduring of subjects taught in schools. It is an essential foundation for learning almost all other school subjects—literature, social studies, science, math. It is essential for most jobs in an advanced, technological society.

When reading does not develop as it should, when it lags behind the age and cognitive development of the individual, it brings serious personal frustrations and loss of confidence. It brings equally serious losses to society. In fact, the importance of reading for society and the individual seems to have grown even during the years I have studied it. We are reminded almost daily by leading economists in the United States that we may slip from our status as a world class nation if our work force does not achieve a higher level of literacy. They remind us that when we were a manufacturing nation fewer people needed to be highly literate. But a high-tech society—one that produces and disseminates knowledge and symbols—needs more people who are highly literate. There seems to be a growing mismatch between workers and jobs—with jobs that cannot be filled because workers are not literate enough. But it is not for work alone that there is a mismatch. Responsible citizenship also requires higher literacy, and personal literacy needs seem also to grow with time. The labels on food and medicine packages require considerable reading ability. Add to this the growing numbers of children reported to have reading and learning disabilities, and the low levels of literacy found among minority students. Further, if one considers the low reading scores on the National Assessment of Educational Progress and the failure to significantly raise the verbal scores on the Scholastic Assessment Test, it is not difficult to see why I have stayed with reading and literacy.

There is still one other reason. The field of reading is so rich and varied that I have been able to change my focus within it, making it ever more interesting and challenging.

Studies in Readability

My first research efforts were in readability and in vocabulary, an interest I acquired from Edger Dale, my teacher and mentor at the Bureau of Educational Research at Ohio State University. I worked with him on the development of the Dale-Chall Readability Formula and on various studies of vocabulary during the four years of my graduate study at Ohio State. These formative years were followed by nearly forty years of collaboration on research and writing. In fact, one of our works, *Readability Revisited and the New Dale-Chall Readability Formula* (Dale & Chall), was published in 1995.

I found readability a fascinating subject for research and for application. It was an excellent vehicle for studying reading development—through the changes that take place in the texts that can be read by readers of growing proficiency.

Readability drew its knowledge from many disciplines—the humanities, psychology, statistics, language, semantics—and in turn could be applied to textbooks, newspapers, and magazines, comic books, radio, and so forth.

The four years of working closely on readability and vocabulary with Edgar Dale also taught me lessons about research that still remain with me. One of these first lessons was the value of past research—why it is important and how to use it.

After a year as research assistant, Dale suggested that I write an article on readability, a review of research. Although I had been assisting him for a year, I did not feel quite ready to write such an article. To be more accurate, I was terrified. I protested that I didn't know enough. "That is why you should write it," he said. "You will learn from your writing."

I started the research with much anxiety, fear, and agony. Why should I do this? I thought. Reviewing the past research is not original. I wanted to get on with the new. But after all the fussing, I finally finished it and had to admit it had been a good assignment after all. I gained familiarity with the past research on readability and an ease in working with the ideas of earlier researchers. I gained different viewpoints on the topic—some that were unpopular at the time they were first proposed were later accepted and became the dominant view. I felt I knew the researchers whose work I reviewed, and I knew how they thought. When I met several of the researchers during the ensuing years, I felt that we had been friends for many years.

I had beginner's luck with that first article. "This Business of Readability" was reprinted in two digest journals (Chall, 1947). But more valuable was the taste for historical synthesis that I developed. My love for this style of research lead to my books, *Readability: An Appraisal of Research and Application*(Chall, 1958), *Learning to Read: The Great Debate*(Chall, 1967), and *Stages of Reading Development* (Chall, 1983). Each received strong research reviews. When I undertook *The Great Debate* (1967), many of my colleagues were skeptical. The research I planned to review was so confused, they said, how could I find anything by going over it again? But I had confidence, from my earlier experiences, that if I stuck with it and found a structure, I would find something useful. Syntheses of past research were out of fashion for a long time but have recently come back in favor. *Becoming a Nation of Readers*(Anderson, Heibert, Scott, & Wilkonson, 1985) is a more current research synthesis by a commission, of which I was a member.

Dale knew that one has to know what scholars of the past knew on a subject if one is to make useful contributions to that subject. He never assumed that what was done in the past was no longer useful or worth knowing. He also knew that the new research does not always clear up all the problems of the past research. Indeed, the results of the new can be more confusing than the old.

Knowing the past research keeps one from being too much within the current fashion. One can see trends in ideas in a field only from a deep grounding in its past theories, research, and writing. It is sad, therefore, to see that current publications tend to refer only to recent writings, omitting even the classic research on a topic (Herber, 1988).

Have we decided to lose our past? If we do not know the past, and if we do not use it well in formulating practice and new research, are we not in danger of repeating the past—the bad as well as the good?

I learned another important lesson from Edgar Dale—the importance of knowing the related research from fields other than one's own. When we planned a project he asked if I had checked it out with the psychologists, the statisticians, the sociologists, and the linguists. Before sending out an article for publication he asked again if I had checked with those in other disciplines who might pick up inconsistencies, conflicts, and errors.

Today, there seems to be little reference in the field of reading to the work of those rooted in other disciplines. This is not difficult to understand, for the reading field is rich in research and writing—richer perhaps than any other field in education. No one person can keep up with all of it.

In the reading field, we seem to have at least five bodies of research—basic research (usually done by educational researchers, cognitive psychologists, and linguists); research on reading methods, materials, and classroom procedures (usually done by educational psychologists, reading specialists, and teachers); research on reading difficulties (by psychologists, neurologists, and special educators); research on the relationship of literature, writing, and reading (by linguists and students of literature and English language arts); and research on reading tests (by psychometricians). There seems to be a tendency for individuals in each of these groups to talk almost exclusively with, and to write for, others within their own field. Seldom does one group refer to the work from the others.

Recently I read an excellent longitudinal study of children's reading in grades 1 to 4. The authors reported that phonemic development was of first importance in early reading without referring to similar findings by leading researchers on language and learning disabilities at least 15 years earlier; and by educational psychologists in the 1930s for beginning reading.

Ignoring the relevant research of others is not uncommon in other areas of education. Can we afford to repeat research studies when our funds are so limited, unless of course the research is a deliberate replication? And can we afford to ignore the relevant research that exists in our field and other disciplines?

Another important lesson I learned from Edgar Dale was to ask for whom one does educational research. For Dale the answer was always clear. All of his studies, including his most theoretical, were designed to be useful in the practice of education—in schools and out of schools. I remember vividly how he helped me realize this. It was after I had written one of my early research reports. He read it, made several editorial suggestions, then said, "Very nice Jeanne. It is very scholarly. What do you think it will mean to the superintendent in Winnetka, the fifth-grade teacher in Oklahoma City, the English teacher in Cleveland?" I knew then that I was far from finished. I had much rewriting to do.

This incident served almost as an imprinting. No matter how theoretical or statistical the research study may be, I try to write it also for teachers, administrators, and others who practice.

Reading Difficulty and Its Prevention

In 1950, when I joined the faculty of the City College in New York, my focus shifted from the readability of texts, in relation to readers' abilities, to the study of the readers, in relation to the texts they read. For 15 years, my interests were concentrated on the teaching of reading and ways of assessing it. I also examined the causes and treatments of those who experience special difficulties in spite of their adequate intelligence—about 10 to 15 percent of the population.

In collaboration with my colleague and Director of the Reading Center, Florence Roswell, I carried out numerous research and development projects. The projects concerned auditory blending and its effects on reading achievement, and why children of low-income families have difficulty and what could be done to remediate their difficulties. We developed tests to help teachers adjust instruction to students' needs. Similar to my collaboration with Dale, Roswell and I have continued our collaboration to the present.

It was at The City College in 1950 when I started to concentrate on the diagnosis and treatment of children, young people, and adults with reading problems. It has continued until today. Indeed, the time I have spent diagnosing and treating individuals with reading problems, and teaching and supervising teachers in this work, has been extremely absorbing and enriching. It influenced not only my teaching and research on reading difficulties, but most of my other research, particularly the research I undertook in the early 1960s on beginning reading methods. Concerned with prevention of reading problems, I sought to find whether there was any evidence that certain beginning reading methods produce better results and help prevent reading failure. This research, which was carried out when I was at The City College, became the book *Learning to Read: The Great Debate* first published in 1967, and later updated in second and third editions in 1983 and 1996.

The study, funded by the Carnegie Corporation, had many facets. It was a synthesis of the past research on beginning reading from the classroom, the laboratory, and the clinic. I also analyzed more than 20 beginning reading programs, including the two most widely used basal readers and their teacher's manuals. I interviewed authors and editors of various reading series. I observed in hundreds of classrooms and talked to as many teachers and principals. I was fortunate again, as I had been with my first synthesis article on readability, to get an almost immediate response. Although many of the reviews in the reading journals were not favorable, most that appeared in the general educational and scholarly journals were very favorable. Even more satisfying was the study's early acceptance by educational publishers in revising their reading programs and its appearance on required reading lists for courses on methods of teaching reading and reading research. Twenty years later the satisfaction was mixed with pain. Despite the fact that my update in 1983 confirmed my earlier conclusions and that my findings were confirmed by the research of linguists, cognitive psychologists, and child development specialists (Adams, 1990). misunderstandings and an attack on its findings and conclusions appeared (Carbo, 1988; Chall, 1988).

My 25 Years at Harvard University's Graduate School of Education

My move to Harvard in 1965 was marked by another shift in my concerns with reading. Much of my attention was focused on building and directing a graduate program for master's and doctoral students which had a dual purpose—training in scholarship and in practice. The Harvard Reading Laboratory was established as a training, research, and service center.

My teaching reflected the dual concerns of the program—research and practice. Through the years I taught the doctoral seminar on reading research—a historical overview of the research on reading and practice. I also taught the courses in the diagnosis and treatment of reading disabilities and, with the assistance of doctoral students, supervised the testing and teaching in the Harvard Reading Laboratory. I taught a general course on reading for non-reading majors that focused on social policy and, in earlier years, taught the general course on the teaching of reading, as well.

I have also had the great pleasure of directing and advising the dissertations of doctoral students and of directing the research training of the many doctoral and master's students who worked with me on various research projects.

My research continued to be concerned with issues of theory and practice, but it moved over, somewhat, to theory and social policy. Among my studies of reading and social policy was the one commissioned by the Panel on the SAT Score Decline and the College Board on the relationship of textbooks to SAT scores, published in 1977 (Chall, Conard, & Harris, 1977). It was extended to a larger study, *Should Textbooks Challenge Students: The Case for Easier or Harder Books* (Chall & Conard, 1991). My interests in the medical aspects of reading failure became even stronger. I attended lectures at Harvard Medical School on neurology and language, and I edited, with Allan Mirsky, the National Society for the Study of Education Yearbook, *Education and the Brain* (Chall & Mirsky, 1978).

The unanswered questions in *The Great Debate* brought me to a theoretical study of the reading process, *Stages of Reading Development* (Chall, 1983, 1996), a work on how reading changes qualitatively as it develops. This was an important study for me since many of the controversies on methods and materials seemed to stem from two theories of the reading process—a single-stage theory or a multi-stage theory. From my synthesis of the relevant theory and research on how reading develops and from my experience in teaching reading at all levels, I concluded that a developmental multi-stage theory fit the data better and was instructionally more useful.

In *The Reading Crisis: Why Poor Children Fall Behind* (Chall, Jacobs, & Baldwin, 1990), we attempted to find out why the literacy of low-income children begins to decelerate around grade 4 and how the deceleration can be prevented. The theoretical basis for the study came from my *Stages of Reading Development*. The work was further enriched by collaboration with linguists, faculty, and graduate students at Harvard.

My interests in social policy brought me to studies of the trends in the reading scores on the National Assessments of Educational Progress. I have tried to explain these trends by relating them to methods and materials used in the schools and to community support for reading (Chall, 1989).

As I reflect on my various professional interests and activities, I am aware of different concentrations at different times. During my early years I concentrated on psychology, statistics, and research design—on objectivity in searching for knowledge about reading. Later, I focused on problems in learning to read and took on the concerns of the teacher and clinician—why certain individuals had difficulty, how to help those individuals learn, and how to prevent such problems. Thus my concerns with the science of reading turned to teaching and healing, and I delved into the neurosciences as well as into the art of teaching. More recently I have been concerned with the broad social, cultural, and educational issues that are related to our reading problems and to their solution and prevention.

Examples of this concern are found in my research on textbooks and publishing, on the trends in scores on the national assessments of reading and writing, and on the methods and materials that work with children from low-income families.

I have gained much from the people I have met and worked with. I have gained great satisfaction from my teaching and have reached the age when my former students are now full professors with students of their own. I have especially gained from my work in the diagnosis and treatment of reading disabilities. Helping children, young people, and adults overcome their reading difficulties has always given me direct and immediate rewards which are especially welcome when the research on which I work reaches a frustrating point. While one cannot always move ahead in research and writing, one can always help a child learn to read.

Current Concerns

In the more than 50 years of my work in the field of reading, I have observed much growth in research and in professional activities. The public has become more conscious about the importance of literacy, for children and for adults.

With these advancements have come many problems. The reading achievement of too many children, young people, and adults is not up to what it should be. This has been reported by the National Assessment of

Educational Progress, by the College Board for SAT verbal scores, by school systems throughout the nation, and by industry, which has long complained that employees are lacking the literacy skills needed for work.

I recognize that this sad state is not the sole responsibility of the reading field or of teachers, yet our efforts, particularly those concerned with the methods and materials of reading instruction, may not be fruitful because we are paying too little attention to our hard-won knowledge and experience. We seem to be so pressed by the low literacy achievement of the nation that many of us tend to drop those procedures that are backed up by research and experience for largely untested solutions.

There also seems to be less confidence now than in the past in the power of research and analysis to find better solutions. A single case study or a classroom observation or a "bright idea" is often considered equal or superior to the hard-won knowledge from research and experience.

There is also a loss of confidence in how we can best assess and evaluate reading achievement and progress, thus making it still harder to base practice on objective evidence. Often it seems as if the tests are being criticized because the results are not those we hoped for. Thus, we seem to kill the messenger, hoping it will turn the bad news to good. While there is a need for better assessment instruments, it is hard to believe that better assessments will find that the state of literacy in the United States is substantially better than it is now being reported.

Perhaps my concerns are colored by my long, positive experiences with the power of research to inform and serve practice. Do I see the past in a more ideal state? Perhaps, but I think we are going through a less analytic time at the present and that it may in the long run lead to even lower levels of reading achievement. Many of the proposals for educational reform are made with little evidence of their probable success based on theory, research, and practice. Indeed, many of the proposed changes have been used in the past, under different labels, and were found wanting.

With the loss of confidence in research has come a heightened emotionality and stridency in the dialogues among teachers, parents, and researchers. The education journalists may have caught the essence of the rhetoric by the label "reading wars." The "wars" have spilled over to teachers, to parents, and to the press who oppose and accuse each other about the uses and non-uses of best methods for the benefit of children. The rhetoric seems more heated than what I had experienced during earlier debates and controversies. There have been differences of opinion about reading instruction during the 50 years of my life in reading. But the almost religious fervor of the present rhetoric seems to go beyond what existed in the past. One asks how it is possible, when the research in reading has grown so considerably. Perhaps this vast research base, while contributing to better practices, has also contributed to the loss of faith in its use. Perhaps it is too vast and confusing and not sufficiently interpreted and synthesized.

It is sad to think that we go through the same debates over and over again and that we seem to learn so little from the past. The tendency of researchers to use ever new labels for old concepts also seems to cut us off from the tested knowledge of the past. Thus the research and writing on phonological awareness seems to cut itself off from the earlier research on phonics. Adult literacy seems to cut itself off from child and adolescent literacy, and emergent literacy is cut off from the vast knowledge and experience on reading readiness. Why, one wonders, do we need to "invent" new terms for existing and valid ideas? It may earn immediate attention and interest, but it cuts one off also from teachers who are urged to do the "new" thing when they may already be doing it, but under an old label.

Where Do We Go From Here?

My present concerns, which are many, have not shaken my strong commitment to research and theory, to the value of analysis, and to experience. In the long run, the methods and materials that will prove to be most effective will be in line with research, theory, and experience. In the meantime, many children, particularly those at risk—the children of low-income families and children of all social levels who are predisposed to having reading difficulty—are not doing as well as they can. Such children benefit most from a reading program that has been proven over the years. They need excellent teachers. They need extra help when they fall behind (Chall, Jacobs, & Baldwin, 1990). Children of middle class families are not affected as much by the reading methods and materials used by their teachers since their parents often supplement their child's reading instruction by their own teaching or by obtaining a private tutor.

To improve reading achievement I would hope that we can look more to what we know works and apply it wisely and well. For the past decades, study after study has found that certain classroom practices produce significantly better results—e.g., high expectations and books that challenge, frequent assessment and instruction based on it. A strong beginning reading program that includes systematic instruction in the alphabetic principle, and attention to word meanings in the intermediate grades and later are also important (Chall, 1987).

Unfortunately, some in the reading field act as if the solutions to our pressing problems lie mainly in changing the old, usually tested methods to untested methods—with their ensuing debates and polarities. One wonders why we do not invest that energy and time into doing better, and more widely, what does work. Indeed, research study after research study has found that students need to read widely to grow in reading. Why then don't we put our energies into better school, classroom, and community libraries? Indeed, these services seem to be declining nationally. Also, while we gain ever stronger evidence that extra instruction keeps children from falling ever more behind, the schools tend too often to underfinance this special service. There is also considerable knowledge about the kinds of programs that are effective with kindergarten and first grade children that help prevent low achievement and reduce reading problems. Why do we not look to broad applications of these programs to improve the reading of our children and young people instead of seeming always to be on a search for a single, charismatic solution?

Teachers need to know and understand this body of knowledge in reading and how it is best implemented. But much of it they already know and need only the resources and encouragement to use it.

There is also a need to look into the education of our researchers. If learning to do research is learning more than knowledge and skills, if it consists also of attitude, values, and commitments learned from an experienced researcher, which I think it does, then we must improve how we educate the next generation of researchers.

There is a need, also, for a greater simplicity in what we do. Our theories, research, and practice are becoming more complex and technical, requiring more explanations to translate to other researchers and teachers. The manuals of the major basal reading textbooks, for example, keep getting larger and heavier, suggesting that the teaching of reading to 6-year-olds requires ever more exacting directions and guidance. And the many suggestions made regularly to differentiate instruction for most children make one wonder whether it is humanely possible for a classroom teacher to carry them out. With all of these growing complexities, one wonders how a teacher can survive. Even more, one wonders how it was possible for anyone to have learned to read before all the new methods and materials were invented. Indeed, we may ask, how did Thomas Jefferson, Abraham Lincoln, or John Dewey become such superb critical readers and writers? I think those of us who are professors, scholars, and researchers of reading must try to simplify it so that it can be understood and used.

And finally, who is to bell the cat? Who is to be responsible? Can teachers use whatever procedures they prefer without being accountable for the results they produce? If the results of standardized tests are not to be accepted, what other objective devices can be used in their place?

What is the responsibility of textbook publishers? They work in a highly competitive atmosphere, but does that mean they can use any procedures and materials that sell?

To what extent should professional organizations take responsibility? And, perhaps foremost, what is the responsibility of the scholar? Is it toward searching for new basic knowledge about the reading process? Or should it also include the responsibility of helping to solve the grave literacy problems facing us today?

An earlier version appeared in D. Burleson (Ed.), Reflections. *Bloomington, IN: Phi Delta Kappa, 1991.*

References

Adams, M. (1990). *Beginning to read: Thinking and learning about print.* Cambridge: MIT Press.

Anderson, R. C., Heibert, E. H., Scott, J. A., & Wilkinson, I. A. G. (1985). *Becoming a nation of readers: The Report of the Commission on Reading.* Champaign: University of Illinois, Center for the Study of Reading.

Carbo, M. (1988).Debunking the great phonic myth, *Phi Delta Kappan, 70,* 226-240.

Chall, J. S. (1947). This business of readability, *Educational Research Bulletin,26,* 1-13.

Chall, J. S. (1958). *Readability: An appraisal of research and application.* Columbus: Ohio State University Press.

Chall, J. S. (1987). The importance of instruction in reading methods for all teachers. In R. Bowler (Ed.), *Intimacy with language: A forgotten basic in teacher education.* Baltimore: The Orton Dyslexia Society.

Chall, J. S. (1988).Learning to read: The great debate 10 years later—a response to 'Debunking the great phonics myth,' *Phi Delta Kappan, 70,* 521-538.

Chall, J. S. (1989). Could the decline be real? Recent trends in reading instruction and support in the U. S. In Haertel, E., et al, *Report of the NAEP Technical Review Panel on the 1986 reading anomaly, the accuracy of NAEP trends, and issues raised by state-level NAEP comparisons* (pp. 61-74). Washington, DC: National Center for Education Statistics and U.S. Department of Education.

Chall, J. S. (1996). *Learning to Read: The Great Debate* (3rd ed.). Fort-Worth, TX: Harcourt Brace.

Chall, J. S. (1996). *Stages of Reading Development* (2nd ed.). Fort-Worth, TX: Harcourt Brace.

Chall, J. S. & Conard, S. S. (1991). *Should Textbooks Challenge Students? The Case for Easier or Harder Textbooks.* New York: Teacher's College Press.

Chall, J. S., Conard, S. S., & Harris, S. H. (1977). *An analysis of textbooks in relation to declining S.A.T. scores.* New York: College Entrance Examination Board.

Chall, J. S., Jacobs, V. A., & Baldwin, L. E. (1990). *The reading crisis: Why poor children fall behind.* Cambridge: Harvard University Press.

Chall, J. S., & Mirsky, A. F. (Eds.) (1978). *Education and the Brain.* Chicago: University of Chicago Press.

Dale, E. & Chall, J. S. (1948). A formula for predicting readability, and instructions. *Educational Research Bulletin 27,* 11-20, 37-54.

Dale, E. & Chall, J.S. (1995). *Readability revisited and the new Dale-Chall Readability Formula,* Cambridge, MA: Brookline Books.

Herber, H. (1988, May). *The heritage of our profession.* Paper presented at the Reading Hall of Fame, International Reading Association Annual Conference, Toronto, Canada.

A SOCIAL-CONSTRUCTIVIST VIEW OF FAMILY LITERACY

Susan B. Neuman

Temple University

Susan B. Neuman is an Associate Professor in the department of Curriculum Instruction and Technology in Education at Temple University. She is Coordinator of the Reading and Language Arts Graduate program. She received her doctorate at the University of the Pacific in Stockton, California. Dr. Neuman's research focuses on literacy and technology, family literacy and early literacy development. She has studied the relationship between television and reading for many years, documenting this work in Literacy in the Television Age.

Her most recent co-edited book is Single-subject experimental research: Applications for literacy. *In addition, she has co-authored* Language and literacy learning in the early years: An integrated approach *and has over 50 articles in* American Education Research Journal, Reading Research Quarterly, Reading Teacher, *and* Early Childhood Research Quarterly. *In addition, Susan has been co-editor of the* Journal of Reading Behavior. *Her newest co-edited book is* Children Achieving: Instructional Practices in Early Literacy *to be published by International Reading Assocation.*

Research supporting the crucial role of the family and early literacy experiences on children's later success in reading and writing has led to an increasing number of programs conceptualized around the family as a unit (Connors, 1993; Shanahan & Rodriquez-Brown, 1993; Winter & Rouse, 1990). Known widely as intergenerational or family literacy, these programs have been designed to improve the education of the mother or other caregivers in order to improve the quality of family life and the achievement of the child. Though varying in design and form (Nickse, Speicher, & Buchek, 1988), programs focus on training parents in literacy and effective parenting skills, assisting children in reading and writing skills, and providing opportunities for parent-child experiences. Consequently, these programs address not only the parent or the child as literacy learners, but the parent-child relationship. It is presumed that the skills learned and practiced by the adult and the child produce an intergenerational and/or reciprocal transfer of skills.

A primary challenge for family literacy researchers, however, has been to understand the process of transmission of behaviors from parent to child and child to parent, particularly as it applies to families from diverse economic, educational and cultural backgrounds (Connors, 1993). For example, although many program developers support a "family strengths model" which recognizes the importance of respecting cultural differences in child-rearing practices (Darling, 1989), Auerbach (1989) has argued that these programs continue to perpetuate a "transmission of school practices model." She suggests that the unifying assumption underlying these programs is school-based: parents are taught to transmit the culture of school literacy through the vehicle of the family.

Yet what characterizes the homes of successful literacy learners, both middle and lower income, is the sheer range of opportunities to use literacy-related practices as an integral part of daily family life (Anderson & Stokes, 1984; Auerbach, 1989). Children and adults experience reading and writing not as isolated events but as part of the social activities with family and friends in their homes and communities. Literacy-related activity, therefore, often occurs in cultural contexts for action that is constructed by people in interaction with one another (Laboratory of Comparative Human Cognition, 1983). Teale's ethnographic study (1986), for example, reported that for almost 90% of all reading and writing activities observed in 22 households, the focus of the activities was not on literacy itself; rather, literacy occurred as aspects of activities which enabled family members to organize their lives.

I argue that family literacy programs should be viewed within the cultural context, a way of thinking, behaving and responding to one's environment. Consequently, this article will show that there is great variability among programs reflecting the specific needs of the participants and the community. Several key features, however, appear common to each of the three following models.

Three Models
A Community-Based Program:
Family Intergenerational Literacy Lab

The Family Intergenerational Literacy Lab (FILL) is a community-based program in Alabama designed to serve families with an average income of $4500. The program aims at moving away from the traditionally General Equivalency Diploma (GED) or child-centered focus of many family literacy programs to one that is more holistic. Typically, reading instruction for adults is centered on the goals established by each individual. For the first two hours of the day, children attend a preschool program while parents attend classes which focus on the ability to solve problems through reading and writing skills and strategies. Time is set aside each day for parents and children to spend time together, working on computers, playing games, and making snacks for the children in preschool. The program also focuses on common family activities such as trips to grocery stores, pharmacies and the library, and social activities like musical plays and performances.

FILL is the product of a dynamic collaboration among community organizations. Vista volunteers help to recruit and organize activities. The local book store donates books. Other agencies conduct workshops, with the transit system providing tokens for all to attend in various locations. The senior center helps by supporting child-care and making meals for special occasions. In this small Alabama town, family literacy has become a community effort bringing people from businesses, schools, and agencies together.

A Head Start Family Literacy Program:
The Ramah Navajo Family Literacy Pilot Project

In this isolated area of the Navajo nation, the Ramah Head Start program has set out to establish a program that strengthens both the native language and traditions of families as well as English language literacy skills. Sensitive to the Navajo tradition, family literacy sessions begin with a 'talking circle,' a custom during which people articulate family and community concerns and arrive at decisions that benefit both families and the community. These concerns form the basis for a participatory reading curriculum, which involves parents and extended family members in using literacy to solve community concerns. In addition, on a regular basis, project leaders provide informational workshops ranging from "How to be your child's advocate in the school/service agency system," to making "toys from junk around the house." Traditionally, families join together with project staff for meals and social occasions.

Since the Navajo tradition gives childrearing roles to the extended family, the family literacy team developed a mobile lending library with multicultural books, toys, and developmentally appropriate learning materials. These materials provide opportunity for all those involved in the young children's lives to participate in playing, talking, and teaching in the context of family life. The project has appeared to lay a firm foundation for continuing family literacy approach in the larger community, creating greater awareness and knowledge about holistic approaches to family and early childhood development.

A School-Based Program:
Parents and Children Reading Together

The Book Club (Neuman, 1996) is a weekly get-together of parents from early childhood classrooms to talk about and read children's storybooks. Designed to be a meeting place for conversations about children's books and a time for parents and children to read together, book clubs are held weekly at schools for about 12 weeks. Sessions follow a similar format and are co-facilitated by a parent leader and a bilingual teacher from the community. Parents are free to select either an English or Spanish version of the story.

Each week begins with a choral reading of a children's book. The facilitator dramatizes the action, emphasizes repetitive phrases, and sometimes stops to ask questions as she reads. Following the reading, the facilitator then engages parents in a discussion of the story, focusing on three key questions:

1. What would you want your child to take away from this book? Acting as a recorder, the parent leader lists common themes, distinctive qualities about the book, descriptive phrases, and unusual vocabulary.

2. What kinds of questions or comments would you use to stimulate a discussion of the story? Various question types, (e.g., recall, prediction, and questions that related to other experiences), and other books are recorded.

3. How would you help your child revisit this book? Parent suggestions like rereading or activity extensions such as visiting a zoo, making cookies, or going for walks together are described.

Conversations are designed to engage parents in analyzing events and ideas presented in the story, relating stories to their own personal experiences as well as helping to bridge these experiences to their children's early educational needs. In this respect, the discussion format assumes that parents had rich experiences to share with others that could be applied to children's literature selections.

Library pockets and small index cards are provided so that parents can write down questions they believe most useful for guiding discussions with their children. Following the discussion of approximately 40 minutes, parents then visit their child's classroom and read their new book together for about 15 minutes, depending on the level of interaction. For those less proficient parent readers, they may read the story to their child, or ask him or her to pretend to read it to them; or they may tell the child the story as they remembered it using the pictures as guides. Parents are given a new book each week to add to their home libraries.

Pre- and post-test scores for children in these Book Clubs compared with a control group indicate their effectiveness in enhancing children's concepts of print and receptive language skills. These results provide strong support that smaller-scale, as well as comprehensive family literacy programs, can enhance children's achievement in schools.

Common Features of Programs

Although each of these models approach family literacy differently, there are several common features. For example, these programs:

1. Offer literacy instruction to families, broadly defined, to include parents, caregivers, siblings, extended family and young children,
2. Include strong participant involvement in curriculum planning and development,
3. Create a supportive environment, where achievements (both short and longer-term) are recognized and celebrated,
4. Provide opportunities for family and social networks to be formed through activities in classrooms and communities, and
5. Know the community, its resources and seek active collaborations with other social and educational services.

Providing educational support to families is an awesome challenge. In the process of seeking the mechanisms for supporting literacy development, researchers have redefined literacy as a far more complex process than was ever conceived in the past. The challenge facing us today is to understand how we can help to support collaborative relationships among schools, families and communities to aid children's literacy development.

References

Anderson, A. & Stokes, S. (1984). Social and institutional influences on the development and practice of literacy. In H. Goelman, A. Oberg, & F. Smith (Eds.), *Awakening to literacy* (pp. 24-37). Portsmouth, NH: Heinemann.

Auerbach, E. R. (1989). Toward a social-contextual approach to family literacy. *Harvard Educational Review, 59,* 165-181.

Connors, L. J. (1993). *Project Self Help: A family focus on literacy* (No. 13). Center on Families, Communities, Schools & Children's Learning.

Laboratory of Comparative Human Cognition. (1983). Culture and cognitive development. In W. Kessen (Ed.), *History, theory and methods.* Vol. 1 of P.H. Mussen (Ed.), *Handbook of child psychology.* New York: Wiley.

Neuman, S. B. (1996). Children engaging in storybook reading: The influences of access to print resources, opportunity and parental interaction, *Early Childhood Research Quarterly, 11,* 495-514.

Nickse, R., Speicher, A. M. & Buchek, P. C. (1988). An intergenerational adult literacy project: A family intervention/prevention model. *Journal of Reading, 31,* 634-642.

Shanahan, T. & Rodriquez-Brown, F. (1993). *Project FLAME: The theory and structure of a family literacy program for the Latino community.* Paper presented at the American Educational Research Association Conference, Atlanta, GA.

Teale, W. H. (1986). Home background and young children's literacy development. In W. H. Teale, & E. Sulzby (Eds.), *Emergent literacy* (pp. 173-206). Norwood, NJ: Ablex.

Winter, M. & Rouse, J. (1990). Fostering intergenerational literacy: The Missouri Parents as Teachers program. *The Reading Teacher, 43,* 382-387.

FINDING COMMON GROUND:
A REVIEW OF THE EXPERT STUDY

Rona F. Flippo

Fitchburg State College
Keynote Address
Presented to the College Reading Association,
November 6, 1997, Boston, MA

Rona F. Flippo is Professor of Reading Education at Fitchburg State College, in Massachusetts. She has authored six books and numerous articles. She is an active member in the International Reading Association, the National Reading Conference, and the Massachusetts Association of College and University Reading Educators. She serves on the editorial advisory boards of The Reading Teacher, Reading Psychology, *and the* Journal of Adolescent & Adult Literacy.

Rona is currently working on several new books: the Handbook of College Reading and Study Strategy Research; What Do the experts Say? Contexts and Practices for Classroom Reading, *and* Reading Researchers in Search of Common Ground.

Rona indicates that in retrospect, "I've been speaking out and writing for more rationality in what we do or mandate in schools to children and to teachers for a good portion of my professional life. Now, I'm writing about the need for some common ground in the reading profession in response to the ridiculous policies, mandates, and decisions we've all seen in our legislatures and media." Rona's expression of this need and her "expert study" was the topic of her Keynote Address at the College Reading Association's conference in 1997. Pulling ideas from her publication in the Phi Delta Kappan *(Flippo, 1997), "Sensationalism, politics, and literacy: What's going on?" Rona asks us to continue to seek a "common ground" and to share our agreements publicly.*

When I was a young child, growing up in Brooklyn, NY, there were certain words that I wasn't supposed to say; if I did say them, I was told that my mouth might be washed out with soap (this was a common threat to children in that culture and time). The bad words then, in my "home community" on East 48th Street, were very different from the words some thought were bad when I presented my study (December, 1996) in my "professional community" at the National Reading Conference. The really bad word there was "consensus." Because I was admonished by some for use of "the word," I intentionally tried not to use it during my next presentation of this study at the International Reading Association (IRA) Convention (May, 1997a), and I left it out entirely from the title of this College Reading Association presentation, as well as out of the papers and book proposals I subsequently wrote about my study.

The argument against "consensus" was that it would dampen the combustive sparks of intellectual discourse and intellectual growth and that it could squelch productive debate and discussion.

Now, after almost one year, I'm gratified to see that others in our reading community are beginning to call for some "consensus" or common ground. For example, in this month's *Reading Today* (October/November 1997), I noted that Jack Pikulski, IRA's new President, is warning that the very persistent Reading War is getting "dangerous," and the field does need to engage in discussion that achieves some "consensus," of some kind, soon.

Just listen to some of these headlines which I'll highlight from my Kappan article (Flippo, 1997b, pp. 301-302) to remind you about what has been going on in the media and in the political arena:

- "The Great Debate Revisited" (Levine, 1994, December, *Atlantic Monthly*),
- "As Reading Scores Plummet, States Get Hooked on Phonics" (Walters, 1996, April 18, *Christian Science Monitor*),
- "Parents Report on America's Reading Crisis: Why the Whole Language Approach to Teaching Has Failed Millions of Children" (Levine, 1996, October, *Parents Magazine*),
- "Phonics Boom: Proponents Say Any Other Approach to Reading Only Spells Trouble" (Kastor, 1996, November 15, *Washington Post*),
- "Why Kids Can't Read in California" (Saunders, 1996, January 12, *San Francisco Chronicle*) (of course they don't mention that as of 1990, more than 137 different languages were represented in California, see California Commission on Teacher Credentialing, 1996, as cited in Flippo, 1997b),
- "California Leads Revival of Teaching by Phonics" (1996, May 22, *New York Times*),

- "State Embraces Phonics in Approving New Texts" (Colvin, 1996, December 13, *Los Angeles Times*), and, I love this one:
- "State Rejects 2 Texts; Citing Phonics Law" (Gunnison, 1996, December 13, *San Francisco Chronicle*).

And within the reading community things are equally as volatile. If you don't think so, again take a look at this month's *Reading Today* (October/November 1997), where many IRA members respond to Dick Allington's commentary "Overselling Phonics," which appeared in the August/September 1997 issue.

What started out as a mostly intellectual, research question to find some areas of agreement in our field (because I saw a need for some common ground eleven years ago when I started my study), has obviously tapped into a raging battle within our profession and amongst the media, politicians, and public. Because of this, the political implications of the study are now as important as the data and the findings themselves. Therefore, much of what I'm going to talk about tonight will reflect this political tone (or tenor).

Basically, it appears that reading instruction has moved from "a concern" amongst interested parents, teachers, administrators, and others interested in education, to a "big" ticket item. In my December 1997 *Kappan* article, I point out that, in essence, the politicians have seized upon the ongoing reading debate (within our profession) as an opportunity to promote their positions and to draw attention to themselves as leaders of educational reform.

In fact, I believe that the political interest and "fire" behind the reading debates have actually further fueled "the fires" to the point that many within our profession are debating in a warlike manner—*attack, defend position, attack again.*

Rather than continue to polarize ourselves by continually focusing on our disagreements, I feel it is time to stop and really focus on the agreements that we do share as a profession. That is what I tried to do with my study.

So, where can we start? Maybe with an answer to the question, "What do reading researchers know?" We know that decisions about reading instruction should not be set up as extreme "either/or" positions. We know that phonics and other necessary skills instruction can be taught by teachers who have whole language philosophies. We also know that neither "phonics" nor "whole language" is a method, and we know that teachers should not be required to teach by one approach alone (Flippo, 1997b, pp. 302-303).

Finally, we know that even though each of us has an individual set of beliefs and philosophies regarding teaching, most of us would agree with certain practices and contexts concerning learning and environments for learning. In the remainder of this presentation I wish to report some major agreements among experts in the field of literacy and reading research. I suggest that these agreements, which span philosophies, and others we will find if we look, rather than the much publicized disagreements, should be considered by state boards and politicians as they propose, shape, and mandate their legislation (Flippo, 1997b, p. 303).

My study of experts spanned ten years. To gather these data I employed a Delphi technique, which involved asking selected reading experts, who represented the major schools of thought in literacy education, to specify what they believed teachers "should do" and "shouldn't do" in their classrooms to promote reading development. Each of the selected experts generated his or her own list of items anonymously, and the remaining experts agreed or disagreed, again anonymously, with each item on these lists. Each round was followed up with queries and interviews as needed (Flippo, 1997b, p. 303).

The experts involved in my study include Richard Anderson, Brian Cambourne, Edward Fry, Yetta Goodman, Jane Hansen, Jerome Harste, Wayne Otto, Scott Paris, P. David Pearson, George Spache, and Rand Spiro.

After four complete rounds, I found that there were 33 practices and contexts that the experts agreed would tend to make learning to read difficult for children; they also agreed on 19 things that teachers might do to facilitate the children's learning to read (Flippo, 1997b, p. 303). Please note that this is not about getting agreement on any "method"! This is about finding out what people would agree to—people from many different philosophies.

For the first round of the study, I sent the experts Frank Smith's (1973) list of "Twelve Easy Ways to Make Learning to Read Difficult," and the experts responded to those, either agreeing or disagreeing, or editing. The experts also then began to develop their own lists during this first round. Smith's list of statements had been cited fairly often in the literature, and it seemed to furnish an adequate starting point to stimulate interest and discussion among the experts.

The lists of agreements are lengthy, and some seem more important and central to the current hot issues than others. Therefore, for this presentation I will highlight the findings and generalize the agreements that seem most significant to the debates reported in the media and to what the state boards and legislatures have been acting on.

Practices that the experts agree would tend to make learning to read difficult for students include:

- emphasizing only phonics instruction,
- drilling children on isolated letters or sounds,
- making sure that children do it correctly or not at all,
- focusing on the single best answer,
- making word-perfect oral reading the prime objective of your classroom reading program,

- focusing on reading skills rather than on interpretation and comprehension,
- using workbooks or worksheets with every reading lesson;
- grouping readers according to ability,
- following a basal program without making modifications,
- teaching letters and words one at a time and making sure each new
  letter or word is learned before moving on to the next letter or word,
  and
- expecting students to be able to spell correctly all the words they can
  read.

Practices that experts agree would tend to facilitate learning to read include:
- bringing opportunities for reading, writing, talking, and listening together so that each feeds off and into the other,
- talking about and sharing different kinds of reading,
- focusing on using reading as a tool for learning,
- making reading functional and purposeful,
- developing positive self-perceptions and expectations concerning
  reading,
- using a broad spectrum of sources and a variety of real books for
  student reading materials,
- providing multiple and repeated demonstrations of how reading is
  done or used, and
- using silent reading whenever possible and whenever appropriate to
  the purpose (Flippo, 1997b, p. 304).

Some have criticized my study, saying that these items are too simplistic—"too common sensical," or "too non-common sensical," depending on
whether you're talking about the desirable or undesirable contexts and practices—so that, they say, the conclusion, that there is some agreement, is flawed.

I'm not saying that these items aren't simplistic, and I'm not saying that
they are necessarily the most important ones to focus on, but this study does
clearly show that experts from different camps can agree on practices that
are at the very least, related to teaching reading. And some of them are very
important and relevant. Additionally, I think that these agreements are very
important because people in the media, people in state legislatures, and even
some of those in our field, espousing one position or another, do not think
there is anything that all camps do agree on.

Here's another criticism: others have criticized my study, saying that it
isn't possible to discuss these practices and contexts across philosophies,
because these experts come from different discourse communities and really speak different languages. For instance, the critics say, these experts would

define "reading" differently, so how can they even approach the idea of consensus on anything?

I say, if we can't even agree on a common language, how can we communicate with other people outside the field of reading about what we are talking about? How can we expect politicians, parents, teachers, and the media to understand us? Are they (the critics) trying to say that our differing philosophies limit us so much that we can't understand each other and others really cannot understand us? Frankly, I find this criticism as even more evidence that we must seek some common ground.

Even men and women these days are learning to speak the others' language, as books like *Men Are from Mars, Women are from Venus* (Gray, 1992) have shown us. And we better learn to speak the same language soon, to intelligently discuss our agreements, or here's what can happen: A recent article in the *U.S. News & World Report* (Toch, 1996) illustrates how we are perceived by the media and the real need we have for more professional unity and political awareness:

> In the reading debate, as in other school reform issues, many progressives and traditionalists seem more eager to fight than to find common ground, routinely misrepresenting each other's views and needlessly polarizing debates at students' expense. It is left to the rest of us to break through the overheated rhetoric, finding in both sides important pieces of a national solution. (p. 64)

Do we really want the media and politicians to piece together *their* solutions because we're fighting and arguing so much with each other that we can't "get it together"?

By the way, did you take notice, as I did, of the study done by Cassidy and Wenrich, reported in the February/March 1997 issue of *Reading Today*? They researched the "hot" and "not hot" topics today in reading research, and found that "hot" topics—in other words, topics that are receiving current, positive attention—are phonics, phonemic awareness, and skills instruction. But, listen to this, the "not hot" topics (the ones that are receiving negative or little attention) are *comprehension, schema theory,* and *word knowledge/vocabulary!* This is, of course, the result of what has been going on politically inside and outside our field.

Here's more Brooklyn street culture: We, my friends and I, boys and girls alike, were very protective of our street. We lived on East 48th Street between Avenues L and M. If any other kids ever set foot on our block, we aggressively protected our turf, even if we had to throw stones, rocks, and bricks at them to scare them away. Such has also become the custom among those of us who protect turf in our field. Because people seem afraid that agreement and consensus may weaken or neutralize the power of their ideas, many don't want to allow anyone else on their block. They would resort to the old Brooklyn way of throwing rocks to prevent it, even if this behavior causes the neighborhood to get a bad reputation.

Let's stop throwing rocks at each other. Let's "hang together" in our literacy neighborhood. I think we can take these agreements and other agreements that the reading community will hopefully generate in the near future from across philosophies and say to the media and politicians that the field of reading professionals are standing on a common ground, and we do not believe that the political solutions now being pushed are good for children or conducive to reading development. In fact, if you carefully review these agreements among these diverse experts, you will see that the political solutions offered in California and other states where politicians are jumping on the "back to phonics" bandwagon are often counter to what literacy experts across philosophies believe to be facilitative practices and contexts (Flippo, 1997b, p. 304).

I believe we need balance between agreement and disagreement, just like we need a balance of reading approaches. Since all we've focused on in the past is the disagreements, it is the model we've become most familiar with in our field. I feel that we need to begin looking at agreement in some way very soon.

And, for those of you who feel that we've seen the worst, and surely things will get better; Nicholas Lemann in the new *Atlantic Monthly* (November 1997) article, entitled "The Reading Wars" predicts that (a) efforts to establish greater quality control in public education (translating to "more central authority") will go on constantly for the next few decades, (b) schools all over the country will be hard pressed by parents and politicians to move toward imparting skills, without considering development of a joy of learning, and (c) as long as the US continues in its current prosperous and peaceful condition, the more that the politicians and the press will keep school curricula issues in the fore of American politics.

In closing, and on a more positive note, I do want to say that since doing my last presentations, I do now see evidence that more people are talking more about the need for "common ground." Whether we call it "common ground," "agreement," or yes, that bad word "consensus," others now seem to be looking for it, and I applaud that idea.

We don't give up anything by being a respectful community. Growth in our field will not be sacrificed or diminished just because we aren't arguing publicly with each other. And, we don't need to agree on everything either. We already acknowledge our differences. Now, let's acknowledge some common ground.

References

Allington article draws praise, nays. (1997, October/November). *Reading Today,* *15* (2), 17.

Allington, R. L. (1997, August/September). Overselling phonics. *Reading Today,* *15* (1), 15-16.

California Commission on Teacher Credentialing (1996). *Standards of program quality and effectiveness for professional teacher internship programs for multiple and single-subject teaching credentials with a (bilingual) crosscultural, language, and academic development (CLAD/BCLAD) emphasis.* Sacramento, CA: California Commission on Teacher Credentialing, State of California.

California leads revival of teaching by phonics. (1996, May 22). *New York Times,* p. B8.

Cassidy, J., & Wenrich, J. K. (1997, February/March). What's hot, what's not for 1997. *Reading Today, 14* (4), 34.

Colvin, R. L. (1996, December 13). State embraces phonics in approving new texts. *Los Angeles Times,* p. A1.

Flippo, R. F. (1996, December). *"Seeds of consensus": The beginnings of professional unity.* Paper presented at the annual meeting of the National Reading Conference, Charleston, SC.

Flippo, R. F. (1997a, May). *Reaching consensus: Findings from the expert study.* Paper presented at the annual meeting of the International Reading Association, Atlanta, GA.

Flippo, R. F. (1997b). Sensationalism, politics, and literacy: What's going on? *Phi Delta Kappan, 79* (4), 301-304.

Gray, J. (1992). *Men are from Mars: Women are from Venus.* New York: Harper Collins.

Gunnison, R. B. (1996, December 13). State rejects 2 texts, citing phonics law. *San Francisco Chronicle,* p. A1.

Kastor, E. (1996, November 15). Phonics boom: Proponents say any other approach to reading only spells trouble. *Washington Post,* p. D1.

Lemann, N. (1997, November). The reading wars. *Atlantic Monthly, 280,* 128-130, 132-134.

Levine, A. (1994, December). The great debate revisited. *Atlantic Monthly, 274,* 38-44.

Levine, A. (1996, October). Parents report on America's reading crisis: Why the whole language approach to teaching has failed millions of children. *Parents Magazine, 71*(10), 63-68.

Pikulski, J. J. (1997, October/November). Beginning reading instruction: From "The Great Debate" to the reading wars. *Reading Today, 15* (2), 32.

Saunders, D. J. (1996, January 12). Why kids can't read in California. *San Francisco Chronicle,* p. A23.

Smith, F. (1973). Twelve easy ways to make learning to read difficult. In F. Smith (Ed.), *Psycholinguistics and reading* (pp. 183-196). New York: Holt, Rinehart, and Winston.

Toch, T. (with Daniel, M.). (1996, October 7). Schools that work. *U.S. News & World Report, 121* (14), 58-64.

Walters, L. S. (1996, April 18). As reading scores plummet, states get hooked on phonics. *Christian Science Monitor,* pp. 1,4.

EARLY
LEADER

Reflections on the Early Years of CRA and the Focus of Reading in the 1950's and 1960's

Robert C. Aukerman, Ph.D.

Professor Emeritus
University of Rhode Island
President CRA 1965-1966

Dr. Robert C. Aukerman was a teacher in Detroit public schools for 11 years. He was a visiting professor in a number of colleges and universities, and he served as dean at the Northeast Missouri State Teachers College. He has lectured at many universities and has spoken at International Reading Association Conferences. A member of IRA, CRA, New England Reading Association, Phi Delta Kappa, and the APA, he also has published several books concerning reading.

Introduction

My role has been cast by the program committee as that of the historian—not only for the early beginnings of the CRA, but as an observer of the focus of reading during those first two decades . . . the 1950's and 1960's.

Beginnings of the College Reading Association

The idea for an association of professionals in reading education in colleges and universities in the middle Atlantic States came in the late 1950's, soon after the advent of the National Reading Conference and the Southwest Reading Council, neither of which included colleagues from Pennsylvania, New Jersey, Maryland or Delaware.

Getting reading professors together for a conference in a particular spot at a specified time to brainstorm the possibilities was, in those years, a difficult task. At times it was discouraging, but, chiefly through the continuing faith in the idea and effort of Dr. Al Mazurkiewicz and the support of his administration at Lehigh University, the fledgling CRA was saved from early demise.

It proved to be a great and viable concept. For the first time on the East Coast, it brought together a group of professionals who were not struggling for power and fame but treated each other as colleagues. Those were the times when most were mounting programs for training classroom teachers in reading materials and methods and developing advanced programs for teachers who sensed the need and opportunity for becoming reading specialists. Ideas were to be shared. No one was in competition; we operated as friends. I feel that same camaraderie here today, after more than forty years.

Other reading associations predate the formation of CRA (1958). The New England Reading Association had been organized by Donald Durrel, his associates, and loyal Boston University graduates ten years earlier (1948). Seven years later (1954), the International Reading Association was organized by some of the big names in the basal reading business. Neither reading organization served the needs of the university professors but encouraged any and all (teachers, parents, bookmen, publishers, authors and students) to become members, to subscribe to journals, and to attend annual meetings.

I believe it was about the time of my presidency that we tried several co-sponsored sessions with the IRA, but, because of the generic nature of that group, our efforts were not successful. The reason was that we were interested in developing programs for educating teachers and in developing college reading clinics.

Eventually, the CRA came to encompass a wider geographic area while remaining a friendly group of first-name colleagues. Because of the dedication of countless numbers of like-minded colleagues, its future is assured from now (1997) far into the 21st century. Even though most of its originators are no longer with us, their ideas remain as valid and viable as a half-century ago.

Reflections on the Focus of Reading 1950's-1960's

In the early decades of the 20th century, reading research was a natural outgrowth of psychological research by university psychologists who were concentrating on studies of the variables in human learning. Psychologists most frequently used the various facets of reading as the media for those psychological investigations. That research supported the fact that reading is a very complicated galaxy of innate and learned behaviors. Briefly stated, the relationship of psychological research and reading is apparent with the mention of such concepts as repetition; drill; phonics; look-say; speed of perception; cognition; associative learning; past experience; the bell curve; individual differences; maturation; readiness; growth curves; graded basals; incremental learning, etc. Those were the variables that were the focus of reading at the beginning of the 1950's.

Basal readers were, with few exceptions, the most significant focus in reading in the 1950's and 1960's. They were a gold-mine for the fifteen major publishing houses in spite of the enormous outlays of money necessary to mount each series. To acquire accurate information for my book, *The Basal Reader Approach to Reading,* I was able to establish a confidential relationship with the managing editors of each of those series. I learned that between $15,000,000 and $20,000,000 were required to plan for the methods and materials that comprised each of the graded readers, the accompanying workbooks, teachers' manuals, and ancillary commissioning of gorgeous illustrations done by dozens of top artists. Such sums of start-up money would exceed the equivalent of $50,000,000 today. Huge investments necessitated big promotions.

Big-name so-called "editors" were acquired from among the movers and shapers of the International Reading Association. The names of those leaders assured respectability and authenticity to the series, even though those under contract acted in most instances only as advisors. In some cases they did produce stories for the first few levels of the series, but in at least one instance, the well-known "editor" and former IRA president conscripted his graduate students as ghost writers of the story lines, using prepared controlled vocabulary lists for each level. There was also a formula for controlling the number of times that each new whole-word was to be used. Whole-word learning, was supposedly assured through controlled repetition and progressive increments as the children progressed through the levels of the basal series.

Big money was to be made through state-wide adoptions of a particular series. A barrage of promotions ensued, and exposure at the annual IRA conventions was impressive. Classroom teachers welcomed basal readers as great tools to use, inasmuch as the teachers' manuals provided packaged lesson plans and elaborate suggestions for expansion and enrichment of each day's segment of learning. Student workbooks and other ancillary materials proved to be a boon to classroom teachers who were faced with a curriculum crowded with demands in arithmetic, social studies, writing, science, health, music, art, holidays, programs, parental conferences, assessments, etc.

In the early 1960's it was apparent that a significant shift was beginning in the focus of reading. There arose some challenges to the supremacy of basal readers as the main media of reading instruction in America's schools. The beginning of decades of chaos and confusion had arrived.

"Phonics-First" enthusiasts, represented collectively by the Reading Reform Foundation, promoted phonics instruction as the essential basis of reading. Naturally, they were portrayed as radical reactionaries and stuffy "has-beens." Jeannie Chall's *Learning to Read: The Great Debate* (1967) attempted to encourage the profession to use impartial basals, as well as direct phonics instruction, and to espouse some of the newer fads beginning to appear. The result was that teachers-in-training received little or no training in the uses of basal readers or phonics.

Holistic learning became a popular theme, perhaps based on the German "Gestalt" psychological school, in which it was recognized that "the whole is greater than the sum of its parts." That movement eventually evolved into the currently-popular buzz-word, "literacy," promoted by Dr. Marie Clay at one of the IRA meetings and wholeheartedly accepted by many who were grasping for something new and, therefore, better. It seems to have brought forth the idea of "whole language." Theorists seemed to have the idea that children utilize the same innate means for reading as they do for oral language.

Similarly, attention to the gifted child encouraged the notion that, inasmuch as many gifted children developed their own "systems" for reading before being formally instructed in the classroom, why not have all children "learn to read by reading?" "Just do it." Another challenge was launched when "Sesame Street" appeared on daytime TV, and many children arrived at kindergarten with some basic reading skills. "What to do now?"

Moreover, the U.S. Office of Education sidetracked excellence in reading instruction by hiring a huge staff of federal and state bureaucrats, most of whom were totally ignorant of the methods, materials or research in reading instruction. Their jobs were to run the quickly-devised mechanism for doling out the tens of millions of federal dollars that had been voted to "encourage the development of innovative programs." I met the head of the entire program in Washington. He was a history professor and questioned me, "What is all this about reading? . . . Don't the schools teach reading? Hasn't everyone learned to read when they get out of school?"

Our rich Uncle Sam was just what was needed, and at an opportune time, to satisfy the urge for something different and "innovative" by financing the most fantastic, imaginative, worthy-and-unworthy schemes ever to appear in the world of education, the majority of which were in the field of reading. Hundreds of proposals, seeking federal monies, were quickly devised. To briefly describe a few should illustrate the carnival of hucksters that hit the road to school; each hawking his own panacea. This was when the focus of reading instruction became totally fractured. The result: NO focus at all!

The butcher, the baker and the candlestick maker suddenly appeared as reading specialists: Glenn Doman, a physiotherapist, made national headlines with his book for parents, "Teach Your Baby to Read." It created an uproar and more division between many schools of thought. "Progressive education" had, by the 1950's, been in vogue for long enough to illustrate some of its shortcomings in the meager attention to what were considered to be basics, especially in reading. These shortcomings became fertile territory for old-time reactionaries such as Mae Carden, who left her center of operations in New Jersey and hit the road, promoting "co-rec-tuh pro-nun-cee-ay-shun," thereby stirring up a storm. Fueling the reactionary movement were two best-sellers, "Educational Wastelands" (Arthur Bestor, 1953) and "Tomorrow's Illiterates" (Charles C. Walcutt, 1961). Many ridiculed the Carden System as stilted and archaic. Nonetheless, the Carden System found acceptance in a number of school systems in California and elsewhere, perhaps a foreunner of the reactions that are currently rocking California schools today.

Would you believe that the "archaic" notion of formally teaching phonics is presented in one of the highlighted articles as part of the special issue entitled, "What Makes a Good School?" in last week's TIME magazine! And, as might be expected, another debate has begun with the IRA Board of Directors doing a jig around the subject. We have come around full circle. "Back to the Future."

Romalda Spalding, another product of the "old school" also toured; demonstrating the features of her "Writing Road to Reading." My research and observation of her system in operation leaves me convinced of its effectiveness, providing a teacher is dedicated enough to follow its rigid routine. In one sense, it was a "whole language" approach based on correct pronunciation, spelling and writing as logical components of excellence in reading. The last time I spoke with Mrs. Spalding was in Hawaii in 1993. I observed that she had already progressed through several of the first stages of Altzheimers. Consequently, it is my prediction that her approach may not survive without her enthusiastic demonstrations.

Another "innovative" idea (although it had been tried decades before) was revision of our 26-letter alphabet to accommodate our 44 sounds. One of the most innovative of all was the "Initial Teaching Alphabet," better known as i/t/a. It was an amalgamation of earlier works by Britons, especially Sir Isaac Pitman. When it finally was imported to America, it attracted the attention of reading specialists who recognized its logic; our own Al Mazurkiewicz being one of them. In 1964, the Ford Foundation for the Advancement of Education funded the experiment and eventually it was adopted by school systems such as Reading (Pennsylvania). Other fonetic-alfabet systems were tried, but the dream of a perfect, regular, predictable language continues to remain a dream.

Many newcomers to education surfaced in the 1960's as instant reading specialists. Nancy Rambush, a self-described "pushy Catholic parent," strongly and successfully promoted the revival of the highly-structured Montessori

Method that she had discovered during a sojourn in Europe. DISTAR (Direct Instruction Systems for Teaching Arithmetic and Reading) was the brainchild of Dr. Carl Bereiter, a psychologist at the University of Illinois. Siegfried Engelmann, an advertising and promotion man, saw its glamorous possibilities as a showmanship bonanza. The system was exclusively a teacher-centered, structured, canned approach through which all children learned simultaneously, under directions read from an easel by the teacher. Engelmann, a fast talker, put on great shows for teachers and fielded their objections like a pro.

"Reading readiness" had become a popular buzz word. Many schemes were developed to fill the "need" for readiness training such as establishing left-to-right directionality for reading in English. Maverick plans surfaced claiming to be effective reading-readiness activities; among them were those popular with physiotherapists. Children were soon structured into programs designed to train them in left-to-right directionality as a reading-readiness skill. Systems to achieve that visionary goal were mounted to have children creeping, crawling, walking beams, and crossing themselves from left-to-right. It seemed logical that Catholic children would just naturally become better readers than Protestants.

Perhaps the most innovative of the many gaining attention was the "Talking Typewriter" experiment by Dr. O. K. Moore, a social psychologist at Yale. His program was called a "responsive environments approach." His typewriter with its computer-like screen and visual and verbal response systems was, without a doubt, a dream fulfilled by today's classroom computer. It used interactive programmed visual and verbal responses to help children learn to read. His research was funded by a grant from the Navy. This was an innovation that apparently escaped serious attention by educators.

The large sums of Federal monies and interest in machines as teaching aids spawned a dozen or more bits of electronic hardware. One example is the "Tachistiscope" (Greek word, takhos-speed) through which a film travels carrying the script of a story. Its speed could be controlled. Similarly, the "Tach-X" carried phrases and the "Flash-X" supplanted flash cards with flash words. Overhead projector programs were tried with little success. Eye-movement studies became routine as part of testing children with reading disabilities. "Speed Reading" was developed originally for older students, but it eventually was taken over and promoted commercially for adults. Mobile reading labs were housed in large vans that visited a school one day, pulled up anchor, and moved to a different school the next day. Their large cost and personnel and upkeep were easily financed, as were packaged reading centers equipped with the latest hardware and software. These and scores of other plans were the multi-focused reading scene that faced CRA members in those first two decades.

Money became the motivation for reading gimmicks and gadgets in those years, and we, as professional teacher educators, were in a quandary to know how to deal with them in the elementary reading curriculum. Moreover, the United State Office of Education (USOE). was also offering us plenty of money to set up conferences and institutes in our colleges and universities. The offers of those federal grants gave rise to the term "grantsmanship" to describe those individuals clever enough to plan proposals, many of which contained themselves as the directors of the proposed operations. Those conferences and workshops frequently resulted in the creation of instant reading specialists after 6 weeks exposure.

At one such institute in which I participated in Appalachia (reading for the disadvantaged) it seemed that the institute promoted more confused teachers and, moreover, offered them amazing machines to take back to their schools in the hills and hollers . . . many of which had no electricity to run the mechanical wonders.

Dyslexia became another buzz-word in the 1950's and 1960's. It was used frequently to shield the possibility that, just perhaps, the "dyslexic" child had never been in an effective reading program, or in one of continuity. Many teachers tossed the word "dyslexic" around carelessly, creating concerned parents and "identifying" scores of children as dyslexic.

Another buzz-word that created a stir was "linguistics." Publishers of basal readers quickly changed the covers to assure selection committees that their materials were "linguistically based." . . . not aware of the fact that there are several kinds of linguistics. Summer reading conferences, as well as the IRA conferences quickly devised sections on linguistics. Even teachers began glibly speaking in linguistic terms. At the New England Reading Conference (Fall, 1963) Dr. Henry Lee Smith, the featured speaker from Buffalo University, advised me that he was America's foremost linguistics scholar. His scholarly presentation on linguistics was over the heads of most, if not all, in attendance. Nevertheless, many went away thrilled at the thought of having been exposed to linguistics and thinking they could speak authoritatively on that new fad. Thus, linguistics soon became another structured sequence of phonograms, just about as senseless as anything devised previously: "Dan. Dan can. Dan can fan. Dan can fan Ann."

New fads, schemes, buzz-words, gimmicks, and gadgets continued to appear annually with the opening of every yearly reading conference. Some lasted only until the next year . . . some until the demise of their originators. Others continued until it became apparent to some CRA members that it was expedient to get with each new and currently-popular tune being played by each new Pied Piper.

Some Conclusions

Are these "Reflections on Reading in the 1950's and 1960's" to remain just a parade of gimmicks, new patent medicines, snake oils, machinery, and classroom voodoo, whose originators guarantee success? It is my opinion that these reflections will remain just such interesting trivia unless some "lessons of history" are derived from them. First, is the fact that thousands of teachers took advantage of federal money to attend workshops, conferences, and seminars on reading. This was a significant turning point in the world of reading. Teachers became thinkers, rather than followers of pre-planned reading materials and methods. Some became innovators. Most were better for the experience. Second, reading became an important subject for discussion and concern, not only among educators, but at local school budget hearings, with political pow-wows and with the media. Third, it should be significant that 25,000 studies and research investigations have been done on reading methods and materials, yet most of the new fads that paraded across the reading stage ignored research. Fourth, most of the "innovative" schemes were promoted by honest people who sincerely believed that each material and/or method was the best, and each deserved to be tried. Fifth, and perhaps, most important, is the fact that the field of education and reading in particular, was wide open in the 50's and 60's to each and every huckster who surfaced. The reading world welcomed each regardless of logic; regardless of research; regardless of proof.

So, that's the way it was.

If the lessons of history tell us that history repeats itself . . . that the mistakes of the past are bound to be repeated in the future, can it be possible that the 1950's and 1960's foretell the future?

A note of thanks to Estill Alexander and to Susan Strode for their untiring work.

Reference

Aukerman, R. C. (1971) Approaches to beginning reading (1st ed.). New York: Wiley.

Aukerman, R. C. (1981). *The basal reader approach to reading.* New York: Wiley.

Bestor, A. (1953). *Educational wastelands.* Urbana: University of Illinois Press.

Chall, J. S. (1967). *Learning to read: The great debate.* New York: McGraw-Hill.

Doman, G. (1964). *How to teach your baby to read.* Philadelphia: Better Baby Press.

How to save our schools. (1997, Oct. 27). *Time, 150*(7).

Spalding, R. (1969). *Writing road to reading.* New York: Morrow.

Walcutt, C. C. (1961). *Tomorrow's illiterates: The state of reading instruction today.* Boston: Little, Brown.

RESEARCH
AWARDS

FIRST AND SECOND GRADERS CONSTRUCT LITERARY UNDERSTANDING DURING READALOUDS OF PICTURE STORYBOOKS

Dissertation Award

Lawrence R. Sipe
University of Pennsylvania
Dissertation Award

Abstract

The literary understanding of first and second graders was studied as picture storybooks were read aloud to them. Over seven months, field notes and transcripted audiotapes of 83 readalouds were collected; 45 representative transcripts were selected for intensive analysis. There were five types of literary understanding: (a) textual analysis, (b) intertextual connections, (c) personal connections, (d) becoming "lost" in the story, and (e) using the text as a platform for creative expression. Teachers' scaffolding roles including reading; managing/encouraging; clarifying/probing; wondering/speculating; and extending/refining. Children learned illustration conventions, using all the visual stimuli of the picturebook. Two-thirds of the conversational turns took place during the readalouds, suggesting the importance of allowing children to talk during the reading of the story. Intertextual connections proved to be pivotal in enabling children to make various interpretive moves.

Reading stories aloud to children is a common practice in both home and school. Researchers have accumulated a great deal of knowledge about how these readalouds of storybooks enhance children's development of literacy (Sulzby & Teale, 1991). Cited benefits include the development of a love of books (Holdaway, 1979); understanding the difference between oral and written language and the acquisition of "book language" (Baker &

Freebody, 1989); and development of a sense of story and story structure (Meyer & Rice, 1984). Through storybook readalouds, children may also learn the conventions of print and "how books work" (Clay, 1991). Storybook reading also enhances vocabulary development and listening comprehension (Dickinson & Smith, 1994), as well as contributing to independent reading and writing ability in general (Morrow, 1989). One aspect of young children's literacy development that has received much less attention from researchers is literary understanding and interpretation.

This article reports on part of a qualitative descriptive study (Sipe, 1996) of the construction of literary understanding of picturebooks by a class of first- and second-grade children as suggested by their responses before, during, and after storybook readalouds. The purpose was to describe richly what constituted literary understanding for the children in one literature-rich classroom.

The research questions were: (a) What is the nature of the literary understanding of young children, displayed by their talk during readalouds of picture storybooks? and (b) How do adults (the classroom teacher and the researcher) scaffold the children's developing literary understanding during storybook readalouds?

The study was framed with the theory of social constructivism (Gergen, 1985; Schwandt, 1994). The following principles summarize the theory in relation to discussion during storybook readalouds:

1. Human beings socially construct their understanding of the world (and of literature) by social interaction. Oral language is the primary component of social interaction (Vygotsky, 1978, 1986; Wertsch, 1985). Therefore, one important way of investigating children's literary understanding is to analyze their talk about stories.

2. Children's talk about stories is always situated in a particular social context, and the natural setting of the classroom is the most appropriate place to study it, rather than a clinical setting (Gumperz, 1986). In this case, the social context was the familiar storybook readaloud situation in the classroom.

3. Children's developing understanding is enabled by scaffolding from adults and more capable peers (Wood, 1989). Scaffolding involves solving problems jointly; arriving at shared understandings through discussion; warmth and responsiveness; engaging children in tasks they could not perform for themselves, but which they can perform with assistance; and promoting self-regulation (Berk & Winslor, 1995). Therefore, it is important to investigate the teacher's role in discussion during storybook readalouds.

4. Children and their teachers construct the rules and conventions of

what counts as literary understanding within the context of their classroom interpretive community (Culler, 1975; Fish, 1980).

Researchers have established that storybook reading is an important contributor to young children's emerging literacy development. The significance of the study reported here lies in its focus on a less-researched aspect of literacy development: how young children interpret, analyze, and respond to literature, developing "literary competence" (Culler, 1975) during the reading of stories. Most research on literary understanding deals with children in home or preschool settings (Cochran-Smith, 1984; Crago & Crago, 1983; Wolf & Heath, 1992); or children who are in third grade or older (Cox & Many, 1992; Galda, 1982; Wiseman, Many, & Altieri, 1992; Zarillo & Cox, 1992). This study concerned first and second graders, whose literary responses have been less frequently researched. Moreover, most research on literary understanding deals with children's discussions *after* a story has been read, in literature discussion groups, literature circles, books clubs, or "grand conversations" (Daniels, 1994; Eeds & Wells, 1989; McGee, 1992; McMahon & Raphael, 1997; Short & Pierce, 1990). The study reported here concerned children's talk with each other and with the teacher *during* storybook readalouds. Sharing and talking through their ideas assisted the children in reaching higher levels of literary understanding. The study supports the view that such free exchanges about literature during storybook readalouds should be encouraged in primary classrooms.

Methodology

The study took place over a period of seven months in a first- and second-grade classroom in a school with a long history of using children's literature in creative ways. The choice of site was an instance of "intensity sampling" (Patton, 1990), since the phenomenon to be studied was likely to be intensely manifested in such a literature-rich school. The school's population came from mostly blue collar families. The class of 27 children constituted a racial and cultural mix that included Euro-American, African-American, and Native American children, with a strong representation of children with Appalachian backgrounds.

The classroom teacher's philosophy of teaching and learning was, like that of the entire school, based on the model of the British Primary Schools (Brown & Precious, 1968; MacKenzie & Kernig, 1975). She valued (a) informal learning situations, where the children had a great deal of choice in determining their own focus; (b) an integrated approach, where activities were given unity around a common theme; and (c) the active and social nature of the learning that took place as children spoke freely to each other and worked on projects in small groups. Reading, writing, listening, and speaking permeated the school day, as children engaged in these projects. The teacher had a well-developed knowledge of children's literature, and used trade books to teach reading. She read stories to the children twice daily, and her reading style was interactive: she encouraged discussion during the reading of the stories.

Three literary genres were represented in the study: folk/fairy tales; realistic fiction; and contemporary fantasy. These genres were chosen because they formed part of the series of thematic units the teacher had planned for the year. Decisions about the specific books to be read were made jointly between the teacher and the researcher.

Although response to literature permeated the classroom in creative play, drama, art, writing, and many other ways (Hickman, 1981), the focus of the study was the *talk* before, during, and after storybook readalouds. The study considered this talk in three contexts: (a) in readaloud sessions by the teacher with the whole class, (b) in readalouds done by the researcher with two small groups of five children each, and (c) in one-to-one readalouds done by the researcher with each of the ten children in the two small groups. The small group and one-to-one readalouds were conducted in the hallway immediately outside the classroom. The children were accustomed to using this space for various activities, including individual and small group work.

During the large group readalouds, the researcher sat with the children as the teacher read, making observational field notes. During the small group and one-to-one readalouds, the researcher assumed the role of the reader of the story, closely following the teacher's interactive style. The researcher's stance, therefore, ranged on the continuum of participation-observation (Spradley, 1980). The read-aloud discussions (35 whole-group, 28 small group, and 20 one-to-one) were audiotaped and transcribed by the researcher.

A representative sample of 45 complete transcripts was chosen for intensive analysis. The sample was chosen so that it included data (a) from the beginning, middle, and end of the study, (b) from all three literary genres, and (c) from each of the three contexts (the one-to-one readalouds, small group readalouds, and readalouds to the whole class). The data were analyzed recursively and iteratively, according to the constant comparative method (Glaser & Strauss, 1978; Lincoln & Guba, 1985), by assigning codes and categories and modifying them as the analysis proceeded (Bogdan & Biklen, 1992), proceeding according to the three-stage model of open coding, axial coding, and selective coding described by Strauss and Corbin (1990). The unit of analysis was the conversational turn.

In *open coding*, descriptive codes were formulated from the collection of the first piece of data, and tested against subsequent data. All the data were used in this stage of coding. In *axial coding*, the 45 representative transcripts were intensively analyzed by coding each conversational turn. As well, a manageable number of conceptual categories was developed through combining codes that had similar foci. In *selective coding*, the conceptual categories were used to describe what Strauss and Corbin refer to as the "core category," the overarching construct of the research. In this case, the overarching construct was the children's literary understanding. In this way, a grounded theory (Glaser & Strauss, 1978) of this classroom's construction of literary competence (Culler, 1975) emerged through "data-theory bootstrapping" (Richards & Richards, 1994), as the conceptual categories were modified according to the developing theory. In all, two complete passes were made through the data set, with further passes through parts of the data that seemed especially rich.

Findings and Discussion
Research Question 1: The Children's Construction of Literary Understanding

It was found that the children's responses fell into five conceptual categories. Each conceptual category corresponded to a different type of literary understanding. Thus, the literary understanding of these children had five components or aspects. They were: (a) *the analytical*, (b) *the intertextual*, (c) *the personal*, (d) *the transparent*, and (e) *the performative*.

Category 1, *The Analytical*, comprised responses that seemed to be aimed at dealing with the text as an opportunity to construct narrative meaning. For example, children discussed the media used to produce the illustrations; the structure and meaning of the verbal text; the illustration sequence; the ways in which the verbal text and pictures related to each other; conventional visual semiotic codes; and the traditional elements of narrative (setting, characters, plot, and theme), as well as narrative techniques such as foreshadowing. Also included in this category were responses which dealt with the book as a made object or cultural product, as well as discussion about the relationship between fiction and reality. This category was by far the largest, comprising approximately 73% of the children's conversational turns in the coded data.

A strong example of the children's analytical skills may be seen in their discussion of the structure of *The Napping House* (Wood, 1984), a cumulative tale in which a series of animals and people join a "sleeping granny" on a bed until they are finally awakened in the morning by a flea. The children noticed that "it gets smaller and smaller" because each of the successive characters is smaller than the one before. They also noticed that each page contains "more and more" words, concluding that "The words go from small to big, and the animals go from big to small." The children were making observations about the structure of the entire story. They also noticed that the illustration sequence represents a change in point of view. In the opening illustrations, the viewer seems to be on the same level as the bed. In subsequent illustrations, the viewer seems to be positioned further and further above the bed. As Terry commented, "It's like you're standing on the floor, and then you kind of walk up the wall backwards. Because, first you are looking straight at it, and then you're starting to go up and you're looking down a lot."

The front and back endpages of *The Napping House* also occasioned some analytical discussion. In this book, the front endpages are a shade of dark blue-gray, and the back endpages are light blue. After noticing the difference in the endpages, Sally and Gordon interpreted the change:

Sally: That makes sense, because it's dark when the story starts, so there's a darker endpage, and it's lighter when the story ends. So the endpage is lighter, back there.

Gordon: Yeah, that makes sense! Darker, then lighter. That's different, like most books, the endpages are the same on the front and the back.

A final example of responses in the analytical category is Brad's comment about the flea in *The Napping House*: "The flea is the alarm clock in this story!" When the teacher asked him to say more about his idea, Brad amplified: "Well, the flea wakes 'em all up, they're all sleeping, and the flea's their alarm clock because he wakes 'em up." Brad was making an interpretive comment about the function of one of the story characters.

Within the analytical category, analysis of illustrations (as in Terry's comments on perspective in the example above) was an important part of the children's meaning making. Twenty-three percent of the children's conversational turns in all the coded data concerned this type of *visual* analysis, showing that the children were paying close attention to the visual aspects of the picture storybooks.

Of special note was the interpretive use children made of elements unique to the picturebook format. The peritext (Higonnet, 1990) of the picturebooks (all the visual and textual information *other than* the actual text and illustrations for the story itself) was very important in adding to the children's experience of the picturebook. The children discussed the semiotic significance of the front and back covers, dustjacket, front and back endflaps, endpages, half-title and title pages, dedication pages. The children also developed an understanding of how illustrators portray the illusion of three-dimensional space in a two-dimensional illustration; interpreted the semiotic significance of colors; and interpreted the various conventions for portraying movement in illustrations.

Category 2, *The Intertextual*, indicated that the children were making connections between the text being read aloud and other texts: other books; the work of other artists and illustrators, movies, videos, advertisements, TV programs, or the writing or art of classmates. In this category, the text at hand (the story being read aloud) was linked to other texts with which the children were familiar; thus the text was understood or interpreted in the context of a matrix of related texts. This category comprised approximately 10% of the children's conversational turns in the coded data, indicating their familiarity with a wide range of literature.

For example, during the reading of *The Napping House*, Mickey commented that it reminded him of *The Sweetest Fig* (Van Allsburg, 1993), "because there's a lot of dreaming in that one, too." Mickey was connecting the two stories by their similarity of content. The discussion continued, with an observation that the illustrations in *The Napping House* are gently indistinct or "hazy":

1. Mickey: And *The Sweetest Fig* has kind of hazy illustrations, too.
2. Teacher: Yes, I think it does. Hazy, and indistinct colors.
3. Mickey: But in *The Sweetest Fig*, it's because of the dots.
4. Teacher: Because of the dots?
5. Mickey: Yeah, it's done the same way that French painter, what's his name? Seurat, with lots of little dots, and remember we talked about how it looks sort of hazy?
6. Teacher: Oh yes, pointillism, like in Seurat. Thank you for making that connection, Mickey.

In this vignette (at 1), Mickey makes another intertextual connection between *The Napping House* and *The Sweetest Fig*; not only do they both concern the topic of dreaming, but the illustrations in both books resemble each other in their hazy or indistinct quality. At 3 and 5, having compared the illustrations, Mickey proceeds to contrast them: in *The Sweetest Fig*, the haziness is due to the grainy texture of the illustrations that look like they are composed of "lots of little dots." Mickey then goes on to make a connection to another "visual text," a painting (or paintings) by Seurat, the French pointillist artist. Thus, Mickey has made a series of interesting intertextual connections, not only between the plots and illustrations of *The Napping House* and *The Sweetest Fig*, but also between *The Sweetest Fig* and the art of Seurat.

Intertextual connections seemed to be of pivotal importance for the children, as shown by the many ways in which they used these links:

1. They interpreted personal experiences in the light of intertextual connections.
2. They used intertextual connections to make symbolic interpretations of elements of the text.
3. Intertextual connections assisted children in predicting what might happen in the narrative.
4. Intertextual connections figured largely in the children's creation and modification of schemata for stories.

5. Intertextual connections allowed the children to construct and re-fine their ideas about illustration style.
6. Intertextual connections were utilized to interpret story characters' feelings, motivations, or actions.
7. Children used intertextual connections to position themselves above the dynamics of the narrative; to stand outside and above, as it were, in order to take on new interpretive perspectives in relation to the story.
8. Lastly, intertextual connections tended to beget other intertextual connections. The process gathered momentum like a rolling snow-ball, until a critical mass was reached that enabled the children to achieve a higher level of interpretive understanding or predictive power.

In this study, children's ability to make these intertextual links was likely facilitated by the reading of many versions of some traditional tales. For example, many versions of the Cinderella tale (traditional European; Chinese; African; modern gender-reversed variants, and others) formed a rich interpretive context upon which the children could draw when experiencing a new version. As cognitive flexibility theory (Spiro, Coulson, Feltovich, & Anderson, 1994) suggests, the children were able to build up their knowledge across a number of cases.

Responses in Category 3, *The Personal,* suggested that the children were connecting the text being read aloud to events and situations in their own lives. As in the work of Cochran-Smith (1984), there were two types of personalizing responses. A life-to-text connection was one in which the children utilized some experience from their own lives to understand or illuminate the text being read aloud. A text-to-life connection was one in which the children used the text in order to understand or illuminate something in their own lives. The responses in this category were thus essentially personal in nature, and the text seemed to act as a stimulus for a personal connection. This category comprised approximately 10% of the children's conversational turns in the coded data.

For example, during the reading of *Owl Moon* (Yolen, 1987), Jane Yolen's poetic story of a girl who goes out at night with her father to search for owls, the children made many personal connections to times they had been out at night or in the forest:

Bill: It reminds me when I was four years old, and I went camping.
Alice: When I went camping, I was closer to the woods.
Sally: I remembered at Christmas time, when we were out driving around looking at the lights.

Thus, the children were personalizing and interpreting the story by connecting it to similar occasions in their own lives. These types of connections were text-to-life connections.

The children also made life-to-text connections by using stories to interpret experiences in their own lives. For example, Peggy observed that she had gone on a walk while camping, and entered a "moon-filled tunnel" that was full of graffiti and beer cans; she wished it were as clean and unspoiled as the forest in *Owl Moon*. Thus, Peggy was remembering an experience in her life and using the literary text of *Owl Moon* to reflect on its meaning.

In Category 4, *The Transparent*, the responses indicated that the children had momentarily become so engaged with the story that they had "entered" it and become part of its "secondary world" (Benton, 1992). The word "transparent" is used to describe this category because the responses indicated that the world of the story and the children's world became transparent to one another. Talking directly to the story characters or "talking back to the story" was taken to be an indication of this transparency. Verbal responses in this category were rare, providing only evanescent traces of what was possibly happening as the children had a "lived-through" experience (Rosenblatt, 1978) of the story. This category comprised approximately only 2% of the children's conversational turns in the coded data, possibly because the children's *silence* was the strongest indicator of the lived-through experience.

An example of a verbal response in the transparent category was Rose's comment during the reading of *Owl Moon*. Seeing the illustration of the owl flying, she said very quietly and happily, "Here she comes! Here she comes!" If the researcher had not been seated next to Rose, he would not have heard her; she did not seem to be speaking to the group, but simply thinking aloud, and having a lived-through experience of the owl's flight.

Category 5, *The Performative*, comprised responses which suggested that the children were manipulating the text in order to use it for their creative purposes. In Category 4, the children were, so to speak, manipulated by the text; in Category 5, responses suggested that the text was being manipulated by the children. The text seemed to function as a launching pad for the children's own creativity or imagination; or the text became a playground for a carnivalesque romp (Bakhtin, 1984). The children took some situation or event in the story and used it as the basis for a flight of their own imagination, a type of playful performance or "signifying" (Gates, 1988). This category comprised approximately 5% of the children's conversational turns in the coded data.

An example of performative response occurred at the beginning of the reading of *Piggybook* (Browne, 1986), when the teacher showed the children the book's front cover, with its illustration of a woman carrying a man and two boys on her back. Krissy responded:

"Give me a piggy ride," said the big brother. "Give me a piggy ride," said the little one. "and me a piggy ride," said the dad. "Give me a piggy ride," said everybody. And mom carried dad and mom carried the brothers, I mean the little, the two childs.

In making this comment, Krissy was less interested in interpreting the possible significance of the front cover illustration than in using it as a platform or catalyst for the expression of her *own* creativity. She was, in fact, using the illustration to make up her own story. The story constituted a little performance.

Performative responses could include elements of the carnivalesque (Bakhtin, 1984) and the subversive, as in the following vignette from the reading of *The Stinky Cheese Man* (Scieszka, 1992). The teacher was reading the text on the front endflaps:

1. Teacher [reading]: Only $16.99! 56 action-packed pages. 75% more than those old 32-page "Brand-X" books. 10 complete stories! 25 lavish paintings! New! Improved! Funny! Good! Buy! Now!

2. Terry: I don't wanna go "bye" now. I don't wanna go bye-bye now!

3. Gordon: Me neither!

4. Several children: Bye-bye! Bye-bye!

5. Terry: I don't want to go to the bathroom and be the stinky cheese man!

Terry's performative response to the frenetic style of the endflap text is to use it (at 1) to make a pun ("bye" for "buy"). At 3 and 4, Gordon and several other children join in this amusing performance, but Terry tops them all at 5, with his subversive bathroom humor. This playfulness is reminiscent of some deconstructive criticism (Derrida, 1989), where the text is considered a collection of signifiers that can be manipulated to produce an infinite number of interpretations, including the display of wit (Hartman, 1975).

To summarize: these five categories describe what literary understanding meant for this group of children as suggested by their verbal responses: what they (and their teacher) had constructed as the appropriate ways of responding to and interpreting stories. The children:

1. Engaged in textual analysis.

2. Connected the text with other texts and cultural products.

3. Linked their own lives to events, situations, and characters in the text.

4. Engaged in a "lived-through" experience of the story, merging the world of the story with their own world.

5. Playfully (and sometimes subversively) manipulated the text for their own creative purposes.

Research Question 2: The Scaffolding Functions of Adults

It was found that the talk of the teacher and the researcher represented five different scaffolding functions. In other words, the adults assisted the children's developing literary understanding in five different ways. They acted as (a) *readers* of the text, *(b) managers and encouragers*, (c) *clarifiers and probers*, (d) *fellow wonderers and speculators*, and (e) *extenders and refiners*.

As *Readers* of the text, the adults read the text of the story as well as the publishing information, book jacket flaps, and other printed text. They acted as tour guides for the book, pointing out noteworthy features such as the endpages or the dedication page: "And here are the endpages." "Here's the title page." Approximately 28% of the adults' conversational turns were classified in this category. There were several aspects of the scaffolding function present in this type of adult talk. By focusing the children's attention on a selected aspect of the book, adults were indicating its importance. As readers, adults interpreted and mediated the text for the children; what the children were responding to was not the text itself, but rather the teacher's interpretation of the text. By dividing the story into segments as they read, adults were also scaffolding the experience by presenting it in manageable and coherent parts.

Adults functioned as *Managers and Encouragers*, controlling the discussion during the readaloud by calling on children, asking them to wait, dealing with disturbances, or directing their attention to an aspect of the story or to another child's comments. They praised the children and echoed what the children said as a way of encouraging further response. For example, when *The Napping House* (Wood, 1984) was read to the whole group, the teacher followed her custom of showing the front and back covers so that the children could comment on whether they constituted one continuous cover, or if the front and back covers were separately designed. In the case of *The Napping House*, there is not one continuous illustration. The following is the beginning of this readaloud:

1. Teacher: I'm going to wait until every single person is ready.
2. Teacher: [showing front cover and reading] *The Napping House*. By Audrey Wood. Illustrated by Don Wood.
3. Charles: Shhh! Shhh!
4. Teacher: Yes, shhh! [shows front and back covers together]
5. Unidentified child: It's not a double spread.
6. Sean: It's a split cover.
7. Teacher: That would be a neat term for it, Sean, a split cover. If it were a double page spread, the illustration would continue on the back.
8. Unidentified child: I have this story at home.
9. Teacher: Do you?

The teacher's comments at 1, 4, 7, and 9 are examples of the mangaging/ encouraging function. She asks for attention (at 1); validates children's comments by repeating them (at 4) or responding with the polite interrogative "Do you?" (at 9); and praises a child for coming up with an interesting name ("split cover") for a book in which the front and back covers do not constitute a continuous illustration (at 9).

This category comprised about 36% of the adult conversational turns. The scaffolding function represented by this type of adult talk was two-fold. First, adults created an atmosphere of responsiveness and acceptance that supported the children's risk-taking. Second, adults modeled the ways in which a discussion can proceed productively.

As *Clarifiers and Probers*, adults linked children's remarks to each other and pointed out how a comment may have supported, amplified, extended, or contradicted what had been previously said. They asked children to explain what they meant or to provide further information. They asked clarifying and probing questions, questions for which they probably already knew the answer, or general questions such as "What do you think might happen?" For example, during the reading of *The Napping House*, the teacher showed the illustration of the "sleeping granny" on the third opening of the book. The illustration prompted Charles' comment, "She looks like she's having a baby." The teacher responded, "A little chubby, isn't she?" In this exchange, the teacher was *clarifying* Charles' comment by supplying the reason for his interpretation; in the illustration, the granny's stomach is comically swelled up. The readaloud of *The Napping House* also provoked some personal connections from Kenny about his experiences of taking naps during preschool day care. The teacher asked the *probing* question, "When did you use to go to daycare?" in order to find out more about his experiences. About 28% of the adult conversational turns were classified in this category. The scaffolding function of this type of adult talk was to supply the concepts and logical reasoning that might not be supplied by the children, and to develop the children's reasoning by probing questions.

When they acted as *Fellow Wonderers or Speculators*, adults situated themselves as members of the interpretive community in a non-authoritative way. They expressed puzzlement or confusion, or they offered their own personal associations. During the reading of *Owl Moon* (Yolen, 1987), for example, the children observed that the story takes place at night, yet it seems quite light outside, due to the reflection of the moon on the snow. The teacher agreed that it looked like daylight, commenting, "When I go out at night sometimes, like at midnight, when the moon is high, I can see just like it was daylight." This category comprised about 3% of the adult conversational turns. The scaffolding function represented by this category of adult talk is the stance of allowing the children to function more independently and simply entering the conversation as another listener and responder. The relatively small percentage of conversational turns in this category is not surprising, since the adults' *silence* also contributed to the children's independence. In other words, they frequently allowed the children to talk rather than sharing their own opinions, personal connections, or observations.

The fifth way in which adults scaffolded the children's literary understanding was by acting as *Extenders and Refiners* of the children's responses. Adults listened to the children's conversation with an analytical ear, identifying possible "teachable moments" (Eeds & Wells, 1989). They used the children's ideas as opportunities to introduce new literary terms or to amplify on what the children said so as to make higher-level generalizations. In this category, adults also summarized groups of responses so as to achieve closure. About 5% of the adult conversational turns were classified in this category. The scaffolding function of this type of adult talk is the teaching of new information and concepts in the context of the continuing conversation about the story. Over the course of the study, new elements (like the concept of foreshadowing) were added to the children's "literary tool kit" in this manner.

For example, during the discussion of how bright the forest seemed in *Owl Moon*, the teacher took the opportunity to explain, "It does look very light, because any light that's coming from the night sky reflects off the light snow. If it were black ground, it would soak up any light, but the white reflects light, and it makes the whole outside seem brighter at night."

Notably *absent* in the data were teacher questions on the literal level, such as "What color was Grace's Peter Pan costume?" or "Who told Grace that she couldn't be Peter Pan because she was black?" Questions were not aimed at testing the children's comprehension of stories, but rather at enabling them to interpret the story to relate it to their own lives, to make links with other texts, or to encourage further thought about the illustrations or the verbal text of the story.

The findings in this study about the various roles played by the teacher during storybook readalouds relate most directly to the work of McGee and her colleagues (McGee, Courtney, & Lomax, 1994), who studied the role of teachers in literature discussions with first grade children. McGee found that teachers played several roles, including that of "facilitator" (by managing turn-taking, for example); "helper/nudger" (by summarizing, restating or asking for clarification); "responder" (by introducing, expanding, or elaborating topics); "literary curator" (by extending literary understandings during "teachable moments"); and "reader" (by reading the story). It is clear that these roles are quite similar to the findings in this study. McGee's "facilitator" role is similar to the role of *manager and encourager*, her "reader" compares to the role of *reader* in this study; her "literary curator" role is similar to the

extender/refiner role; and her "helper/nudger" and "responder" roles correspond to the *clarifier/prober.* The studies therefore support each other to a
great extent on their interpretations of the roles that adults play in talking
about literature with young children.

The adult teachers thus played a very active role in scaffolding and enabling the children's developing literary understanding. This study therefore
provides support to social constructivist theory (Vygotsky, 1978, 1986; Berk
& Winslor, 1995; Tharp & Gallimore, 1988; Wood, 1989) in its assertion that
the scaffolding of "expert others" is critical in enabling children's learning. It
also supports the call for both active students and active teachers (Cazden,
1992; Clay, 1991).

Pedagogical Implications

In this study, two-thirds of the children's conversational turns took place
during the reading of the story; one-third of the turns took place after the
story had been read. This suggests that allowing children to talk during the
readaloud may result in a richer socially constructed meaning for the story,
and a wider range of responses. In the case of young children, asking them
to hold their response until the story is finished may simply result in the
suppression of the response. The storybook readaloud situation was an
important site for the formation of a literary "interpretive community" (Fish,
1980) in the classroom. Teachers may want to reflect on how their own
storybook readaloud practices, rules, and routines assist in the formation of
an interpretive community in their own classrooms.

In most literature circles, literature discussion groups, and classroom book
clubs (Daniels, 1994; McMahon & Raphael, 1997), the discussion takes place
only after the story is read. Storybook readalouds offer the possibility of scaffolding the children's meaning construction as it is in the process of being
constructed. Just as physical scaffolds are of most use when buildings are
being built, the scaffolding provided by the teacher is perhaps most powerful when the children are in the midst of the literary experience.

The typology of children's responses suggests that there are at least five
aspects to children's literary understanding. Teachers can consider how they
may increase their students' repertoires to include a greater portion of this
spectrum. The richness and depth of literary discussion may be determined
by the variety of stances the children assume; the variety of actions they take
in relation to literary texts; and the range of literary functions texts may have
for them. For example, when children make *analytical* responses, they are
situating themselves so that they interpret from within the boundaries of the
text. They are taking the action of analyzing; and the text functions as an
object for "close reading." When children make *intertextual* responses, they

are situating themselves across texts, so as to perform the action of linking or relating texts with other texts; thus, the text functions as an element in the contextual matrix. When children make *personal* responses, they are drawing the text to themselves and drawing themselves to the text, so as to perform the action of personalizing; and the text functions as the stimulus for their personalizing connections. When children make *transparent* responses, they are situating themselves so that the story world and their world are transparent to each other; thus the action they perform is to merge with the text, and the text functions (momentarily) as their identity. When children make *performative* responses, they are situating themselves, as it were, on texts, using them as platforms from which they enact performances.

The importance of the peritextual features of picturebooks, as well as the illustration sequence, should not be underestimated. In order to understand the potential for meaning-making offered by these aspects of picturebooks, teachers may need to refine and extend their own understanding of art, illustration, and picturebook theory. By according illustrations equal importance with the text, teachers can encourage a richer diversity of interpretation, and facilitate children's ability to integrate visual and verbal information.

Because intertextual connections were found to be pivotal in many interpretive moves, teachers can encourage children to make these connections by (1) reading many variants of one story; and (2) directly asking, "What other stories does this story remind you of?"

The study identified five ways in which teachers scaffolded children's literary understanding. Teachers may reflect on their own scaffolding roles, and ask how their own comments and questions may assist children in achieving higher levels of literary understanding. Teachers should be aware of the potential of "teachable moments" in order to extend and refine children's understanding.

Implications for Further Research

Research is needed that makes clear the connections between literary understanding and the broader cognitive processes involved in learning to read and write, and that places the literary understanding of young children in the wider context of emergent literacy learning. We know that narrative literature is highly motivating for children; but what other qualities make literature a powerful tool in learning to read?

The connection between literature and children's writing seems to be very powerful. As we expand our view of what constitutes literary understanding beyond the traditional "elements of narrative," this broader view may reveal more connections between literary understanding and writing ability. How, for example, would a child's aptitude for performative response impact on the ability to write forcefully and with strong rhetorical purpose? Of what use are intertextual connections in learning to present a cohesive argument? How might the development of the personal response assist children in generating written text that "speaks" to its readers?

Longitudinal studies of the developing literary understanding of the same children over two or more years would be extremely useful. Researchers could investigate how new elements are added to the children's "literary tool kit" and utilized in increasingly complex ways.

The five types of literary understanding represented by the five conceptual categories of children's responses in this study need to be tested across many cases in order to validate, extend, and refine them. What modifications or refinements are necessary in order to characterize the literary responses of older children? How would the use of other literary genres or formats affect the formulation of conceptual categories for children's responses? Is there evidence for the importance of intertextual connections in other classroom contexts?

The integration of visual and verbal sign systems is one of the most salient characteristics of picturebooks. Thus, children's learning of illustration codes and conventions deserves more attention by researchers.

Conclusion

This study shows that children in first and second grade can be sophisticated literary critics, displaying a wide range of interpretive strategies, forging connections to their own lives, and responding to stories in aesthetically creative ways. These children's developing literary understanding blurred the sharp distinctions between their world and the world of stories, making it possible for literature to be both an informing and transforming experience for them. Thus, understanding stories and how they work may help children to understand and give meaning to their lives.

References

Baker, C. D., & Freebody, P. (1989). *Children's first school books*. Oxford: Basil Blackwell, Inc.

Bakhtin, M. M. (1984). *Rabelais and his world* (H. Iswolsky, Trans.). Cambridge, MA: MIT Press.

Benton, M. (1992). *Secondary worlds: Literature teaching and the visual arts*. Buckingham, UK: Open University Press.

Berk, L., & Winsler, A. (1995). *Scaffolding children's learning: Vygotsky and early childhood education*. Washington, DC: National Association for the Education of Young Children.

Bogdan, R. C., & Biklen, S. K. (1992). *Qualitative research for education: An introduction to theory and methods.* Boston: Allyn and Bacon.

Brown, M., & Precious, N. (1968). *The integrated day in the primary school.* London: Ward Lock.

Browne, A. (1986). *Piggybook.* New York: Alfred A. Knopf.

Cazden, C. (1992). *Whole language plus: Essays on literacy in the United States and New Zealand.* New York: Teachers College Press.

Clay, M. M. (1991). *Becoming literate: The construction of inner control.* Portsmouth, NH: Heinemann.

Cochran-Smith, M. (1984). *The making of a reader.* Norwood, NJ: Ablex.

Cox, C., & Many, J. (1992). Toward an understanding of the aesthetic response to literature. *Language Arts, 69,* 28-33.

Crago, H., & Crago, M. (1983). *Prelude to literacy: A preschool child's encounter with picture and story.* Carbondale: Southern Illinois University Press.

Culler, J. (1975). *Structuralist poetics: Structuralism, linguistics, and the study of literature.* Ithaca: Cornell University Press.

Daniels, H. (1994). *Literature circles: Voice and choice in the student-centered classroom.* York, ME: Stenhouse.

Derrida, J. (1989). Structure, sign, and play in the discourse of the human sciences. In D. H. Richter (Ed.), *The critical tradition: Classic texts and contemporary trends* (pp. 959-971). New York: St. Martin's Press.

Dickinson, D. K., & Smith, M. W. (1994). Long-term effects of preschool teachers' book readings on low-income children's vocabulary and story comprehension. *Reading Research Quarterly, 29,* 105-122.

Eeds, M., & Wells, D. (1989). Grand conversations: An exploration of meaning construction in literature study groups. *Research in the Teaching of English, 23,* 4-29.

Fish, S. (1980). *Is there a text in this class? The power of interpretive communities.* Cambridge, MA: Harvard University Press.

Galda, L. (1982). Assuming the spectator stance: An examination of the responses of three young readers. *Research in the Teaching of English, 16,* 1-20.

Gates, H. L. (1988). *The signifying monkey: A theory of African-American literacy criticism.* New York: Oxford University Press.

Gergen, K. J. (1985). The social constructivist movement in modern psychology. *American Psychologist, 40,* 266-275.

Glaser, B., & Strauss, A. (1978). *The discovery of grounded theory.* Chicago: Aldine.

Gumperz, J. J. (1986). Interactional sociolinguistics in the study of schooling. In J. Cook-Gumperz (Ed.), *The social construction of literacy* (pp. 45-68). London: Cambridge University Press.

Hartman, G. (1975). *The fate of reading and other essays.* Chicago: University of Chicago Press.

Hickman, J. (1981). A new perspective on response to literature: Research in an elementary school setting. *Research in the Teaching of English, 15,* 343-354.

Higonnet, M. (1990). The playground of the peritext. *Children's Literature Association Quarterly, 15,* 47-49.

Holdaway, D. (1979). *The foundations of literacy.* Sydney: Ashton Scholastic.

Lincoln, Y. S., & Guba, E. G. (1985). *Naturalistic inquiry.* Beverly Hills, CA: Sage.

MacKenzie, M., & Kernig, W. (1975). The challenge in formal education: Extending young children's learning in the open classroom. London: Darton, Longman, and Todd.

McMahon, S., & Raphael, T. (Eds.) (1997). *The book club connection: Literacy learning and classroom talk.* New York: International Reading Association and Teacher College Press.

McGee, L. (1992). An exploration of meaning construction in first graders' grand conversations. In D. Leu & C. Kinzer (Eds.), *Literacy research, theory, and practice: Views from many perspectives* (pp. 177-186). Chicago, IL: National Reading Conference.

McGee, L., Courtney, L., & Lomax, R. (1994). Supporting first graders' responses to literature: An analysis of teachers' roles in grand conversations. In C. K. Kinzer & D. J. Leu (Eds.), *Multidimensional aspects of literacy research, theory, and practice* (pp. 517-526). Chicago, IL: National Reading Conference.

McMahon, S. I., & Raphael, T. E. (1997). *The book club connection: Literacy learning and classroom talk.* Newark, DE & New York: International Reading Association and Teachers College Press.

Meyer, B., & Rice, G. E. (1984). The structure of text. In P. D. Pearson (Ed.), *Handbook of reading research, Vol 1* (pp. 319-351). New York: Longman.

Morrow, L. M. (1989). Literacy development in the early years: Helping children read and write. Englewood Cliffs, NJ: Prentice Hall.

Patton, M. Q. (1990). *Qualitative evaluation and research methods* (2nd ed.). Newbury Park, CA: Sage.

Richards, T. J., & Richards, L. (1994). Using computers in qualitative research. In N. K. Denzin & Y.S. Lincoln (Eds.), *Handbook of qualitative research* (pp. 445-462). Thousand Oaks, CA: Sage.

Rosenblatt, L. M. (1978). *The reader, the text, the poem: The transactional theory of the literary work.* Carbondale: Southern Illinois University Press.

Schwandt, T. A. (1994). Constructivist, interpretivist approaches to human inquiry. In N. K. Denzin & Y. S. Lincoln (Eds.), *Handbook of qualitative research* (pp. 118-137). Thousand Oaks, CA: Sage.

Scieszka, J. (1992). *The Stinky Cheese Man and other fairly stupid tales.* New York: Penguin.

Short, K., & Pierce, K. (Eds.). (1990). *Talking about books: Creating literate communities.* Portsmouth, NH: Heinemann.

Sipe, L. R. (1996). *The construction of literary understanding by first and second graders in response to picture storybook readalouds.* Unpublished doctoral dissertation, The Ohio State University, Columbus, OH. UMI #9710658.

Spiro, R. J., Coulson, R. L., Feltovich, P. J., & Anderson, D. K. (1994). Cognitive flexibility theory: Advanced knowledge acquisition in ill-structured domains. In R. B. Ruddell, M. R. Ruddell, & H. Singer (Eds.), *Theoretical models and processes of reading* (4th ed.) (pp. 602-615). Newark, DE: International Reading Association.

Spradley, J. P. (1980). *Participant observation.* New York: Holt, Rinehart & Winston.

Strauss, A., & Corbin, J. (1990). *Basics of qualitative research: Grounded theory procedures and techniques.* Newbury Park, CA: Sage.

Sulzby, E., & Teale, W. (1991). *Emergent literacy.* In R. Barr, M. Kamil, P. Mosenthal, & P. D. Pearson (Eds.), *Handbook of reading research, Vol. II* (pp. 727-757). New York: Longman.

Tharp, R. G., & Gallimore, G. (1988). *Rousing minds to life: Teaching, learning, and schooling in social context.* Cambridge: Cambridge University Press.

Van Allsburg, C. (1993). *The sweetest fig.* Boston: Houghton Mifflin.

Vygotsky, L. S. (1978). *Mind in society: The development of higher psychological processes.* Cambridge, MA: Harvard University Press.

Vygotsky, L. S. (1986). *Thought and language.* Cambridge, MA: The MIT Press.

Wertsch, J. V. (1985). *Vygotsky and the social formation of mind*. Cambridge, MA: Harvard University Press.

Wiseman, D. L., Many, J. E., & Altieri, J. (1992). Enabling complex aesthetic response: An examination of three literary discussion approaches. In C. K. Kinzer & D. J. Leu (Eds.), *Literacy research, theory, and practice: Views from many perspectives* (pp. 283-289). Chicago, IL: National Reading Conference.

Wolf, S. A., & Heath, S. B. (1992). *The braid of literature: Children's worlds of reading*. Cambridge, MA: Harvard University Press.

Wood, A. (1984). *The napping house*. San Diego: Harcourt Brace.

Wood, D. (1989). Social interaction as tutoring. In M. H. Bornstein & J. S. Bruner (Eds.), *Interaction in human development* (pp. 59-80). Hillsdale, NJ: Lawrence Erlbaum Associates.

Yolen, J. (1987). *Owl moon*. New York: Philomel.

Zarillo, J., & Cox, C. (1992). Efferent and aesthetic teaching. In J. Many & C. Cox (Eds.), *Reader stance and literary understanding* (pp. 235-249). Norwood, NJ: Ablex.

The Enhancement of Literacy Development in an Adult Beginning Reader Through Creating Texts to Accompany Wordless Books

Thesis Award

Melissa L. Brock

Vanderbilt University
Thesis Award 1997

Abstract

This study explored the growth of an adult beginning reader's literacy development during participation in a program designed to build upon her oral language habits. A descriptive case study is presented to discuss the benefits of focusing on adult students' strengths as language users as opposed to the difficulties they experience. Specifically, this study investigated the effects of this instructional activity on a reader's developing fluency in oral reading as well as the opportunities the participant was given to obtain ownership of her literacy through decision making and risk taking. In addition, this study explored alternative ways of learning about the literacy development of an adult beginning reader before instruction begins.

Powerful metaphors are used to describe the "problem" of adult illiteracy. The person who cannot read is often viewed as a "victim," a "societal burden" or as "sick." The condition is described as a "tragic epidemic" or a "disease." Illness and a lack of capital in the banking system are used as extended metaphors to describe the problem, and military terminology refers to it as a "national enemy" (Isley & Stahl, 1993, p. 22). This "dramatic, emotion-laden language" conveys "a sense of urgency" and the need to "advance an agenda" (Isley & Stahl, 1993, p. 25) by the educational, social, political and corporate arenas.

The real problem is that the use of these medical, military and banking metaphors—even while directing attention to the problem—builds a reliance on "a belief in systems, techniques, and professional expertise—not in the mission, the purpose, or the human processes of learning" (Isley & Stahl, 1993, p. 25). Assumptions that adults who cannot read are ill or are suffering victims promote inaccurate generalizations which "provide a disservice to society because such statements keep us from identifying the real issues" (Richardson, 1993, p. 31). These obstructions block the exploration of such important issues as what criteria adults are seeking in their literacy instruction and what factors adults perceive as facilitating or impeding their progress. Consequently, "renewed efforts to improve adult literacy have not brought the dramatic gains that have been hoped for by policy makers and the public" (Wagner, 1993, p. 10).

Some adult literacy programs, such as the 100,000 Level Program of the 1960s and the Project Literacy of the United States (PLUS) of the mid-1980s, have sought drastic reading improvement in many adult students within a short period of time (Richardson, 1993). Such "quick fix" (p. 29) programs often recruited instructors/tutors who had little knowledge about methods of reading instruction or the processes of adult learning. Although these result-oriented plans were fueled by the best of intentions, they ignored the reality that learning to read is a gradual process, particularly for individuals who bring years of frustration and difficulty to that process. Wagner (1993) points out that National Educational Goal #5 perpetuates the "quick fix" philosophy in claiming that illiteracy in America will be eradicated by the year 2000. Such a goal implies that illiteracy can be cured, much like a disease. Once we, as a nation, pinpoint the skills in which these adults are *deficient*, we can teach them the necessary skills to make them *proficient*. Then, illiteracy will be eliminated as a "problem" in our country.

Of course, the creators of this goal probably did not mean to imply such simplistic ideas; however, a "deficient view" of adult beginning readers does not promote a view of learning as a process or recognize the wealth of knowledge already acquired by these learners. Richardson (1993) asserts that this "deficit view" is not restricted to the adult beginning readers' low performance in reading, but instead extends to the view of the whole person; it denies that "many adult beginning readers are very successful personally, socially and economically. The only deficit they have is a lack of literacy" (Richardson, 1993, p. 31).

Focusing on the weaknesses and perceived failure of adult beginning readers can lead to the dangerous misconception that these adults have nothing to offer to their own learning. Thus, the life experiences and strengths of the students are omitted from the learning process. Norton and Moore (1993) state that "literacy programs are generally organized around the acquisition of skills, which often equate decoding with reading" (p. 232). In such programs, meaning is presented as the icing on the cake rather than as one of the ingredients that goes into making the cake. Thus, a need exists for more adult literacy programs and activities which focus on the construction of meaning and depend upon the thoughts and experiences of the students.

The pursuit of an instructional activity for adult beginning readers that emphasizes the process of meaningful learning and invites the use of prior knowledge to generate text serves as the purpose of this investigation. During this study, the use of wordless books as a mechanism for providing meaningful learning experiences to adult beginning readers was explored. Specifically, the focus of the study was the growth of an adult's literacy development during participation in a reading program which not only utilizes, but builds upon her oral language habits and personal experiences. In order to establish a basis of support for this study, two specific bodies of literature were reviewed: literature related to adult literacy activities which focus on meaning and literature related to the use of wordless books for developing literacy. A review of these two areas is followed by a summary of their implications.

Meaningful Learning for Adult Beginning Readers

"Most reading materials published for adult basic education (ABE) students are bits and pieces selected to teach specific reading skills such as finding the main idea, recognizing details and understanding inference" (Schierloh, 1992, p. 137) rather than on complete selections. Picture books are seldom selected as "instructional fare for adult learners" (Norton & Moore, 1993, p. 233) due to the fact that they often are not viewed as age appropriate. Yet the strong pictorial elements of such books "provide ready clues for understanding to all learners" (Norton & Moore, p. 234) not just to children. Danielson (1992) states that picture books can enhance visual literacy and critical thinking, develop vocabulary and give opportunities for integrating reading and writing. The variety exhibited in the genre of picture books renders them adaptable to the needs of different adult learners.

Variety in instructional activities is imperative if the possibility of drudgery or student failure is to be avoided. Many students in adult basic education programs have found that they are forced "to run someone else's ideas in someone else's language through their own heads" (Stasz, Schwartz & Weeden, 1991, p. 31). In an effort to provide students with more meaningful learning, several studies have focused on giving students a chance to conduct their learning in their own language (Stasz et al, 1991; Garfield, 1993; Purcell-Gates, 1993; Rhoder & French, 1995). Rhoder and French (1995) identify a main purpose in using participant generated text with adult beginning readers: "Reading and writing about topics that they have chosen, that they care about, puts them on another level of literacy. They can *perceive themselves* as literate" (p. 115).

Wordless Books as a Means of Instruction

The merit of using wordless books to facilitate the beginning reading process of young children, linguistically and culturally different students, and middle and secondary students (Ellis & Preston, 1984; Lindauer, 1988; Flatley & Rutland, 1986; McGee & Tompkins, 1983; Read & Smith, 1982) applies to adult beginning readers. We live in a visually oriented and dominated culture (McGee & Tompkins, 1983; Read & Smith, 1982). Turbayne's (1970, p. 19) comment (as cited in Read & Smith, 1982) emphasizes the universality of symbols: "The visual world is a script we all have to learn to read." Carrying this point further, Read and Smith define "visual literacy" as "the comprehension of visual stimuli in the environment" (p. 929). The process of becoming visually "literate" involves using "line, shape, and color to interpret actions, recognize objects and understand the message of symbols" (p. 929). The skills necessary to make use of such visual clues are similar to reading skills. Hence, skills which can be taught through the use of wordless books include sequencing, noting details, determining main ideas, making inferences and judgments, noting cause and effect relationships, drawing and predicting conclusions, developing a sense of story and sharpening observation skills and visual discrimination (Read & Smith, 1982; Lindauer, 1988). On an even deeper level, beginning readers can use wordless books to practice discovering literal and inferential messages, evaluating a character's actions, and understanding relationships between concepts (Ellis & Preston, 1984).

Summary

Researchers support the value of more holistic approaches to literacy instruction for adult beginning readers, as well as the advantages of using wordless picture books in the development of literacy. However, applications of methods to use wordless picture books with adult beginning readers are absent from the literature. In reference to middle and secondary students, McGee and Tompkins (1983) assert that older readers "who have experienced repeated failure in reading also may respond more favorably to nontraditional reading materials (McWilliams & Smith, 1981)" (p. 121). Rather than focusing on the letters and sounds which have always been problematic for adult beginning readers, wordless books offer the opportunity for adults to create their own stories. While composing their own texts, adults are able to practice the reading skills that are, as research shows, evident in wordless books. They are able to move beyond the arduous task of decoding toward the ultimate goal of constructing meaning.

Purpose

The purpose of this investigation was to explore the literacy development of an adult beginning reader as she engaged in composing and reading her own text to accompany a wordless book. The underlying theory for writing this study was that holistic approaches and generative learning activities grounded in one's experiences can lead to a meaningful development of literacy in adult beginning readers. Case study methodology was chosen to provide an indepth analysis of an adult's participation in such instruction.

As a means of supporting the general focus of the study, the following guiding questions were developed: (a) What can be learned about the literacy development of an adult beginning reader before instruction begins? (b) How will this approach to literacy development influence a reader's developing fluency in oral reading? (c) How will this approach lend itself to opportunities for the participant to obtain ownership of her literacy, specifically what opportunities for decision making and risk taking will arise?

Methodology

Qualitative methods based upon case study research methodology were chosen as the most appropriate for this study which focused on the process of emergent reading and writing in an adult. Although a set of questions guided the course of the research, quantified answers were not the main concern. Instead, the primary focus was the evolving process of literacy the participant experienced as she immersed herself in creating text to accompany a wordless picture book. The role of the primary researcher was to explore the participant's initial literacy strengths which could be built upon throughout the study, to facilitate the emergent reading and writing processes, and when necessary, to make decisions which guided instruction. Yin (1989) explains that the topics of "decisions" and "processes" are among the major foci of case studies. Data was collected throughout the study to illuminate the processes of this approach and the decisions which followed.

The Participant and Setting

The participant was drawn from a group of parents who participated in the parent workshop program at the elementary school which served as the setting for this study. The participant, who is referred to as Mary throughout this report, is the mother of three children, ages 15, 12 and 8. She completed the eleventh grade and then dropped out of school to become the primary care-giver for her mother who had suffered paralysis after a stroke. Mary had not been involved in any other literacy programs in the interim between her last year of completed schooling and the beginning of this project. However, she had tried twice to enter a GED program, but had received no response from the persons she attempted to contact.

This investigation took place in a public elementary school in the Southeastern United States. The school, identified as a Title I school, is located in a low-income, inner city neighborhood and serves primarily economically-disadvantaged students.

Data Collection Techniques and Recording

Data were collected through a variety of sources. During the initial assessment, Mary's previous literacy experiences were revealed through her responses to a series of interview questions. This interview was audiotaped and later transcribed. Her reading of a short 32-word book was also audiotaped in order to document her reading accuracy as well as other reading behaviors. In addition, Mary's storytellings of wordless books were audiotaped and coded as a means of analyzing her ability to describe main ideas, provide supporting details, make inferences, summarize and reason while telling a story. The storytelling discussed in this study was read and coded by an independent rater. Interrater reliability between the primary researcher and the independent rater was 90% agreement. During instruction, approximately 75% of the instructional sessions were audiotaped and transcribed. Running records were taken throughout the study while Mary read aloud the text she had created. These running records were used to calculate her reading accuracy and to analyze the reading behaviors she employed. Structured and spontaneous interviews were conducted frequently throughout the course of instruction. Complete transcriptions of instructional sessions were coded and analyzed to evaluate how Mary's language reflected her risk-taking behaviors as a literacy learner and her sense of ownership in the learning process. In addition, field notes were written during instructional sessions and then expanded upon after each session in order to provide a thicker description of what occurred.

Data Analysis Techniques

The constant comparison method (Glasser & Strauss, 1967; Lincoln & Guba, 1985) was used as a framework for analyzing data. This method was appropriate for the open-ended exploratory nature of the study and allowed data to be analyzed without an a priori design. The method was employed early in the study, when data collection began. Thus, the identified and analyzed patterns within the data guided and facilitated the emergent design of the study. Three of the data collection techniques used—the transcriptions of storytellings of wordless books, oral readings, and transcriptions of instructional sessions—were subjected to specific coding systems in order to organize and interpret the data in a meaningful way. These coding systems are defined more explicitly in the discussion section of this paper.

Procedure Followed: Using Wordless Books as Teaching Tools

Instruction occurred in three phases. The first phase, *organization and preparation for writing,* began after the initial assessment was completed. Mary was provided with four wordless books that contained clear, sequential story-lines. She perused the books and *selected* the wordless book *Carl* by Alexandra Day. After making her selection, she *previewed* the book and *brainstormed* ideas. During the brainstorming process, Mary and I (as the primary researcher) discussed answers to such questions as "What is this book about?", "Who are the main characters in the story?", "What happens?". We later progressed to a more inferential level through the discussion of "Why" and "How" questions. Mary *generated a list of key words* that might appear in a written story to accompany the wordless book. I transferred these words to flashcards, forming a word bank that Mary practiced at the beginning of each session.

The second phase of instruction focused on the *composition of text.* We progressed through the book page by page, creating a rough draft of the story. The keyword list created during the first phase of instruction helped Mary to create text to accompany each picture. I emphasized throughout this phase that she was creating a context for these words which she practiced in isolation at the beginning of each session. Since Mary was very reluctant to write, she dictated sentences about each page while I wrote, similar to the Language Experience Approach. I modeled such conventions as beginning each sentence with a capital letter and ending with some mark of punctuation. I left Mary's language intact and did not put her nonstandard dialect into the form of standard English so that she could gain a better understanding of the print-sound connection. Time was allotted during the beginning and end of each lesson for Mary to *reread the generated text.* Words that were particularly difficult for Mary during these repeated readings were written on notecards and added to her word bank. *Mini-lessons* based on difficulties Mary experienced within the text (e.g. letter-sound relationships, punctuation, word endings) often followed these repeated readings.

The third phase of instruction consisted of *revising and editing the rough draft* in order to reach the ultimate goal of *publication.* Revisions occurred throughout the process of composition and repeated readings. For example, if she continually stumbled on a portion of the text, we discussed rewording the text so that it was less problematic (one of the main goals of using wordless books as instruction is to promote confidence in reading fluency). Since we were planning to publish Mary's story, we discussed standard writing conventions and edited the draft so that it complied with such conventions. To publish her edited rough draft, Mary used a Brother label maker to type sentences of the text. She then secured the typed sentences to the appropriate pages of the wordless book. Once the publishing process was completed, Mary read the finished product to family members and friends.

I modified and adjusted these instructional phases in accordance with Mary's life events. Flexibility was crucial. Our usual meeting time was on Tuesdays and Thursdays from 11:00-12:30, directly following the school's Family Workshop meeting which Mary attended. However, we often needed to reschedule our meetings. Mary's lack of transportation complicated our task of scheduling instructional sessions. Although she lived within walking distance of the school where we met, other responsibilities in her life required her to make transportation arrangements. Her literacy difficulties affected her comprehension of bus schedules, so taking advantage of public transportation was not a simple solution. Since rides from friends could be hard to come by, our schedule often revolved around her transportation plans. As a result, we scheduled sessions around her visits to doctors, social agencies and the schools of her two other children. The Family Service Coordinator advised me to anticipate scheduling difficulties at the beginning of each month when aid checks are issued and recipients are busy paying rent, buying groceries and taking care of other household business. I found that scheduling was also difficult during the entire month of November when Mary spent a lot of time traveling to stores to make payments on Christmas presents she had put on lay-away.

The flexibility necessary in scheduling instructional sessions extended to the procedure of the lessons. I learned early that I could not become too attached to my lesson plans. During several lessons, we discussed difficulties Mary was facing in communicating with neighbors, landlords, social workers and teachers. These discussions took precedence over my lesson plan for that session. However, even these discussions provided opportunities for Mary to focus on her literacy skills. Mary developed written plans of action (e.g., how to handle a meeting with her landlord, questions to ask at her child's M-team meeting) which I wrote down, and she practiced rereading. Although during such lessons Mary did not practice reading the text that she had created to accompany the wordless book, she still was engaged in the activity of reading ideas she, herself, had composed.

Discussion of Findings

This study examined the developing literacy of an adult beginning reader through the process of writing and reading text to accompany a wordless book. A restatement of the initial guiding questions is useful in illuminating the findings.

What can be learned about the literacy development of an adult beginning reader before instruction begins?

The findings of this study demonstrate that even though an adult beginning reader may not be able to decode enough words for a thorough reading miscue analysis to be conducted, useful information about who she is as a literacy learner can still be gathered. The picture book used as part of the initial assessment consisted of 32 words. Of those 32 words, Mary recognized six. Rather than discontinuing assessment at that point, alternative forms of assessment were explored in an effort to learn more about Mary's literacy.

Mary's responses during an interview revealed that she often participated in literacy activities with her children and that she learned to compensate for her difficulties during such shared experiences, "And I just go through the pages with him. And then he'll read it to me and then I just put it in my mind what the words are—as he's saying them to me. I just let it concentrate in my mind. Then next day, I go and read it to him and then he'll read to me." Her belief that she could protect herself with more proficient skills in reading and writing was evident in her responses, "You might sign something you ain't got no business signing." Yet her motivation to improve her literacy skills—not only as a protective measure but as a means of enjoyment—came through in the following comment: "I know there's a lot of parents out there, don't know how to read. So, I think, to me, it's very fun, something that people really need to know how to do. You know, if they don't know how, then they should get somebody to teach them."

Mary's oral storytelling to the wordless book *A Boy, a Dog, a Frog and a Friend* by Mercer and Marianna Mayer yielded more specific information. Lytle's (1985) system of analyzing think-aloud protocols was modified in order to inform and guide the process of coding and analyzing Mary's storytelling. A listing of these codes is presented in Table 1.

Table 1. Coding System for Transcription of Storytelling of Wordless Book

Monitoring Clarity (M) includes units indicating that storyteller is attempting to explain what she previously said by:
M1 providing information which helps listener understand referent of previously uttered pronoun
M2 correcting word in order to improve clarity of storyline

Reporting of Picture (R) includes units in which storyteller describes picture without adding inferences or personal judgments
R1 unit that is a literal description of a picture

Elaborating on Picture (E) includes units in which storyteller provides information that is not a literal report of a picture by:
E1 using dialogue
E2 inferring a character's emotional or physical feelings and/or thought processes
E3 giving a character a proper name
E4 inferring an action signaled by a verb or adverb choice that seems to go beyond a literal restatement of the picture

Analyzing Features of Book (A) includes units in which storyteller appears to view book as an object and comments on particular features of the book by:
A1 referring to process of progressing through a book by beginning the book, turning pages and ending the book
A2 making aside comment to listener about a particular page

Signaling Understanding (S) includes units in which storyteller signals current understanding of the book's meaning by:
S1 summarizing several previously stated ideas into one unit

Reasoning (r) includes units which indicate that the storyteller is attempting to interpret storyline and engage in problem-solving approaches by:
r1 attempting to explain "why" a particular character behaved in a certain manner
r2 predicting future events and/or consequences as signaled by the use of the future tense
r3 resolving story problems through making hypotheses or assumptions about the progression of the storyline

Digressing From Storyline (D) includes units which indicate storyteller is straying from the storyline by:
D1 reporting about events, characters or objects that do not logically coincide with the pictures of the book

Repeating Idea (*RE*) includes units in which storyteller repeats previously stated idea by:
RE1 using the same words in the same order
RE2 using slightly different words but revealing no new information

An indepth analysis of the transcripts of this storytelling, as reported in Table 2, revealed Mary's ability to describe what she sees, make inferences, summarize, draw conclusions and reason. The low occurrence of repetitions in her story showed an ability to generate multiple ideas about a story. Her tendency to monitor and correct what could have been confusing to the listener as well as her occasional comments to the listener about particular features of the book exposed her sense of audience. Her ability to stay with the storyline without digressing indicated that she was capable of developing a cohesive story from beginning to end.

Table 2. Distribution of Codes for One of Mary's Storytellings

Code	Number of units scored as code
Monitoring Clarity	3
Reporting of Picture	24
Elaborating on Picture	25
Analyzing Features of Book	5
Signaling Understanding	3
Reasoning	11
Digressing from Storyline	0
Repeating Idea	2

How will this approach to literacy development influence a reader's accuracy in oral reading?

Prior to instruction, Mary's oral reading accuracy was calculated as 18% for the 32 word book *Rosie's Walk* by Pat Hutchins. Once instruction began, Mary's fluency in oral reading did increase as she read the text that she, herself, composed. Marie Clay's (1975) technique of documenting reading miscues in the form of running records was used to code patterns in Mary's reading and calculate her level of accuracy across eight oral readings. Data for these oral reading records are presented in Table 3. During instruction, Mary read passages that ranged from 72 to 283 words (substantially more words than appeared in the 32 word book *Rosie's Walk*). Across these passages, she maintained a high level of accuracy, 87% or above, on passages under 200 words. Even her lowest calculated accuracy of 67% was judged as adequate for a student who could recognize only 6 words a few weeks earlier.

Table 3. Summary of Mary's Running Records

Date	no. words in passage	no. of miscues	no. of words read correctly	% accuracy	no. of self corrections	no. of repetitions	no. of omissions
10-30-95	72	5	67	93	2	2	1
11-3-95	72	4	68	94	2	1	1
11-8-95	109	8	101	92	2	4	1
11-9-95	122	16	106	87	4	8	8
11-30-95	271	57	214	79	6	29	25
12-1-95	271	57	214	79	14	51	17
12-7-95	283	84	189	67	5	16	42
12-14-95	196	18	178	91	8	15	3

As Mary attempted to read longer passages, her reading fluency decreased. In addition to a decrease in reading fluency, her reliance on such reading behaviors as repetitions and omissions increased. When faced with an abundance of text, even text she had composed, she became flustered and stopped reading for meaning. In response to these difficulties, instruction was adjusted to focus on smaller portions of text. Through pacing and the reading of texts of increasing lengths, Mary was able to concentrate more on constructing meaning and, consequently, experienced a higher level of reading fluency. Yet it should be noted that despite the difficulty she experienced in reading passages containing more than 200 words, her level of accuracy for the reading of texts that she composed was never calculated below 67%.

How will this approach lend itself to opportunities for the participant to obtain ownership of her literacy?

Paulo Freire (1970) emphasizes the importance of the adult literacy process occurring within "the context of authentic dialogue between learners and educators as equally knowing subjects" (p. 214). Halliday's (1978) work on seven functions of language guided the development of the coding system used for this analysis. Halliday's functions were modified for the purposes of this study. Specifically, Mary's use of regulatory, personal, heuristic and informative language was explored.

The coding of Mary's comments during instructional sessions revealed that Mary most often engaged in personal language. The category of personal language included comments in which Mary made a decision based on her own interpretation of the story, comments in which Mary responded to the literature by expressing a personal judgment, and comments in which Mary evaluated her own performance (e.g. "This is where I messed up, right here . . . I skipped that one.") Mary's use of personal language indicated her developing sense of herself as a reader and writer.

Mary relied on regulatory and informative language equally. Her use of regulatory language as exhibited in the comment, "Okay, let me read this whole thing," demonstrated her ability to guide the path of instruction and assume initiative in the learning process. Her ability to justify and support the decisions she made were revealed through her use of informative language. For example, when creating text to accompany a picture in which Carl, the dog, is carrying the baby on his back, Mary waivered on which verb, "bringing" or "helping" to use in the sentence. After much thought, she explained her decision to use "bringing" in the sentence, "'Cause 'helping' really like he's, like the baby...couldn't get out, that's what you call 'help'. But that's 'bringing' him." Although the wording of Mary's explanation is somewhat convoluted, her intent to convey the reasoning behind her choice is evident.

In later instructional sessions, Mary began to experiment with words, as revealed in this example of heuristic or problem-solving language, "Let's try to put these words together and see what it sound like." Even though she engaged in heuristic language the least, it cannot be overlooked that as Mary's confidence in her literacy increased, she began to develop her own questions rather than merely responding to prompting, instructional questions. Mary's language during instructional sessions communicated her growing strengths as a literacy learner as well as her increasing awareness of her role in the literacy process.

Conclusions

This study shows how wordless books can enhance the literacy development of an adult beginning reader. Through the process of exploring this approach, three conclusions can be drawn: (a) although the adult student's decoding difficulties may be so severe that a reading miscue analysis yields little information, data from a coded storytelling and information revealed in an interview can provide a rich portrait of the individual as a literacy learner; (b) repeated readings of text composed by the adult student promote reading fluency; and (c) such an approach provides the adult student with opportunities to make decisions, take risks, and assume initiative and ownership in the learning process. Thus, the methodology used in this study supports the view of the adult learner as a whole person with multiple contributions to her own literacy growth and mitigates the "deficit view" that Richardson (1993) warns against.

The instructional approach described in this study is a long process. The issues of time, the building of rapport, and the impact of the participant's life events on instruction must be factored into the planning of such a program. A structured series of rigid lesson plans would not be a useful guide for instructional sessions based on this approach. Flexibility in instructional design and the use of multiple and alternative measures to collect information about developing abilities must be accounted for in the implementation of such a program. The process described in this study gave the participant the opportunity to read connected text while simultaneously experiencing the writing process. As her confidence and sense of ownership in this process increased, she began to perceive herself as both a reader and a writer. The initial instruction described in this study could serve as a springboard to additional texts which are authored by others as well as to the exploration of different styles or genres of writing. An implication of the study is that a continuation of this approach will be successful only if the following conditions are satisfied during the initial phase of this process: the participant's initial strengths as a communicator and language user are identified and capitalized upon, and the participant's contributions to the learning process are validated.

References

Clay, M. M. (1975). *The early detection of reading difficulties* (2nd ed.). Portsmouth, NH: Heinemann.

Danielson, K. E. (1992). Picture books to use with older students. In M. C. Radencich (Ed.), *Adult literacy: A compendium of articles from the journal of reading* (pp. 112-115). Newark, DE: International Reading Association.

Day, A. (1986). *Carl*. New York: Green Tiger Press.

Ellis, D., & Preston, F. (1984). Enhancing beginning reading using wordless picture books in a cross-age tutoring program. *The Reading Teacher, 37* (8), 692-698.

Flatley, J., & Rutland, A. (1986). Using wordless picture books to teach linguistically/culturally different students. *The Reading Teacher, 40* (3), 276-281.

Freire, P. (1970). The adult literacy process as cultural action for freedom. *Harvard Educational Review, 40* (2), 205-225.

Garfield, S. (1993). Beyond the barriers: creative writing with adult remedial students. *Journal of Reading, 37* (1), 55-56.

Glaser, B., & Strauss, A. (1967). *The discovery of grounded theory*. Chicago: Aldine.

Halliday, M. A. K. (1978). *Language as social semiotic: The social interpretation of language and meaning*. Baltimore: University Park Press.

Hutchins, P. (1968). *Rosie's walk*. New York: Macmillan.

Isley, P., & Stahl, N. A. (1993). Reconceptualizing the language of adult literacy. *Journal of Reading, 37* (1), 20-27.

Lincoln, Y. S., & Guba, E. G. (1985). *Naturalistic inquiry*. Newbury Park, CA: Sage.

Lindauer, S. (1988). Wordless books: an approach to visual literacy. *Children's Literature in Education, 19* (3), 136-141.

Lytle, S. (1985, April). *Comprehension styles of twelfth grade readers: What verbal protocols can (and can't) tell us.* Paper presented at the annual meeting of the American Educational Research Association, Chicago, IL.

Mayer, M., & Mayer, M. (1971). *A boy, a dog, a frog and a friend.* New York: Penguin Books.

McGee, L., & Tompkins, G. (1983). Wordless picture books are for older readers, too. *Journal of Reading, 27* (2), 120-123.

Norton, D. E., & Moore, K. (1993). Realizing the wednesday surprise: Building adult literacy with picture books. *Reading Improvement, 30* (4), 232-237.

Purcell-Gates, V. (1993). I ain't never read my own words before. *Journal of Reading, 37* (3), 210-219.

Read, D., & Smith, H. (1982). Teaching visual literacy through wordless picture books. *The Reading Teacher, 35* (8), 928-933.

Richardson, J. S. (1993). Fads or substantive changes in the field of adult literacy? In T. Rasinski & N. Padak (Eds.), *Inquiries in literacy learning and instruction: The fifteenth yearbook of the College Reading Association* (pp. 27-37). Pittsburg, KS: College Reading Association.

Rhoder, C. A. & French, J. N. (1995). Participant-generated text: A vehicle for workplace literacy. *Journal of Adolescent and Adult Literacy, 39* (2), 110-118.

Schierloh, J. M. (1992). Using classic novels with adult new readers. In M. C. Radencich (Ed.), *Adult literacy: A compendium of articles from the journal of reading* (pp. 137-143). Newark, DE: International Reading Association.

Stasz, B. B., Schwartz, R. G., & Weeden, J. C. (1991). Writing our lives: An adult basic skills program. *Journal of Reading, 35* (1), 30-33.

Wagner, D. A. (1993). Myths and misconceptions in adult literacy. *Adult Learning, 5* (1), 9-10, 23.

Yin, R. K. (1989). *Case study research: Design and methods.* Newbury Park, CA: Sage.

LITERACY DEVELOPMENT FOR ELEMENTARY, SECONDARY AND COLLEGE STUDENTS

A Literature Based E-Mail Collaborative

Christine A. McKeon

Walsh University

Linda C. Burkey

Mount Union College

Abstract

Based on a constructivist theoretical framework, this paper describes an e-mail collaborative program between pre-service teachers and fourth and fifth graders. The use of electronic mail as a means to enhance literacy learning has the potential to contribute to the social nature of the reading and writing development of elementary students. The project focused on reading comprehension, vocabulary, and word recognition lessons that were designed by university students about literature that was selected by classroom teachers. As correspondences occurred, informal social communication skills were also enhanced. The goals of the collaborative were discussed, sample lessons were given, and considerations for implementing such a project were recommended.

Whole language, literature based reading programs, phonics in context and now, the computer. Current questions about reading and writing have clearly changed over the past two decades and researchers are now asking questions about the social nature of reading and writing (Irwin & Doyle, 1992). As today's literacy teachers strive to provide meaningful language learning and usage in their classrooms, reading and writing are viewed as composing and problem solving activities and as vehicles for thinking within this context (Tierney, 1992). Extensive research suggests the importance of providing authentic language experiences for children (Cambourne, 1995). And so, what about the computer? Technology, specifically the use of electronic mail communication, is one area which holds many possibilities for enhancing this social aspect of literacy learning in today's classrooms (Selfe & Hilligoss, 1994). Communication using e-mail can provide a means for authentic reading and writing experiences (Tuman, 1992).

According to May (1994), Vygotsky's work in the early 1900s provides the theoretical roots for this social constructivist viewpoint. Reading, through telecommunications, is a process of dialogue between the writer and the reader. The goals of telecommunications projects can also be traced to the early work of Piaget (1926) which laid the groundwork for the naturalistic learning perspective of the whole language movement (Goodman, 1989). Proponents of whole language emphasize reading and writing practices that are based on one's innate ability, as well as on one's interaction with the environment and others. Additionally, the work of Dewey (1943) provides the theoretical rationale for considering questions about the learning environment which technology has to offer. Dewey viewed learning as a social process and considered how students relate new information to their personal experiences, as well as to the experiences of others. Telecommunications projects provide a way for learners to share these experiences; these learning opportunities have their roots in constructivist theories of how learning takes place. Jerome Bruner's work (1981) adds to the theoretical basis for electronic discourse as an interaction between the learner and the environment.

Butler (1997) cites numerous research studies (Barker & Kemp, 1990; Gere, 1987; Hillocks, 1986; Moffet, 1968; Slavin, 1983) that contribute to the learning pedagogies involved in collaborative networking in classrooms. These works provide another basis for e-mail projects. Additionally, Selfe and Hilligoss (1994) suggest that technology has the potential to change the definitions and contexts of literacy; Reinking, Labbo, and McKenna (1997) suggest that electronic literacy should be incorporated into language arts curricula. They even recommend that technology be a part of every educational issue related to literacy. Little research, however, has carefully documented the nature of e-mail collaboratives in elementary classrooms. There is a need to describe what they look like and what characterizes them in different contexts on this level (Bowen, 1994).

The purpose of this paper is to offer one context in which e-mail can be purposefully used in elementary classrooms to enhance authentic language learning. Our paper describes the nature of an e-mail collaborative between pre-service teachers and fourth and fifth graders in which literature was used as a vehicle for language and reading enhancement. The goals of the project are discussed, and specific examples of correspondences are given which demonstrate the goals. Additionally, guidelines for initiating a similar project are given with suggestions for implementation.

The Collaborative

This collaborative grew out of an existing program in which future teachers communicated with elementary students through pen pal projects. The pre-service teachers were corresponding with local elementary students in order to gain a better understanding of students' development of writing skills. This e-mail partnership expanded in an effort to offer the future teachers the opportunity to further understand the literacy development of elementary students.

The pre-service teachers, elementary education majors, were enrolled in semester-long reading methods courses at two institutions of higher education. The students were fourth and fifth graders from five local elementary schools in the midwest. These schools were selected based on need, interest, proximity, and on past collaborations with both universities. Representatives from the elementary schools identified a need for reinforcing literacy learning and enhancing technological skills among their students, and grades four and five were selected for the telecommunications project with the intention of expanding to other grade levels and other schools.

The pre-service teachers were informally matched with elementary partners. Communications occurred weekly. The focus of the correspondences was on children's literature that was chosen by the classroom teacher. Literature used in this project included: *Class President* (Hurwitz, 1990), *The War with Grandpa* (Smith, 1984), *James and the Giant Peach* (Dahl, 1961), *A Taste of Blackberries* (Smith, 1973), *Stone Fox* (Gardiner, 1980), and *From the Mixed-Up Files of Mrs. Basil E. Frankweiler* (Konigsburg, 1967), among others. As the pre-service teachers were learning the teaching of reading comprehension, word recognition, and vocabulary, formal lesson plans were written, and the lessons were taught via e-mail. This dialogue was accompanied by informal conversation during which the partners communicated socially.

Goals of the Project

The initial goals of the project were twofold: the pre-service teachers were given the opportunity to develop their ability to teach literacy skills and strategies, and the elementary students were given the opportunity to enhance their literacy skills through authentic dialogue. Additionally, through the socialization process, both the pre-service teachers and the elementary school students had the opportunity to further develop communication and writing skills, as well as to experience purposeful use of the computer.

Sample Correspondences that Support Goals

Effective teachers of reading teach students how to activate prior knowledge and experiences about a topic before and during reading (Vacca, Vacca, & Gove, 1991). The following dialogue about *The Mixed-Up Files of Mrs. Basil E. Frankweiler* (Konigsburg, 1967) is an example of a typical pre-service teacher's attempt to activate a student's schema:

Hi, Joe, I received your letter today. I am glad to hear that you like to read. You wanted to know my favorite movie. I do not have one favorite movie. However, I do like comedy movies. Any movie that is funny, I seem to enjoy watching. I am going to get started on the book we will be reading. The title of the book is "From the Mixed-Up Files of Mrs. Basil E. Frankweiler." It is written by E. L. Konigsburg. The story is about a sister and brother who run away from home. I would like you to answer the following questions before you begin the book, and please send your answers to me.

1. If you wanted to go away without telling anyone you were leaving, where would you go?
2. Why would you go there?
3. How would you get there and what would you take with you? (H. C., personal communication, October 5, 1997)

In response to the e-mail, the fourth grader wrote:

Hi, Miss C. If I ran away I'd go to Sea World, and take lots of money to buy the little fishes. I'd also take a camera and a million picture film. I'd take pictures of all the things there. Then I'd get on one of the water boat things and go across the lake to Geauga Lake and go on all the rollercoasters and other rides. (J. J., personal communication, October 6, 1997).

Cognitive maps (e.g., character maps, story pyramids) help to show key relationships among concepts (Tonjes & Zintz, 1992). Another pre-service teacher attempted to enhance comprehension using a character map in the following correspondence about *Class President* (Hurwitz, 1990):

Hello! You did a very nice job with your second assignment. How do you like the book so far? I hope that you are enjoying it.

Your third assignment is to do what is called a character map. What you are to do is first, list the main character's name at the top, underneath the main character's name, list three (3) characteristics that describe that character. Next to each of these characteristics list two (2) supporting details of this characteristic. Here is an example of what I am looking for:

Cricket

1. Popular
   A. Everyone likes her.
   B. Everyone thinks that she will get class president.

I hope that you understand what I am looking for. This assignment will help you to get a better understanding of the main character in the story. (My example is not necessarily the main character)! (Miss G., personal communication, October 22, 1997)

The following is an exerpt from the student's response:

Dear Miss G ,

Here is my assignment. The main character is Julio.

Julio.
1. Nice.
    A. He is going to help Lucas campaign.
    B. He says that everyone should have a bake sale for new glasses for Arther. (He is showing he cares about Arther).
2. Smart.
    A. He has an idea to suprise his class.
    B. He has an idea to get back playing soccer for the boys.
3. Popular.
    A. He has been in the class since kindergarten.
    B. Everyone knows him. (C. L., personal communication, November 11, 1997)

Story pyramids can also enhance a reader's comprehension (Fowler, 1982). In the following correspondence about the book *Class President* (Hurwitz, 1990), the pre-service teacher attempts a variation of this strategy:

I am really glad that you finished the book and enjoyed it so much. When I started reading it I couldn't put it down either. You made some really good predictions about the book too. Do you have a favorite part?

Now that you have finished the book I would like you to complete a story pyramid. I will explain this to you.
1. Insert 1 word that names a character in the first line.
2. Insert 2 words that describe the setting in line 2.
3. Insert 3 words that describe a character in line 3.
4. Insert 4 words in a sentence that describe one event in line 4.
5. Insert 5 words in a sentence that describe another event in line 5. (Ms. S., personal communication, November 4, 1997).

The student responded:

How are you? I am fine . . . I like when Lucas gets mad. It's funny. Here are the Questions You Gave Me. 1. Julio 2. fifth grade 3. know it all 4. Arthur broke his glasses. 5. class has a bake sale. (B. L., personal communication, November 7, 1997).

A variety of other lesson strategies were attempted including prediction questions, anticipation guides, word searches, crossword puzzles, and word matching puzzles. Worksheet formats were not recommended; the pre-service teachers were encouraged to discuss the stories in a conversational manner. Additionally, it is noteworthy that the pre-service teachers needed to be flexible and to base their successive lessons on the quality of the students' e-mail responses.

Underlying the goal of enhanced literacy, the project provided the partners with a learning environment in which the social nature of the e-mail fostered communication skills.

One partnership included the following conversation initiated by the pre-service teacher about career aspirations: "I am going to be an elementary teacher . . . My dream grade is to teach second grade in a small public school. After graduation I will teach in whatever grade I get a job" (A. K., personal communication, March, 1997).

The student responded, "When I grow up I want to be a teacher!" (A.F., personal communication, March, 1997).

The pre-service teacher wrote back, "I think that it is neat that you want to be a teacher when you grow up! I think we are a lot alike!" (A. K., personal communication, March, 1997).

Other conversations included interest in what the partner actually looked like. One elementary student wrote, "What color is your hair? Mine hair color is light brown" (C. S., personal communication, March 1997).

She received the response, "My hair is light brown too!" (J. L., personal communication, March 1997).

Still other communications indicated that the project was indeed motivating. A fourth grader informed her partner, "Oh! Guess what. I got a brand new computer at home!!!!" (A. T., personal communication, March, 1997).

The pre-service teacher responded, "How do you like your new computer . . . I got a computer as a graduation gift from my parents before I went to college." (R. F., personal communication, March 1997).

The fourth grader suggested, "Maybe we could e-mail each other from our homes!!!" (A. T, personal communication, March 1997).

The reply came back, "If you would like to e-mail me at home that would be great!" (R. F., personal communication, March 1997).

Other social communications included information about favorite hobbies, pets, vacations, and activities going on at school and at home. Each group of students met face-to-face following fourteen weeks of e-mail dialoguing. In many instances the parents participated in this gathering. For several participants, the social interaction continued beyond the project, and the pre-service teachers became personal tutors for the elementary students.

Guidelines for Initiating a Similar Project

The facilitation of this project was dependent upon compatible computer accessibility and usage by all students. There were various levels of accessibility in the schools. Educators who wish to plan a similar project need to be aware of the computer arrangements in the school setting. Some schools had several computers in the classrooms, others had computer labs, and another had only one computer located in a library. In the latter case, access was more difficult. The classroom teachers in all settings, however, needed to arrange sufficient time for students to correspond with their partners during the school day and had to remain flexible in scheduling time on-line when students were absent. Additionally, training sessions needed to be arranged, and a facilitator needed to be available for troubleshooting with the technological connections both at the universities as well as the elementary schools. There were occasions when e-mail was lost in space for several days and when the computers were down; the partners had to be patient with technological difficulties. Issues concerning security access also needed to be addressed to ensure that the correspondences were kept confidential.

The role of the classroom teacher in this project was key. In addition to being a facilitator of computer training, the teacher needed to consider what literature would be read. In some cases, the teachers selected the books based on the genre being studied in the classroom setting. In other classrooms, the teachers allowed the children to choose from a variety of teacher-selected books. The level of teacher assistance for individual student lesson support varied depending on student ability. For example, a non-reader met weekly with his teacher and dictated his e-mail responses. Another elementary student worked closely with a learning disability specialist as he composed his correspondences. Other issues for classroom teachers to consider include whether or not the accuracy of spelling is crucial at all times with young students and whether the format of an e-mail correspondence needs to follow that of a formal letter.

Conclusion

Although telecommunications projects are becoming more and more prevalent between classrooms (Abilock, 1996; Anderson, & Lee, 1995; D'Souza, 1991), this collaborative was unique in its use of literature with school age students and pre-service teachers. During the two years in which this project was implemented, approximately 200 literature-based partnerships developed. The motivation for the project was evident. Classroom teachers from the intial year asked to continue as participants in the project, district administrators supported the effort, and parents were impressed with the students' increased interest in reading and purposeful computer usage. The pre-service teachers developed both skill in motivating students to read, as well as respect for authentic communication with elementary students. One university student wrote in a final essay about the project, "I was thrilled when Fred said that I got him to like reading now" (D. B., personal communication, April, 1997).

The value of the program for the elementary students is evident in still another correspondence:

> I liked the E-mail project because it was fun learning about computers more, and now I can type a lot faster. The best part was when I got to read a new book, and I don't even like to read very much, but now I love to read now since this E-mail project. (D.R, personal communication, April, 1997).

In conclusion, Butler (1997) points out the possibilities for using e-mail to teach critical reading. Though he acknowledges the criticisms and contradictions which some researchers have found when using electronic conferencing, he emphasizes that "we as literacy educators would be remiss not to usher our students into the age of on-line literacy" (p. 564). This project has done just that. Through the correspondences, the elementary students had the opportunity to enhance their critical reading and social skills using the computer, while the pre-service teachers developed their teaching and communication skills. It is suggested that other teacher preparation programs consider using literature based telecommunications projects which allow pre-service teachers to connect with elementary students. It is also suggested that other classroom teachers embrace the possibilities of using e-mail as a way to enhance children's literacy development through authentic communication about literature. Though only fourth and fifth graders experienced this project, other grade levels might explore literature based e-mail collaboratives with pre-service teachers. Since technology is here to stay, constructive implementation needs to be discovered by all of us who touch upon the literacy development of others.

References

Abilock, D. (1996). Integrating e-mail into the curriculum. *Technology Connection 3*(5), 23-25.

Anderson, J., & Lee, A. (1995). Literacy teachers learning a new literacy: A study of the use of electronic mail in a reading education class. *Reading Research and Instruction, 34*(3), 222-238.

Barker, T. T., & Kemp, F. O. (1990). Network theory: A postmodern pedagogy for the writing classroom. In C. Handa (Ed.), *Computers in society: Teaching composition in the twenty-first century* (pp. 1-27). Portsmouth, NH: Boynton/Cook.

Bowen, B. A. (1994). Telecommunications networks: Expanding the contexts for literacy. In C. L. Selfe & S. Hilligoss (Eds.), *Literacy and computers: The complications of teaching and learning with technology* (pp. 113-129). New York: The Modern Curriculum Language Association.

Bruner, J. (1981). The pragamatics of acquistion. In W. Deutsch (Ed.), *The child's construction of language* (pp. 39-55). New York: Academic Press.

Butler, W. M. (1997). Electronic discourse communities: Theory, practice, and research. In J. Flood, S. B. Heath, & D. Lapp (Eds.), *Research on teaching literacy through the communicative and visual arts* (pp. 558-565). New York: Macmillan.

Cambourne, B. (1995). Towards an educationally relevant theory of literacy learning: Twenty years of inquiry. *The Reading Teacher, 49*(3), 182-190.

Dahl, R. (1961). *James and the giant peach*. New York: Penguin Books.

Dewey, J. (1943). *The child and the curriculum and the school and society*. Chicago: University of Chicago Press.

D'Souza, P. V. (1991). The use of electronic mail as an intstructional aid: An exploratory study. *Journal of Computer-Based Instruction, 18*(3), 106-110.

Fowler, G. (1982). Developing comprehension skills in primary students through the use of story frames. *The Reading Teacher, 36*(1), 176-179.

Gardiner, J. R. (1980). *Stone Fox*. New York: Harper-Collins.

Gere, A. R. (1987). *Writing groups: History, theory, and implications*. Carbondale, IL: Southern Illinois University Press.

Goodman, Y. M. (1989). Roots of the whole-language movement. *The Elementary School Journal, 90*(2), 113-127.

Hillocks, G. Jr. (1986). *Research on written composition: Directions for teaching*. Urbana, IL: National Council of Teachers of English.

Hurwitz, J. (1990). *Class president*. NY: Scholastic, Inc.

Irwin, J. W., & Doyle, M. A. (Eds.). (1992). *Reading/Writing connections: Learning from research*. Newark, DE: International Reading Association.

Konigsburg, E. L. (1967). *From the mixed-up files of Mrs. Basil E. Frankweiler*. NY: Simon & Schuster.

May, F. B. (1994). *Reading as communication* (4th ed.). New York: Merrill.

Moffett, J. (1968). *A student-centered language arts curriculum, grade k-13: A handbook for teachers*. Boston: Houghton Mifflin.

Piaget, J. (1926). *The language and thought of the child*. Orlando, FL: Harcourt Brace Jovanonvich.

Reinking, D., Labbo, L., & McKenna, M. (1997). Navigating the changing landscape of literacy: Current theory and research in computer-based reading and writing. In J. Flood, S. B. Heath, & D. Lapp (Eds.). *Research on teaching literacy through the communicative and visual arts* (pp. 77-92). New York: Macmillan.

Selfe, C. L., & Hilligoss, S. (Eds.). (1994). *Literacy and computers: The complications of teaching and learning with technology*. New York: The Modern Language Association.

Slavin, R. (1983). *Cooperative learning*. New York: Longman.

Smith, D. B. (1973). *A taste of blackberries*. New York: Harper-Collins.

Smith, R. K. (1984). *The war with grandpa*. New York: Bantam Doubleday Dell.

Tierney, R. J. (1992). Ongoing research and new directions. In J. W. Irwin & M. A. Doyle (Eds.), *Reading/Writing connections: Learning from research*. Newark, DE: International Reading Association.

Tonjes, M. J., & Zintz, M. V. (1992). *Teaching reading thinking study skills in content classrooms* (3rd ed.). Dubuque, IA: Wm. C. Brown.

Tuman, M. C. (1992). *Literacy online: The promise (and peril) of reading and writing with computers*. Pittsburgh, PA: University of Pittsburg Press.

Vacca, J. L., Vacca, R. T., & Gove, M. K. (1991). *Reading and learning to read* (2nd ed.). New York: Harper-Collins.

Students' Perceptions of Literacy Learning in a Project-Based Curriculum

Jacqueline K. Peck

Cleveland State University

William Peck
James Sentz
Richard Zasa

Parma Senior High School

Abstract

This collaborative classroom study examines high school students' perceptions of their literacy learning in a thematically integrated humanities course using a project approach to instruction. All students in the class were asked to write reflections of themselves as readers, writers, and researchers, and several participated in follow-up interviews. Findings show that students perceived they used multiple texts, revisited texts, and evaluated information through their reading, writing, and researching for the projects. These findings informed continued curricular development.

Two years ago Bill, Jim, and Rich (collectively referred to as "the team") began to redesign their team-taught, traditional, chronological survey of art, music, and literature into a student-centered, thematically integrated course that engaged the students in research of broad issues and presentation of their findings using a variety of print and non-print media. This format was new to them and their students. The first year they were involved with their own perceptions of change. During this time I was an informal observer and evaluator of student projects, and I had many opportunities to talk with the team. I was excited about the students' work, but even more so by the team's insightful comments about what was happening in their classroom. They were already engaged in teacher research, so during the second year I asked if they were interested in taking a look at students' perceptions of their literacy learning. They were ready to collaborate on a classroom research study to gain understanding of their students' perceptions that would inform their ongoing curricular development. Together, we decided to ask the students to reflect on themselves as readers, writers, and researchers (Fedele, 1996).

This collaborative classroom research study of the students' perceptions of their literacy learning emerged through the informal conversations I had with the team over an 18-month period. It is grounded in reflection, inquiry, and action (Patterson & Shannon, 1993). I provided support by frequently observing and responding to student project presentations. In this paper we provide the theoretical framework that grounds the study. We describe the setting, participants, and design, and we present our findings, discuss conclusions, and develop implications for practice.

The Study

Several years ago, the team's school was awarded a state grant to pursue membership in the Coalition for Essential Schools (Sizer, 1992). This rigorous process provided opportunities for them to evaluate the way they were teaching their course and to explore alternative approaches. Dewey (1910, 1938) grounded their decisions to create a student-centered classroom, to pose ill-defined problems, and to engage students in analysis and synthesis of ideas. During the second year of their curricular redesign, Eisner (1997) provided a framework for thinking about multiple forms of representation. Other classroom studies supported their continued curricular development. Rekrut (1997) helped them understand collaborative classroom research, and Schaller and Wenk (1997) supported their continued integration of content.

Setting, Participants, Design

Jim describes the setting as,

a large public high school in an area recently designated "urban" by socioeconomic indicators. Our course, Arts Seminar, has a 40-year history in our school district and is considered to be an honors course. Until only 2 years ago, we taught it with a traditional lecture-style delivery. Poor retention of material and inactive student participation was becoming an increasing concern to us. Through our observations, it became obvious that the traditional approach was no longer a valid way of communicating subject mastery to our students. Therefore, we redesigned the course to a project-based, authentic assessment approach that implements the theory of multiple representations. Students began to actively participate in conceptual topics, such as the meaning of a masterpiece, and to be totally integrated into the classroom setting instead of being passive, sometimes learners.

The participants in this study were high school juniors or seniors. Some chose to take the course for English credit, others for humanities credit. All students in the class provided data in written form. Nine students provided interview data. Four were girls, 5 were boys; 4 were above average readers, 3 were reading at grade level, and 2 were reading below grade level. All of them were Eurocentric students who lived in the local community.

Written data was collected as part of their midterm examination; we asked our students to reflect on their perceptions of learning in a traditional format and in the project-based format. Then at the close of the school year, Jackie interviewed 9 students that we selected to represent a range of involvement in the class—some who showed enthusiasm for the redesigned course, some who were openly resistant, and some who were neutral. Using a critical incident protocol, she asked the students to "think of a time in this class when you really learned a lot and enjoyed what you were doing. Tell me about it. What did you do? Who did you work with? How did it go? What did you learn? Why? Why did you like it?" Using the same format, she also asked students to "think of a time you didn't learn very much and did not enjoy what you were doing. . . ."

Analyzing What the Students Said

The team collaborated with me on the inductive analysis of the midterm written reflections and verbatim transcripts of the interviews. We combed the data for themes and patterns (Lincoln & Guba, 1985); then we refined the tentative categories that emerged using the constant-comparative method (Glaser & Strauss, 1967). We used team observations to provide further support.

Three categories appeared throughout the data. In both the written midterm reflections and the close of the school year interviews, students described instances of using multiple texts, revisiting texts, and evaluating texts. These categories appeared across comments pertaining to students as readers, writers, and researchers.

Using Multiple Texts

In this study, "multiple texts" included print and non-print materials of various forms and genres. In the midterm reflections, students indicated that they "read more than one source," and wrote a variety of texts (e.g., notes on their readings, presentation scripts). In addition to researching traditional printed text, they commented on researching non-print materials. They were aware that "reading printed text was only one way to gather information"; they also described interviewing people with expertise on their project topic and viewing relevant artifacts.

Interview data also yielded comments about use of multiple texts. Students explicitly commented about writing a variety of texts, and their examples were specifically connected to project purposes. For example, students talked about writing lyrics to songs, writing logs of their research process, and writing presentation scripts. As researchers, students perceived interviews as another kind of text. One student articulated this perception when she described her research process: "First I have to think of ideas and talk to other people . . . interview or ask the teachers for their points of view, or part of my family. . . ." Rich confirmed that "research was difficult" for this student, and Jim observed that she had "a difficult time making decisions," but she "got teachers' and family opinions" when beginning a new project.

Revisiting Texts

Students said they revisited texts as readers and writers. For example, in the midterm reflections they said they could "re-look up a quote and a piece's name" or engage in rewriting of texts. One student wrote that "in a group presentation you are forced to remember information because of the writing and rewriting of the script . . ." Similar to segments in the midterm reflections, interview data described revisiting text as "rewriting" and "revising" scripts for presentation.

Evaluating Texts

Evaluating texts was the most prevalent category that emerged across data types. In the midterm reflection data, students considered both the quantity and quality of the information they gathered. They "read to decide if the information was adequate" for their purpose. When reflecting on how they do research in the project-based format, they described a need to evaluate the information they gained and make decisions about what was important to know. One student showed insight into this process by writing, "I used to copy pages and pages of notes and end up using only a tiny fraction of the information. And the information and examples weren't always the most pertinent. So . . . I have learned to be discriminating and use only the most important facts. I have learned to analyze, to think critically, and to search for reasons."

Segments from the interview data indicate that students evaluated during writing. For example, one student said, "I write what I think's going to work best" and "if it looks important, I write it down." Rich observed that this student "already knows where to look," has "lots of prior knowledge," and "reads to confirm what she already knows."

Evaluation comments in the interview data relevant to the role of researcher were numerous and indicated greater depth than those in the midterm reflections. One student described "other research . . . it's more focused, it's not with ideas. Other research is like facts. This is more emotional or personal application." Another student recognized that "you have to be able to explain why. . . ." And another observed that "most of [the projects] were with the ideas of art. . . . I think that's sort of what's always fascinated me about art. I think it adds a depth to art." Students also evaluated information for connections and understood a need "to tie things together, to tie seemingly unrelated things together. . . ." Another student conveyed this idea by relating it to drawing, one of his particular areas of talent: "This class . . . doesn't teach you how to make [art], but it shows you why and how . . . how important it is, why it's so painstaking, how hard it was to do. I find it much more interesting to learn art this way than just to draw. . . ." Bill observed that this student "came to realize all of what he's been doing is suddenly now connected—how, why, why it's important."

Conclusions and Implications

As we continued to discuss the categories yielded through our collaborative analysis of the data, we noticed some interesting features. It became increasingly clear that the students' perceptions about themselves as researchers were more richly detailed than perceptions as readers or writers. This occurred in both the midterm reflections and interview data and could be attributed to the lack of specificity in the midterm prompt and interview protocol; "reading," "writing," and "research" were intentionally omitted to avoid influencing the student perceptions.

At first we puzzled over the lack of comments in the interview data pertaining to students' perceptions as readers. With further thought and analysis, however, we noticed that although the students did not explicitly comment about reading, they frequently embedded references to reading within comments on themselves as researchers.

Our dialogues about the findings yielded three conclusions:

1. As researchers, students used reading and writing as tools to achieve their purposes. The students commented that they read and wrote many kinds of texts, reread texts for clarification of details, rewrote or revised their scripts for presentation. In each instance, reading and writing is used as a tool to accomplish the students' purpose. Often the references to reading and writing were implied or embedded within comments about "research." The students seem to perceive research as a superordinate act that at times subsumes reading and writing. For these students, reading, writing, and research were not discrete processes.

2. As researchers, students engaged in critical thinking, reading, and writing. Critical thinking is an elusive yet longed-for goal of educa-

tion. In this study the students themselves gave many examples of how they used critical thinking and made decisions about what they were reading and writing in the project-based curriculum.

3. As researchers, students engaged deeply with ideas of how and why. Students in this study were accustomed to the traditional schooling cycle of being the audience during a lecture, taking notes, researching and remembering unconnected facts. But in the project-based curriculum they recognized that they worked with more than just facts—they delved deeply into ideas of how and why.

Significantly, the team has already put implications of this study into practice, for the findings have informed their ongoing curricular revision in several ways. In one instance the findings caused the team to question whether the projects they designed gave students enough opportunity to read and write. Now in their third year of the project-based format, the team is encouraging students to engage in more sustained reading and writing. They have designed a project that involves the students in extended reading of a variety of novels, and they are asking the students to do more reflective writing in response to the content of each others' presentations.

In other instances, the team has decided to build upon the students' perceptions of research as critical thinking, reading, and writing by encouraging them to be more selective in their research. Before deciding on a project focus, the students need to demonstrate that it is researchable; they need to evaluate the quantity and quality of relevant sources. The students must also validate their research; assertions regarding their project must be supported by more than one source. The team is also extending opportunities for students to use multiple texts. They are planning to have students complete a project that incorporates multimedia expressions of learning. Jim summarizes nicely, "We continue to monitor the responses and evaluations of our students with the desire to revise the course to emphasize the student as a reader for content, a researcher for detail, and a writer for communicating their reactions and evaluations."

The work Bill, Jim, and Rich have done has also informed practice beyond the limits of their shared classroom. Rich often talks about how he has implemented similar redesigns in the English classes he teaches. As chair of the English department, he recently reported that a grade 9 English team embarked on their first project-based assignment and that most grade 12 English classes are now project-based. Bill has also implemented the project-based approach in other classes, particularly computer graphics. The work of this team emanates outward.

References

Dewey, J. (1938, 1963). *Experience and education*. NY: Collier.

Dewey, J. (1910, 1991). *How we think*. Buffalo, NY: Prometheus.

Eisner, E. W. (1997). Cognition and representation: A way to pursue the American dream? *Phi Delta Kappan, 78,* 349-353.

Fedele, F. (1996). Building a reflective classroom. In Z. Donoahue, M.A. van Tassell, & L. Patterson, (Eds.), *Research in the classroom: Talk, texts, and inquiry,* pp. 36-50. Newark, DE: International Reading Association.

Glaser, B., & Strauss, A. (1967). *The discovery of grounded theory.* Chicago: Aldine.

Lincoln, Y. S., & Guba, E. G. (1985). *Naturalistic inquiry.* Newbury Park, CA: Sage.

Patterson, L., & Shannon, P. (1993). Reflection, inquiry, action. In L. Patterson, C. M. Santa, K. G. Short, & K. Smith, (Eds.), *Teachers are researchers: Reflection and action,* pp. 7-11. Newark DE: International Reading Association.

Rekrut, M. D. (1997). Collaborative research. *Journal of Adolescent & Adult Literacy, 41,* 26-34.

Schaller, S., & Wenk, J. (1997). A humanities class for the twenty-first century. *English Journal, 86,* 75-78.

Sizer, T. R. (1992). *Horace's school: Redesigning the American high school*. Boston: Houghton Mifflin.

A Study of the Reading/Writing Connection in a University Writing Program

Sabiha T. Aydelott

The American University in Cairo

Abstract

A study was initiated in order to gauge the reading levels of students enrolled in a university Freshman Writing Program (FWP). This study was part of the review process undertaken by the Core Curriculum Review Committee. The purposes of the study were to build a profile of students' reading levels, to determine the effect of the required Core Curriculum on their reading skills, and to compare the students' reading levels with the instructors' perceptions of those students' performance in their writing classes.

The study was conducted over a period of four semesters. The study looked at the reading levels of freshmen students enrolled in writing courses, as well as at the reading levels of other students who were enrolled in the Core Seminar course. A comparison was made between the students' reading levels and their performance in their writing classes. The findings suggest that students who scored high on the reading test were those who were considered to be good writers by their instructors.

Beginning Spring 1995, a study was initiated in order to gauge the reading levels of students enrolled in the Freshman Writing Program (FWP) at the American University in Cairo (AUC). This study was part of the review process undertaken by the Core Curriculum Review Committee. The purposes of the study were to build a profile of students' reading levels, to determine the effect of the required Core Curriculum on their reading skills, and to compare the students' reading levels with the instructors' perceptions of their performance in their writing classes. As the University's only Reading Specialist, I was asked to undertake the study, which was conducted over a period of four semesters.

In line with the University's major goals of producing students who think critically, this study was designed to assess students' reading levels, which may be closely connected with their ability to think critically. A profile of the students' reading levels would probably help FWP to review the existing curriculum with the intention of further developing and improving it. Therefore, taking into consideration the need to study the incoming FWP students critically and the need to establish their reading levels, the Nelson-Denny Reading Test (NDRT) was selected.

AUC, established over 75 years ago, is governed by a Board of Trustees. The University is registered in the State of New York, uses U.S. textbooks in its courses and, generally, follows the system of education that one would find in universities in the U.S. The medium of instruction is English. The student body is diverse, as the students come from various countries in Asia, Africa, and from the U.S.; however, predominantly, the students are Egyptians. Students entering AUC are graduates of various educational systems: Egyptian, U.S., British, French, and German; hence, for most of the students English is a foreign language. For many of them it is a third language. None of the students to whom the NDRT was administered was a native speaker of English.

Explanation of Terms

A brief explanation of the various terms used in this paper follows:

1. Nature of Students: This phrase refers to the course in which the students were enrolled at the time of the test administration, or to the course or program they had been through before they took the NDRT.

2. Freshmen Writing Program (FWP): This program consists of two courses—English 112 and English 113—that all students take sequentially in order to meet their English requirements, unless exempted under special circumstances. FWP is housed in the Department of English and Comparative Literature. These courses, both offered each semester, are described in the 1998-1999 AUC Catalog as:

   Composition, Critical Reading, and Library Skills (ECLT 112)
   Sessions are devoted to writing expository prose with special attention to rhetorical methods, discussion, critical reading and thinking, and to instruction in the use of the library. Credit: 4 hrs. Grading in this course is on a Pass/Fail system.

   Composition and Research Paper (ECLT 113)
   Sessions are devoted to analytical reading, methods of research, and the process of research paper writing. The course culminates in the student's production of a research paper on an intellectually worthwhile topic with appropriate attribution of sources. Prerequisite: ECLT 112. Credit: 5 hrs. Grading for this course is on a Pass/Fail system.

3. Intensive English Program (IEP): An intensive program designed to provide students with adequate English skills in order to deal with academic work at the University. Students enrolled in this program cannot take any other course of study as this intensive program is a pre-academic program.

4. English 111: This course acts as a bridge between the courses offered by IEP and FWP. This course is housed in the English Language Institute (ELI), as is IEP.

5. Core Seminar: This is one of the Hard Core courses. The 1998-1999 AUC Catalog describes it as an interdisciplinary course in the humanities, natural sciences, and social sciences. Its goal is to foster the critical interpretation of texts. In this course, students read a variety of texts from different disciplines in an attempt to explore new ideas and new approaches to knowledge. Prerequisites: PHIL 220 and ECLT 113. Credit: 3 hrs.

6. Direct Entrants: This term refers to students who have enrolled in English 112 or English 113, in FWP, i.e., these students have not gone through ELI (through IEP or English 111). More students enroll as Direct Entrants to FWP in fall semesters than in spring semesters.

Limitations

Some of the limitations faced during this study included the following:

1. Current and up-to-date literature pertaining to the study is not available in libraries in Egypt, and, therefore, was not available to the researcher.

2. Collecting data from teachers regarding their perceptions of their students' writing abilities was difficult, as not all teachers responded when asked to provide the data. These data may not depict the students' writing abilities accurately, as perceptions tend to be subjective rather than objective.

3. Another possible limitation could be that the NDRT is designed for native speakers of English, and the AUC students who were tested were not native speakers of English. However, the renormed and revised version (1993) does make allowances for non-native speakers of English by building in an option of extended time for them, thus allowing them additional time in which to complete the test.

Rationale for Selecting the Nelson-Denny Reading Test

The Nelson-Denny Reading Test is primarily a test used for screening and predicting purposes. The NDRT was selected on the basis that

1. it provides a tool for screening students,
2. it provides a tool for predicting students' academic achievement, and
3. it provides the option of extended-time administration of the test for those students whose native language is not English—therefore, suitable for our students.

Review of Literature

In order to provide a rationale for using the NDRT to test the FWP students, a review of available literature related to the subject was attempted. According to Flippo, Hanes, and Cashen (1991), assessing the reading abilities and reading needs of entering university freshmen has become a fairly standard practice, resulting in the growth of college reading assistance programs throughout the U.S. These researchers state that of the incoming freshmen and re-entering students in the U.S., approximately one-third to one-half are in need of reading assistance. Seventy-five percent of four-year public institutions in the US offer developmental and/or remedial programs in reading. Flippo, et al., citing the works of Kerstiens (1990) and Ross and Roe (1986), state that "the need for such programs is likely to increase over the next decade" (p. 118). The existence of learning assistance programs in postsecondary institutions indicates that high schools are not preparing all their graduates for the intense independent learning that is required in colleges and universities. This need for learning assistance "extends from the earliest colleges in the country to the newest, from open admission junior colleges to highly selective universities, and from high-risk students to straight-A students" (Carpenter & Johnson, 1991, p. 29).

In order to determine who needs reading programs, reading tests are the most commonly used instruments. According to Flippo, et al. (1991),

> "Many post-secondary institutions, even those with open admission policies, require incoming students to take tests as part of the admissions process. Reading tests are often among the exams administered. The extent to which reading tests are used varies from institution to institution and from state to state; some states require all students entering postsecondary schools within the state system of higher education to take reading tests" (p. 119).

According to Flippo, et al., reading tests are popular because they provide data for an institution's academic profile of its students, thus providing a measure against which stability or change in the student body can be measured. Reading tests, similar to the Scholastic Aptitude Test (SAT) and the American College Test (ACT), have predictive value; therefore, they have significant standing alongside these more traditional admissions criteria.

Though reading tests have become important as part of an institution's academic profile and as a predictor of academic success, they are not free of problems. The long-standing concern related to most reading tests is that they may not adequately reflect the actual reading demands of academic course work (Wood, 1988). One needs to look at the various tests critically and match the tests to the purposes for their use. Current trends in testing advocate that institutions should develop their own tests; Flippo, et al. (1991), offer a note of caution in such cases: ". . . if a college elects to develop its own test, it should do so with the expertise of a testing and measurement specialist. Such tests must undergo rigorous review and field testing by the content and reading faculty involved" (p. 126). Popham (1975) recommends norm-referenced tests as they are the best measures for looking at one student in relation to others of similar age and educational level. Maxwell (1981), on the other hand, advises institutions to develop their own norms, based on the performance of their students. However, to develop local norms data on test administration findings need to be looked at over a period of at least three to five years.

Several studies and program descriptions have reported that using survey tests for diagnostic and achievement purposes has been useful (Anderson, 1971; Cartwright, 1972; Stewart, 1970). Creaser, et al. (1970), suggested that the NDRT may be useful for screening, prediction, diagnosis, and assessment. However, most researchers caution against using survey tests for diagnostic purposes. Carsello (1982) and Sweiger (1972) profess that the NDRT is the test most widely used by college reading instructors. Raygor and Flippo (1981), and Van Meter and Herman (1986-1987), examining the NDRT, concluded that the test was too difficult for college students with significant reading problems; therefore, though a good predictor of academic success, the NDRT was not considered useful for diagnostic purposes. The NDRT has been reviewed by several researchers (Farr, 1972; Flippo, et al., 1991; Gordon, 1983; Tierney, 1985; Ysseldyke, 1985) in order to examine the test for its weaknesses and strengths. According to these researchers, the NDRT has weakness in three areas:

1. Time constraints appear to be a problem (AUC students were administered the revised version of the NDRT [Forms G & H] which has addressed this weakness by allocating extended time, especially for non-native speakers of English).

2. The difficulty level of the reading passages is a problem for underprepared students.

3. The rate section is a problem (this did not affect AUC students; they were tested using the revised version of the NDRT [Forms G & H] which provides the option of using extended time without being tested for reading rate).

According to the same researchers the strengths of the NDRT lie in the following:

1. The instrument may be a valid measure of the reading efficiency of students in advanced reading courses. It might also be used effectively to measure the reading ability of students preparing for graduate study.

2. A strong attempt was made to norm the revised test on entering college students (Forms G & H). Few other reading survey tests have been normed on a college population; most rely on high school seniors.

3. The test can be administered in a typical college class period.

4. The passages in the reading comprehension section are an attempt to test students' ability to read typical textbook material. However, due to the brevity of all passages except the first, extended reading cannot be measured.

Method

The Nelson-Denny Reading Test was administered over a period of four semesters: Spring 1995, Fall 1995, Spring 1996 and Fall 1996 to students enrolled in English 112, English 113 and the Core Seminar. The test was administered either by individual teachers in their classrooms or by the Reading Specialist. All those administering the test were trained to administer the test and were required to follow the instructions.

The data derived were used to ascertain the grade equivalent scores, percentile ranks, and stanines. A comparison was also drawn between the Grade Equivalent scores of the students and their performance in their writing classes. In order to analyze the data the following variables were looked at:

1. Raw Scores for Vocabulary
2. Raw Scores for Reading Comprehension
3. Total Scores
4. Scaled Scores
5. Grade Equivalents
6. Percentile Ranks
7. Stanines

The data also included the following demographic information which was used in the analysis:

1. Student Name
2. Student ID
3. Student's Date of Birth
4. Gender
5. Instructor's Name
6. Nature/Enrollment Standing (e.g., freshman, sophomore)

Data regarding the nature of a student—whether a Direct Entrant or one who had enrolled in FWP after completing course work in IEP and/or English 111—was obtained from the FWP Administration. In addition to this information, Instructors were asked to rate the class performance of their students as Good, Average, or Weak, in relation to their writing skills.

Analysis

This study tested students in order to ascertain their reading levels and to compare those levels with their performance in their writing classes. Table 1 shows the number of students tested and the courses they were enrolled in during the four semesters. The total number of students tested was 2,522. Of this total, 1,710 students were enrolled in English 112.

Table 1. Students Tested

	Spring '95	Fall '95	Spring '96	Fall '96
English 112	392	467	368	483
English 113	—	—	332	—
Core Seminar	—	—	184	296
Total	392	467	884	779

As data regarding teacher perceptions of English 113 and Core Seminar students is not complete, the discussion presented here will focus only on data pertaining to English 112 students.

Nature/Enrollment of Students

Of the 392 English 112 students tested in the Spring 1995 semester, no breakdown regarding their nature or enrollment standing was attempted. However, during subsequent analysis of the data the enrollment/nature of the students was looked at, as well as their gender and class performance. During Fall 1995 467 English 112 students were tested, however, the nature/enrollment of two students was not identified. Table 2 illustrates the nature/enrollment of students in English 112 who took the NDRT.

Table 2. Nature/Enrollment: English 112

Nature	Fall 1995	Spring 1996	Fall 1996
Direct Entrants	261	95	238
English 111	149	179	179
IEP	55	94	50
Total	467	368	483

Teacher Perceptions

The NDRT results were used in order to compare the reading levels of the students with the Instructors' perceptions of students' abilities in class. At the beginning of each semester, workshops are held to facilitate an understanding of the grading system followed by FWP. These workshops are designed to orient new faculty and reorient the "old" faculty to follow criteria and standards set by the Program. For the purposes of this study, instructors teaching English 112 were asked about their perceptions pertaining to their students' performance in class. These data are illustrated by tables 3 through 5. Table 3 shows that the standing of three students was not identified.

Table 3. Instructor Perceptions: English 112 Fall 1995

Standing	Number	Percent
Weak	148	31.90
Average	169	36.42
Good	147	31.68
Total	464	100.00

Table 4. Instructor Perceptions: English 112 Spring 1996

Standing	Number	Percent
Weak	103	27.99
Average	161	43.75
Good	104	28.26
Total	368	100.00

Table 5. Instructor Perceptions: English 112 Fall 1996

Standing	Number	Percent
Weak	147	30.43
Average	219	45.34
Good	117	24.22
Total	483	100.00

Reading Levels

An analysis of the test scores indicates a pattern of students' reading levels. The majority of students, according to the test results, were reading at the high school level, i.e., at levels indicative of grades 9 through 12. For the Spring and Fall 1995 testing, the data were divided into three groups: middle school level or below; high school levels; and college/university levels.

In order to acquire a better understanding of students' reading levels, the Spring and Fall 1996 data were broken into groups that were indicative of groups elementary school levels (i.e., grades 4.1-6.9); middle school; the first two years of high school; the last two years of high school; and college/university levels. Tables 6 and 7 illustrate the number of students that were reading at the high school levels.

Table 6. High School Reading Levels—Grades 9-12

	Number	Percent
Spring 1995	227	57.9
Fall 1995	301	64.5

Table 7. High School Reading Levels—Grades 9-12

Semester	Grade Equivalent Range			
	9.1 - 10.9		11.1 - 12.9	
	Number	Percent	Number	Percent
Spring 1996	158	42.9	391	24.72
Fall 1996	200	41.40	95	19.60

The data for the 1996 Spring and Fall were further analyzed in order to study the reading levels of the students with respect to their nature/enrollment. In Spring 1996 there were 95 Direct Entrants and there were 179 students who had come through English 111. In Fall 1996 there were 238 Direct Entrants. Of the 179 students coming through English 111, 94 were reading at levels indicative of the first two years of high school, and of the 50 students coming through IEP, 28 were reading at those levels. Summaries of these data are shown in Tables 8 and 9.

**Table 8. Nature/Enrollment & High School
Reading Levels—Spring 1996**

| Nature/ | Grade Equivalent Range | | | |
| | 9.1 - 10.9 | | 11.1 - 12.9 | |
Enrollment	Number	Percent	Number	Percent
Direct Entrants	32	33.7	26	27.4
English 111	74	41.3	52	29.1
IEP	52	55.3	13	13.8
Total	158	42.9	391	24.72

Table 9. Nature/Enrollment & High School Reading Levels—Fall 1996

| Nature/ | Grade Equivalent Range | | | |
| | 9.1 - 10.9 | | 11.1 - 12.9 | |
Enrollment	Number	Percent	Number	Percent
Direct Entrants	78	32.8	60	25.2
English 111	94	48.2	30	15.4
IEP	28	56.0	5	10.0
Total	200	41.4	95	19.6

The Reading/Writing Connection

A general assumption held by most educators is that a good reader will also be a good writer. According to Pearson (1994), reading and writing are inter-related skills which support each other in several ways: the writer is able to construct meaning through reading by understanding the structure and the conventions of language use; the writer learns to read critically in order to improve his/her writing; and the interdependence of the two skills helps the writer to construct meaning while reading. Rosenblatt (1978) states that the transactional view of reading not only "assumes close attention to the words of the text, but it assumes an equal closeness of attention to what that particular juxtaposition of words stirs up within each reader" (p. 137).

She is of the opinion that the interpretation of the text as well as the feelings evoked in the reader should be voiced through writing and through group discussions. This connection between reading and writing has also been advocated by Nancie Atwell (1990) in *Coming to Know*. She encourages educators to examine the "role of writing in helping their students learn about and appreciate the literature they read" (p. xx). Through their writing, the readers are responding to what they found interesting while reading. Anderson (1994) states that he focuses on raising his students' awareness of their own reading processes, as well as their expectations while reading, and the reason(s) for those expectations. When they arrive at this point, they are ready to write. He goes on to state that this

> can only be done satisfactorily by a close reading and analysis of the text. This rhetorical approach, in combination with the reader-response theory, gives students a beginning point. It gives them something concrete to write about and, more importantly, makes better readers of them (p. 312).

Chamblee (1998), discussing her instructional framework, points out that its foundation

> consists of the reader response theories and the process approach to the teaching of writing, but supporting the framework are two very important, yet basic, principles—the importance of connecting the reading and writing processes and the value of helping students bring their own experiences to their reading and writing. (pp.532-33)

Other educators, too, have found that exposing their students to literature has proven to be an effective model for writing. Lancia, discussing the development of his students' writing skills points out that a "literature-rich environment in combination with an interactive writing workshop enabled" them to make "natural connections between their reading and writing through their daily interactions with books" (p.475).

Goodman (1985) considers reading to be transactive and looks at the processes through which a reader constructs meaning. He looks at the role of the writer in creating text, the "interactions and transactions between the reader and the text," (p. 826) and at the unity in reading and writing. Like Rosenblatt, Goodman is of the opinion that the transactional theory takes into consideration that the "knower" as well as the "known" are transformed during the processing of learning and knowing. New knowledge is accommodated and assimilated by the reader, thereby altering the reader's conceptual schemata, which allows the writer to give voice to the new awareness and knowledge. This connection between reading and writing allows for the construction and expression of meaning.

One of the purposes of this study was to compare the writing skills of the students enrolled in the FWP courses with their reading levels. An analysis of the data revealed that those students who were identified as weak writers by their instructors were also weak readers. Those students who were identified as average writers read at levels that reflected middle school reading levels or that of the first two years of high school. The students who were identified as good writers invariably read at levels reflective of high school or higher levels. The latter category of students had a fairly extensive vocabulary as well as good comprehension skills at their command. These skills were reflected in their written assignments, which were of a higher caliber than those of their classmates.

Conclusions

The following conclusions can be drawn from this study:

1. A large number of students enrolled in English 112 were reading at levels appropriate for the first two years of high school.

2. The results of the study show that over the four semesters, the Direct Entrants into FWP consistently scored higher than those students who enrolled in these courses after attending courses in ELI, i.e., IEP and/or English 111. A possible reason for the better performance of the Direct Entrants could be that they were fairly good readers when they entered AUC, and that the students who came through ELI were weak readers when they enrolled at AUC.

Recommendations

The recommendations put forth as a result of the study were:

1. The American University in Cairo should take the responsibility for and provide assistance to those students who score below a specified score (perhaps below the first two years of high school) on the NDRT, or another similar instrument.

2. An option that should be given serious consideration by the University Administration is that of hiring one or more Reading Specialists in order to set up a Reading Center. The Center could offer both remedial and developmental courses in reading.

3. Another option would be that incoming students who score below the specified score on the NDRT should not be allowed to enroll in FWP courses, but should be asked to take courses in ELI until they achieve a proficiency level suitable for academic work.

4. Particular attention should be given to the schooling of the students prior to their entering AUC, in an effort to understand which schools

provide better students. This information could possibly influence future admission policies.

5. A major drive for Reading Across the Curriculum should be set into motion. All disciplines at AUC, as well as the language programs and FWP, should emphasize reading skills.

6. The existence of a problem is obvious from the results of the study. This problem is concerned with the students' inability to read proficiently. According to Flippo, et al. (1991), reading tests provide data for an institution's academic profile of its students, thus providing a measure against which stability or change in the student body can be measured. In order for AUC to address the problem of students' weak reading skills and to find possible solutions, the study should be repeated; this would allow for another look at the students' reading skills, which could help to predict their success in various academic courses of their chosen majors.

Perhaps this study indicates that there is a strong connection between reading and writing and that in order to encourage students to develop and improve their writing skills and abilities, they should be encouraged to develop good reading skills.

References

Anderson, C. A. (1971). "Problems of individualization." In F. P. Greene (Ed.) *Reading: The right to participate.* Milwaukee, WI: National Reading Conference.

Anderson, L. (1994). "Rhetoric: Reader-response theory, and teaching literature." In J. M. Q. Davies (Ed). *Bridging the gap: Literary theory in the classroom.* West Cornwall, CT: Locust Hill Press.

Atwell, N., Ed. (1990). *Coming to know: Writing to learn in the intermediate grades.* Portsmouth, NH: Heinemann.

Carpenter, K., & Johnson, L.L. (1991). "Program organization." In R. F. Flippo, & D. C. Caverly (Eds.), *College reading and study strategy programs.* Newark, DE: International Reading Association.

Carsello, J. (1982, October). *Tests, workbooks, and books being used in college basic skills programs: The latest survey of college and university programs in the U.S.* Paper presented at the Twenty-fifth Annual Conference of the North Central Reading Association, Flint, MI.

Cartwright, C. A. (1971). "Individualization of instruction in a reading and study skills center with junior college and/or open door policy students." In F. P. Greene (Ed.), *College reading: Problems and programs of junior and senior colleges.* Boone, NC: National Reading Conference.

Chamblee, C. M. (1998). "Bringing life to reading and writing for at-risk college students." *Journal of Adolescent & Adult Literacy 41,* 532 - 537.

Creaser, J., Jacobs, M., Zaccarea, L., & Carsello, J. (1970). "Effects of shortened time limits on the Nelson-Denny Reading Test." *Journal of Reading, 14,*167-170.

Farr, R. (1972). *Reading: What can be measured?* Newark, DE: International Reading Association.

Flippo, R. F., Hanes, M. L., & Cashen, C. J. (1991). "Reading tests." In R. F. Flippo & D.C. Caverly (Eds.), *College reading and study strategy programs*. Newark, DE: International Reading Association.

Goodman, K. S. (1985). "Unity in reading." In H. Singer & R. B. Ruddell, (Eds.), *Theoretical models and processes of reading, third edition,*. Newark, DE: International Reading Association.

Gordon, B. (1983). "A guide to postsecondary reading tests." *Reading World, 23,* 45-53.

Lancia, P. J. (1997). "Literary borrowings: The effects of literature on children's writing." *The Reading Teacher 50,* 470-475.

Maxwell, M. (1981). *Improving student learning skills*. San Francisco, CA: Jossey-Bass.

Pearson, P. D. (1994). "Integrated language arts: Sources of controversy and seeds of controversy." In L. M. Morrow, J. K. Smith, & L. C. Wilkinson (Eds.), *Integrated language arts: Controversy to consensus*. Boston: Allyn & Bacon.

Popham, W. J. (1975). *Educational evaluation*. Englewood Cliffs, NJ: Prentice Hall.

Rosenblatt, L. M. (1978). *The reader, the text, the poem: The transactional theory of the literary work*. Carbondale, IL: Southern Illinois University Press.

Ross, E. P., & Roe, B. D. (1986). *The case of basic skills programs in higher education*. Bloomington, IN: Phi Delta Kappa Educational Foundation.

Raygor, A. L., & Flippo, R. F. (1981). "Varieties of comprehension measures: A comparison of intercorrelations among several reading tests." In G, McNirch (Ed.), *Comprehension: Process and product*. Athens, GA: American Reading Forum.

Stewart, E. W. (1970). "Reading improvement program for college students." In G. B. Schick, & M. M. May (Eds.), *Reading: Process and pedagogy*. Milwaukee, WI: National Reading Conference.

Sweiger, J. D. (1972). "Designs and organizational structure of junior and community college reading programs across the country." In F. P. Greene (Ed.), *College reading: Problems and programs of junior and senior colleges*. Boone, NC: National Reading Conference.

Tierney, R. J. (1985). "Review of Nelson-Denny Reading Test, Forms E and F." In J. V. Mitchell, Jr. (Ed.), *The ninth mental measurements yearbook*. Lincoln, NE: University of Nebraska Press.

Van Meter, B. J., & Herrman, B. A. (1986-87). "Use and misuse of the Nelson-Denny Reading Test." *Community College Review, 14*(3), 25-30.

Wood, K. (1988). "Standardized reading tests and the postsecondary curriculum." *Journal of Reading, 32,* 224-230.

Ysseldyke, J.E. (1985). "Review of Nelson-Denny Reading Test, Forms E and F." In J. V. Mitchell, Jr (Ed.), *The ninth mental measurements yearbook*. Lincoln, NE: The University of Nebraska Press.

LITERACY AND
ASSESSMENT

Historical and Philosophical Antecedents of Structural Knowledge: Implications for Assessment

J. Michael Pickle
St. Mary's University of Minnesota

Liqing Tao
Western Kentucky University

Malcolm Lively
Tom Montgomery
The University of Georgia

Abstract

The structural knowledge of readers and of learners is the focus for numerous studies. Despite many investigations, the theoretical definitions for this construct vary widely. The operational definitions of the constructs are further complicated by theoretical and practical differences related to the measurement of structural knowledge. The works of Kant, Herbart, and Bartlett suggested that knowledge was organized and that variations across mental states were possible. The formulation of these ideas into models of structural knowledge is discussed. The abduction of structural knowledge from theoretical and constitutive definitions to operationalization and assessment is also addressed. Elicitation techniques are discussed and evaluated across the dimensions of conscious processing, cued or free recall, and of assumed knowledge structure. A need for alternative assessments of structural knowledge is noted.

Schema theory (e.g., Spiro, 1977) and connectionist models of reading (e.g., McClelland, 1986) depict memory as involving active processing and as organized according to relations among concepts. Structural knowledge is a psychological construct that explains how through active mental processing sensory data and mnemonic representations of concepts are formed into organized, cognitive networks. Rather than existing as discrete datum, models of structural knowledge depict concepts as systems of relations among the sensory input and the instantiated concepts, and the degree of association among these systemic elements varies.

Because structural knowledge can both facilitate and inhibit reading comprehension, teachers may need to assess their students' understanding of a concept prior to instruction. By determining how a concept is represented in memory, teachers may be able to design lessons that activate prior knowledge in a more beneficial way.

We believe that understanding how models of structural knowledge developed is vital for determining the best methods for assessment. In this article, we identify trends in the historical and philosophical development of structural knowledge, and we use these trends to examine current approaches to assessing structural knowledge.

Conceptualizations of Knowledge and of Structural Knowledge

In the Western philosophical tradition, form and organization are characteristics of knowledge. However, a number of different explanations about what produces the pattern of organization and about how concepts become associated in the mind have been suggested. The metaphysical tension between sensation and reason serves as a nexus for theories of knowledge and as a dialectic within epistemological discourse. Within this broad debate, the existence of innate ideation, the essence of mental states, and the elements that organize experience became specific foci. In the following sections, philosophical, psychological, and biological interpretations of constructive and reconstructive cognitive processes and of structural knowledge are addressed. The sections are arranged according to chronology and to field of inquiry.

Philosophical Investigations of Mental Structure and Form

Innate ideation is an important element of the discourse on structural knowledge because it serves as one explanation for the formal and the organizational characteristics of cognitive processes. Within epistemology, questions regarding the presence of innate concepts in humans have been investigated for millennia. A typical problem involves how a perceptual system that repeatedly encounters variability surrounding a phenomenon yields a unified concept. The proposed solution to this problem ranges from anamnesis, Plato's dictum about not forgetting the universal forms stored in the mind (Pappas, 1995), to the tabula rasa, the mind as a blank slate and devoid of innate conceptions (Locke, 1690). Ideas arising from the epistemological debate over innate ideation frame modern discourse on structural knowledge.

During the seventeenth century, Rationalism was the dominant epistemological paradigm in Europe, and innate ideation, concepts that are a part of the mind from birth, was one of its central tenets. The writings of Locke (1690) represented a marked disjuncture from the European philosophical zeitgeist. Locke argued that the human mind was empty at birth; self-awareness and learning resulted from the additive effects of sensation and of reflection. Rejecting innate ideation, Locke became the philosophical progenitor of British empiricism and of associationism.

Historical Antecedents of Schema Theory

Leibniz (1694) represented the initial response of the Rationalistic school to the bellwether of British empiricism. Leibniz accepted the emergence of concepts from the repetition of sensation, but he also argued that the tabula rasa of Locke could not account for integrity of perception. Leibniz posited an innate consciousness with the abilities to process the data collected by the senses and to monitor the mental states and thought processes. Perception was depicted as a passive mental activity where sensations were merely recorded and stored. The combination of sensations into concepts resulted from active mental processes. Two varieties of truth, truths of reason and truths of fact, emerged from these processes and from the disparate ontological origins of each (Reese, 1980).

The ideas of Leibniz foreshadowed three trends in epistemological theories and in modern conceptualizations of structural knowledge. First, a causal agent or a transcendental component that organized sensations into concepts was introduced. Second, variations across mental states were hypothesized. Third, a prototypical form of the dichotomy between analytic and synthetic truths was posited. The works of Kant (1787/1929) and of Herbart (1806) marked the fruition of these principles within the tradition of Rationalism.

Kantian Schematism

Building from the Leibnizian dichotomy of truths, Kant began to consider the relations among judgment, necessity, and informativity. Specifically, Kant was concerned with the essence of truths that were derived from sensation but seemed to possess logical necessity and conceptual unity. To account for these truths, Kant proposed schemata. According to Kant (1787/1929), schemata were the mental substrate that organize experience. He wrote

> Indeed it is schemata, not images of objects, which underlie our pure sensible concepts. No image could ever be adequate to the concept of a triangle in general. It would never attain the universality of the concept which renders it valid of all triangles, whether right-angled, obtuse-angled, or acute-angled; it would always be limited to a part only of this sphere. The schema of the triangle can exist nowhere but in thought. It is a rule of synthesis of the imagination, in respect to pure figures in space. (p. 182)

Although the effects of experience were additive, the unity of perception resulted from the transcendent quality of schemata, and the further development of concepts emerged from the interaction between these innate ideas and cognitive processes.

Kant had created a fairly comprehensive model of thought, but his system was derived from speculation and reflection rather than empirical studies. Despite this limitation, Kant's ideas had a pronounced and continuing influence upon scholarly discourse throughout the next two centuries. His formulation became a focus for educational systems (e.g., Herbart, 1806) and functioned as both a prototype and a foil in epistemological thought. By the dawn of the twentieth century, variants of schematism emerged from schools of philosophy and entered schools of medicine. Although grossly similar in function, the conceptualizations of schema in the later models differed markedly from Kantian notions, and these differences were so pronounced that Bartlett and others bemoaned the selection of schema as a label (Oldfield & Zangwill, 1942; 1943a; 1943b). Psychological interpretations of schematism varied from epistemological explanations in the loci of the instantiation of schema, the investigative paradigms used by the researchers, and the foci of the studies.

Psychological Interpretations of Schematism

During the late nineteenth century, the tenets of associationism promulgated by Hartley, by Mill, and by Bain pervaded the thinking of the scientific community of Great Britain and was gaining proponents on the European continent. Associationism was a variety of empiricism that suggested complex mental processes such as vision, language, and memory resulted from the additive effects of smaller processes (Reese, 1980). Ultimately the elemental processes could be traced to sensory data. However, advances in neurology led to questions about the form and the organization of memory. Schemata became a primary mechanism for explaining the processes of remembering and recall, and Henry Head (1920; 1926) was a pivotal figure in the development of these models.

Prototypes of Schema Theory

As a theoretician, Head was interested in the relations among memory, cortical lesions, vestibular perception, and somatosensory awareness. His primary interest was identifying the mechanisms involved in determining changes in posture. At the time of his work, memory trace theory was one of the principal, and arguably the dominant, model of remembering. According to the tenets of memory trace theory, mnemonic images were reflections of reality and were passively stored in the brain without alteration. Head

(1920) suggested that a static image could not be the basis for the dynamic perception of changes in posture; he postulated the existence of another standard that mediated these perceptions. Head (1920) proposed a schema that operated through

> . . . perpetual alterations in position [so that] we are always building up a postural model of ourselves which constantly changes. Every new posture or movement is recorded on this plastic schema, and the activity of the cortex brings every fresh group of sensations evoked by altered posture into relation with it. (p. 605-606)

Many of the tenets of Head's model became features of later theories of schemata and of structural knowledge. The schemata were conceived as dynamic, as operating below the level of consciousness, as modifiable, and as a mental epiphenomenon of physiological processes (Oldfield & Zangwill, 1942). The neuroanatomical areas associated with vestibular schemata were localized through clinical observations of patients with cortical lesions. Despite these substantial advances, many issues related to schema theory remained unresolved. First, Head did not address the biological instantiation of the physiological processes. Second, his early studies did not address remembering that was mediated by natural language. His student F. C. Bartlett (1932) would complete the seminal studies on the relation between schemata and the processing of texts.

Schemata and the Comprehension of Written Texts

The use of connected discourse in studies of memory (e.g., Bartlett, 1932) represented a dramatic shift in the experimental paradigm of memory research. During the early twentieth century, psychological investigations of memory typically used relatively simple stimuli such as nonsense syllables (e.g., Ebbinghaus, 1913) or ambiguous pictures (e.g., Bartlett, 1916). Connected discourse was considered too complex for empirical study.

Several factors influenced Bartlett's decision to investigate memory phenomena that were mediated by language. First, the results from empirical studies of reading (e.g., Huey, 1904) and from clinical studies of aphasia (e.g., Head, 1920) were creating an interest in the psychology and the biology of language and of language processing. Second, Bartlett was interested in anthropology (Northway, 1940), and language represented the most appropriate stimuli for investigating facilely the effects of social factors on memory. Third, Bartlett was interested in the relations among perceiving, imaging, and thinking (Bartlett, 1916), and the act of reading a text involved all of these operations. Consequently, Bartlett chose narrative and expository texts as the stimuli for his studies.

Bartlett's studies yielded several results of theoretical significance. First, his research participants did not give a verbatim retelling of the experimental texts. Details were omitted, modified, or replaced in the participants' versions. Further, the errors followed systematic patterns. These results demonstrated that memory was more than a reservoir for experiences but rather involved active, constructive processes. Second, memory was affected by organismic variables. Differences in age and in social background yielded differences in recall. Third, Bartlett (1932) argued schemata performed both reconstructive and storage functions. The text-presented information was retained in the schemata. Finally, Bartlett (1932) suggested that schemata could be modified. For Kant, schemata were innate categories of experience that were immutable. Bartlett's conception echoed the plastic schema of Head (1920) and suggested that structures that underlie knowledge are transient. The conclusions that Bartlett derived from his research have been incorporated into later versions of schema theory and into models of structural knowledge.

Current Psychological Representations of Structural Knowledge

Several elements of the epistemological investigations and of the early psychological studies of schemata are incorporated into psychological representations of structural knowledge. First, the formal and the organizational properties of knowledge are emphasized. Second, memory is depicted as constructive and reconstructive rather than as merely a reservoir for sensations and experiences. Third, the effects of organismic variables are recognized. Finally, structural knowledge is treated as relatively intransigent but still modifiable. In the following sections, each of these elements is examined from the perspectives of psychology and of other social sciences.

Formal and Organizational Properties of Structural Knowledge

Form and organization are included in operational definitions of structural knowledge (Jonassen, Beissner, & Yacci, 1992; Diekhoff, 1983). Many representations of structural knowledge posit a network arrangement for this pattern of organization (Goldsmith et al, 1991). Although the organization of these networks is heterarchical (Alexander, 1992; Goldsmith et al., 1991), superordinate and subordinate relations exist among the concepts. Superordination is characterized by centrality in the structure; subordination is associated with more distal positions in the structure (Jonassen et al., 1992). In network models of concepts and of semantic memory, centrality is inversely related to the likelihood of conceptual change (Alexander, 1992). Relations among concepts near the core of the structure are relatively intransigent.

Because structural knowledge is a psychological construct, these spatial relations are metaphorical and may not reflect the cytoarchitectonic arrangement of the brain.

The Cognitive Processes Associated With Structural Knowledge are Active Processes

Studies of category formation (e.g., Rosch, 1973) suggest that the psychological construction of concepts depict learning and instantiation in memory as an active, constructive process. Relations among concepts as mediated by the construct of structural knowledge change as a function of experience (Mitchell & Chi, 1984) and also affect perception (Neisser, 1975). Polar concepts and concepts approaching the poles of a continuum typically are easier to group into categories than concepts that fall towards the medial positions. For concepts in these medial positions, the boundaries between categories may be nebulous or even overlap. A concept may have characteristics of antithetical categories. In these cases, a heterarchical network representation (e.g., Alexander, 1992) yields a higher degree of structural flexibility that would increase an individual's ability to deal with ambiguity. Consequently, the organization of the structural knowledge also changes.

Although this level of flexibility is valuable in terms of adaptation, concomitant problems associated with mnemonic processing errors may result. Nebulous boundaries among concepts increase the difficulties associated with the accommodation of cognitive structures (Spiro, Coulson, Feltovich, & Anderson, 1988). New data that is inconsistent with an extant cognitive structure may be associated with a less appropriate concept or simply subsumed into different concepts. Consequently, structural knowledge may produce ideation and recall that differs from the experience.

Effects of Organismic Variables on Structural Knowledge

Bartlett (1932) demonstrated that organismic variables such as interests and culturally inured expectations affected how texts were interpreted and recalled. Numerous studies related to the effects of culturally transmitted concepts and beliefs on structural knowledge and cognitive structure in general have been completed. Alexander, Schallert, and Hare (1991) reported that sociocultural knowledge affects the construction of meaning, and they suggested that phenomena may be interpreted according to the social and cultural expectations of a society. Evans-Pritchard (1937) described these expectations as the idiom of belief. While studying the culture of the Azande tribe in Africa, he noted

> Within the limits set by their pattern, they [the Azande] show great intelligence, but it cannot operate beyond these limits or to put it another way: they reason excellently within the idiom of their beliefs, but they

cannot reason outside or against these beliefs, because they have no other idiom in which to express their thoughts. (p. 388)

The idiom of belief shares properties of structural knowledge. Concepts are arranged in a highly systemized structure. The premises subsumed in the system are internally consistent, are integrated with perceptual reality, and are relatively intransigent.

Structural Knowledge as a Relatively Stable but Modifiable Rubric

The relative intransigence of structural knowledge results from its internal consistency and from patterns of reinforcement. Within the context of schema theoretic processing, Piaget (1954) noted that accommodation is more difficult than assimilation. Changes in knowledge structures are difficult because expectations (Bartlett, 1932) affect the interpretation of perceptions. Therefore, even unexpected outcomes may become associated with the extant knowledge structures, and even conflicting data, in the form of unanticipated results, may reinforce both the viability of the world view and the concomitant knowledge structure. Because the predicted outcomes also may arise, the world view is reinforced following a randomized, intermittent schedule; learning acquired via this pattern of reinforcement is the most difficult to eliminate (Carlson, 1988).

Although relatively stable, structural knowledge may be modified. Often experiences that create cognitive conflict within individuals by demonstrating the insufficiencies within their explanations or by providing an alternative frame of reference for understanding the concept may be necessary for promoting lasting conceptual change. The overall knowledge structure must be modified. The divergent concepts within the knowledge structure must be replaced, and the links among data must be altered. The most effective method for determining how a student's knowledge is organized and for devising activities that create cognitive conflict is assessment.

Assessing Structural Knowledge

Assessments of structural knowledge require a method for eliciting the data on the underlying structural relations and a method for representing the organizational pattern (Jonassen et al., 1992). The elicitation phase involves getting the examinee to identify relations among concepts. During the representation phase, the structural relations among the concepts are depicted. Differences in the theoretical assumptions that underlie the assessment of structural knowledge are primarily a function of the elicitation phase.

Approaches for Eliciting Structural Knowledge

A previous review of the techniques (Jonassen et al., 1992) addressed several approaches for knowledge elicitation. Although the procedures for educing these data vary, each technique is mediated by language. Four methods for eliciting structural knowledge are reviewed across the theoretical and the philosophical dimensions that are subsumed within different models of structural knowledge. These dimensions include the amount of conscious processing, the involvement of cued recall, and the assumed knowledge structure. The use of similarity ratings, of card sorts, of word association proximities, and of categorical judgments are examined. Each technique is briefly described, and following this introduction, the techniques are compared and contrasted. Jonassen, Beissner, and Yacci (1992), Goldsmith, Johnson, and Acton (1991), and Cooke (1990) provide more extended descriptions of the techniques.

Similarity Ratings. Similarity ratings are among the most widely accepted and the most frequently used approaches for eliciting structural knowledge (Goldsmith et al., 1991; Jonassen et al., 1992). The technique involves having a respondent assign a numerical value that indicates the level of association between a pair of words. Typically a Likert or a modified Likert scale is used for rating the relation between the terms.

Card Sort. The card sort (Miller, 1969; Hirschman & Wallendorf, 1982) is an experimental and a clinical technique that forces a participant to develop organizational framework for a set of stimuli presented on cards. The typical stimuli are words or concepts, but other stimuli have been used. The participant is given a set of cards and instructed to arrange the cards into groups. Contingent on the purposes of the study, participants may or may not be given categories for sorting the cards. After the cards have been arranged, the participant is questioned about the pattern of organization. In assessments of structural knowledge, card sorts serve two functions. First, the relations among concepts are assessed through the categories that the participant develops. Second, the ability to adapt problem solving strategies and to modify conceptual structures may also be assessed.

Word Association Proximities. Word association proximities (Garskoff & Houston, 1963) are free recall measures. A stimulus word is given, and the participant is asked to list as many associated concepts as possible within a given time period. The organization of structural memory is assumed to be represented by the order of response. Highly associated words are reported first; less related words are reported later.

Categorical Judgments. Categorical judgments (Cooke, 1990) are chronometric measures of structural knowledge. The participant is first presented with a category, and subsequently, another word is presented. The participant must determine whether the word is an instance of the category. Response latencies are recorded. Lowered response latencies are expected for words closely associated with the categorical prime.

Theoretical Differences Among Approaches for Eliciting Structural Knowledge

Although each of these techniques is used frequently in studies of structural knowledge, many of their properties are atheoretical or even conflict with theoretical and constitutive definitions of structural knowledge. Consequently, the assumptions that underlie these techniques need to be examined.

Amount of Conscious Processing

Beginning with Leibniz (1694), a discrete dichotomy between conscious and unconscious mental processes has been posited, and the formation of concepts has been depicted recurrently as an unconscious process. Assessments of structural knowledge that involve lesser degrees of conscious processing have been advocated (Goldsmith et al., 1991). The four techniques included in this review differ on the amount of conscious processing. Both similarity ratings and card sorts involve a high level of conscious processing. The results from these two approaches are based on purposeful decisions and involve both declarative and conditional knowledge. In these instances, structural knowledge becomes an epiphenomenon of declarative and of procedural knowledge rather than the intermediary between these constructs. Word association proximities and categorical judgments are less conscious means for assessing structural knowledge. For both word association proximities and categorical judgments, an inverse relation exists between level of association and the amount of conscious, strategic processing. High association as operationalized by decreased response latencies for categorical judgments and by immediacy of recall in word association proximities requires less reflection about potential relations. Lower levels of association involve more systematic analysis to determine categorical inclusion or association with other concepts.

Cued Recall or Free Association

Structural knowledge may be elicited through both cued recall and free association. A pattern identified in this review was that the use of a cuing stimulus was a function of the theoretical definition of structural knowledge used in a study and of the purposes of a study. Cued recall was used to determine relations among specific concepts (e.g., Cooke, 1990). Tasks based on free association (e.g., Garskoff & Houston, 1963) were used to observe the processes subsumed in the formation of categories.

All of the techniques addressed in this review may be adapted for cued recall. The use of cues may affect both conscious and unconscious mnemonic processes. The effects of priming that are associated with centrality (Schank

& Abelson, 1977) and with distinctiveness (Galambos,1986) in network models of mnemonic processes may only be observed in tasks involving cued recall. These effects are most robust for tasks driven by unconscious processing such as making categorical judgments. Card sorts, word association proximities, and similarity ratings involve the conscious processing of cued recall.

Free association is subsumed within some card sorting tasks. In these instances, the participant is not provided with a rubric and must induce categories. Often a self-report measure is included to determine what factors are guiding the formation of categories.

Assumed Knowledge Structure

The arrangement of structural knowledge into heterarchical or hierarchical networks is disputed (Goldsmith et al., 1991). However, the theoretical model that underlies the approaches for eliciting structural knowledge affects the resultant representation. The categorical judgment and the word association proximity approaches imply a hierarchical structure. For similarity ratings and card sorts, neither a hierarchical nor a heterarchical structure is posited.

Discussion

The epistemological assumptions that underlie models of structural knowledge have been discussed for centuries. Although many of the premises are similar, the differences among the assumptions that underlie techniques for eliciting structural knowledge yield divergent theoretical and operational definitions for the construct. Several implications for reading research and for reading instruction emerge from these extant differences.

Structural Knowledge and Reading Research

Differences in definitions of knowledge have been noted in the literature (e.g., Alexander et al., 1991). Studies that involve the assessment of structural knowledge should be grounded within a specific theoretical model of structural knowledge. Without this theoretical base, the appropriateness of the elicitation technique cannot be evaluated.

Rather than selecting an elicitation technique based upon common practice, studies should be based on the elicitation technique that is the consistent with the researchers model of structural knowledge. The dimensions of conscious or unconscious processing, of assumed knowledge structure, and free or cued recall should be considered in these decisions.

The need for alternative approaches for assessing structural knowledge has been identified (Roller, 1990). As new techniques are promulgated, these approaches should be evaluated in terms of construct validity and examined from an epistemological and historical perspective.

Structural Knowledge and Reading Instruction

Models of structural knowledge have a number of implications for reading instruction. First, if a teacher comprehends the difficulties associated changing a student's understanding of a concept, lessons may be adapted to address these problems. For example, prior to reading, students may complete activities to offend their intuition (Hynd, Qian, Ridgeway, & Pickle, 1991) or advanced organizers. Such activities may facilitate the process of conceptual change. Second, assessments of structural knowledge may reveal the central beliefs that a student possesses about a concept. A teacher may use this information to scaffold instruction via analogies or to directly refute naive conceptions. Finally, when used as pretests and posttests, assessments of structural knowledge can be used to demonstrate changes in understanding and in learning.

References

Abelson, R. (1975). Concepts for representing mundane reality in plans. In D. Bobrow & A. Collins (Eds.), *Representation and understanding: Studies in cognitive science*. New York: Academic Press.

Alexander, P. A., Schallert, D. L., & Hare, V. C. (1991). Coming to terms: How researchers in learning and literacy talk about knowledge. *Review of Educational Research, 61,* 315-343.

Alexander, P. A. (1992). Domain knowledge: Evolving themes and emerging concerns. *Educational Psychologist, 27,* 33-51.

Bartlett, F. C. (1918). An experimental study of some problems of perceiving and imaging. *British Journal of Psychology, 8,* 222-269.

Bartlett, F. C. (1932). *Remembering.* Cambridge, UK: Cambridge University Press.

Carlson, N. R. (1988). *Physiology of behavior* (3rd ed.). New York: Allyn and Bacon.

Cooke, N. J.. (1990). Empirically defined semantic relatedness and category judgment time. In R. W. Schvaneveldt (Ed.), *Pathfinder associative networks: Studies in knowledge organization*. Norwood, NJ: Ablex Publishing Company.

Diekhoff, G. M. (1983). Relationship judgments in the evaluation of structural understanding. *Journal of Educational Psychology, 75,* 227-233.

Ebbinghaus, H. (1913). *Memory: A contribution to experimental psychology.*

Evans-Pritchard, E. E. (1937). *Witchcraft, oracles, and magic among the Azande.* Oxford, UK: Calredon Press.

Galambos, J. A. (1986). Knowledge structures for common activities. In J. A. Galambos, R. P. Abelson, & J. B. Black (Eds.), *Knowledge structures*. Hillsdale, NJ: Lawrence Erlbaum Associates.

Garskoff, B. E., & Houston, J. P. (1963). Measurement of verbal relatedness: An idiographic approach. *Psychological Review, 70,* 277-288.

Goldsmith, T. E., & Davenport, D. M. (1990). Assessing structural similarity of graphs. In R. W. Schvanefeldt (Ed.), *Pathfinder associative networks: Studies in knowledge organization*. Norwood, NJ: Ablex.

Goldsmith, T. E., Johnson, P. J., & Acton, W. H. (1991). Assessing structural knowledge. *Journal of Educational Psychology, 83,* 88-96.

Head, H. (1920). *Studies in Neurology, Volume II.* London: Oxford University Press.

Head, H. (1926). *Aphasia and kindred disorders of Speech, Volume I.* Cambridge University Press.

Herbart, J. F. (1806). *General theory of education.* New York: Humanities Press.

Hirschman, E. C., & Wallendorf, M. R. (1982). Free-response and card-sort techniques for cognitive content: Two studies concerning their stability, validity, and utility. *Perceptual and Motor Skills, 54,* 1095-1110.

Huey, E. B. (1968). *The psychology and pedagogy of reading.* Cambridge, MA: MIT Press.

Hynd, C. R., Qian, G., Ridgeway, V. G., & Pickle, M. (1991). Promoting conceptual change with science texts and discussion. *Journal of Reading, 34,* 596-601.

Jonassen, D. H., Beissner, K., & Yacci, M. (1993). *Structural knowledge: Techniques for representing, conveying, and acquiring structural knowledge.* Hillsdale, NJ: Lawrence Erlbaum Associates, Publishers.

Just, M. A., Carpenter, P. A., & Wooley, J. D. (1982). Paradigms and processes in reading comprehension. *Journal of Experimental Psychology: Human Perception and Performance, 17,* 404-421.

Kant, I. (1965). *Critique of pure reason.* (N. K. Smith, Trans.). New York: St. Martin's Press. (Original work published in 1787)

Leibniz, G. W. (1664). *Meditations on knowledge, truth and ideas.* New York: Humanities Press.

Locke, J. (1690/1988). *Essay concerning human understanding.* Penguin Books.

McClelland, J. L. (1986). The programmable blackboard model of reading. In J. L. McLelland, D. E. Rumelhart, & The PDP Research Group (Eds.), *Parallel distributed processing: Explorations in the microstructure of cognition. Volume 2: Psychological and biological models.* Cambridge, MA: MIT Press.

Miller, G. A. (1969). A psychological method to investigate verbal concepts. *Journal of Mathematical Psychology, 6,* 169-191.

Mitchell, A. A., & Chi, M. T. (1984). Measuring knowledge within a domain. In P. Nagy (Ed.), *The representation of cognitive structure.* Toronto, Canada: Ontario Institute for Studies in Education.

Neisser, U. (1976). *Cognition and reality.* San Francisco, CA: W. H. Freeman.

Northway, M. L. (1940). The concept of the 'schema': Part I. *British Journal of Psychology, 30,* 316-325.

Northway, M. L. (1941). The concept of the 'schema': Part II. *British Journal of Psychology, 30,* 22-36.

Oldfield, R. C., & Zangwill, O. L. (1942). Head's concept of the schema and its application in contemporary British psychology: Part I. Head's concept of the schema. *British Journal of Psychology, 32,* 267-286.

Oldfield, R. C., & Zangwill, O. L. (1943a). Head's concept of the schema and its application in contemporary British psychology: Part II. Critical analysis of Head's theory. *British Journal of Psychology, 33,* 58-64.

Oldfield, R. C., & Zangwill, O. L. (1943b). Head's concept of the schema and its application in contemporary British psychology: Part III. Bartlett's theory of memory. *British Journal of Psychology, 33,* 113-129.

Pappas, N. (1995). *Plato and the Republic.* New York: Routledge.

Piaget, J. (1954). *The construction of reality in the child.* (M. Cook, Trans.). New York: Ballantine Books.

Reese, W. L. (1980). *Dictionary of philosophy and religion.* Atlantic Highlands, NJ: Humanities Press.

Roller, C. M. (1990). The interaction between knowledge and structure variables in the processing of expository prose. *Reading Research Quarterly, 25,* 79-89.

Rosch, E. (1973). Natural categories. *Cognitive Psychology, 4,* 328-350.

Schank, R., & Abelson, R. (1977). *Scripts, plans, goals, and understanding.* Hillsdale, NJ: Lawrence Erlbaum Associates.

Smolensky, P. (1986). Neural and conceptual interpretation of PDP models. In J. L. McLelland, D. E. Rumelhart, & The PDP Research Group (Eds.), *Parallel distributed processing: Explorations in the microstructure of cognition. Volume 2: Psychological and biological models.* Cambridge, MA: MIT Press.

Spiro, R. J. (1977). In R. C. Anderson, R. J. Spiro, & W. E. Montague (Eds.), *Schooling and the acquisition of knowledge.* Hillsdale, NJ: Lawrence Erlbaum Associates.

Spiro, R. J., Coulson, R. L., Feltovich, P. J., & Anderson, D. K. (1988). Cognitive flexibility theory: Advanced knowledge acquisition in ill-structured domains. *Technical Report No. 441*: Center for the Study of Reading.

Synthesizing Authentic Assessment Information in Reading and Writing: The Potential of Curriculum Profiles

Gerry Shiel
Regina Murphy

St Patrick's College, Dublin

Michael O'Leary

Boston College

Abstract

An important development in the context of recent moves towards alternative, performance-based assessment in reading and writing has been the emergence of curriculum profiles. This paper has three broad purposes: (a) to describe curriculum profiles and their components, (b) to outline the development of curriculum profiles in reading and writing in an elementary school system, and (c) to report on an evaluation of the profiles by 64 teachers who implemented them in their classrooms. The first and second parts of the paper provide background on the nature and purposes of curriculum profiles; the third addresses the development of curriculum profiles in reading and writing; and the fourth describes the evaluation of the profiles by the teachers who implemented them. The results of the evaluation point to the usefulness of the profiles for a range of formative and summative assessment purposes, including clarifying teaching and learning goals, delivering a sequenced program of instruction, and recording the progress of students. It is concluded that curriculum profiles offer a manageable approach to synthesizing authentic assessment information in reading and writing.

Contexts for Curriculum Profiles

The past decade has seen the emergence of curriculum profiles—cumulative records of students' achievement in one or more areas of the curriculum based on key curriculum objectives—in countries as far apart as

Australia, Great Britain and the United States. These profiles enable teachers to summarize, in a systematic way, the assessment information they gather about students throughout the school year (O'Leary & Shiel, 1997).

In this section, the different contexts, both international and national, in which curriculum profiles in English have emerged are described.

The International Context

In the past decade or so, there has been widespread criticism of standardized tests of achievement. It has been argued, for example, that such tests provide information about a limited range of student learning outcomes and that they exercise a disproportionate and sometimes negative influence on curricula (e.g., Darling-Hammond, 1994; Gipps and Murphy, 1994). In the literacy field, the validity of standardized tests has been questioned on the grounds that they do not tap into 'real' reading or writing (Calfee & Hiebert, 1991). Several U.S. states, including Illinois and Michigan, have responded to such criticisms by developing improved standardized tests that require students to read extended texts, to provide extended responses, to demonstrate metacognitive awareness, and to engage in 'real' reading and writing tasks.

A second response to the difficulties with traditional standardized tests has been to extend the use of performance-based assessments. Now, several states, including Kentucky and Rhode Island, require teachers to administer these assessments, which call on teachers to observe, interpret and record the performance of students engaged in 'authentic' assessment tasks. Performance assessments focus both on the processes of learning (e.g., discussing a story, composing a text) and on completed products (e.g., final drafts of written texts). They are deemed to be more valid than traditional assessments because they reflect a closer alignment between curriculum, teaching and assessment (Calfee & Hiebert, 1991) and more 'authentic' because the performances they call for are more typical of, and relevant to, classroom life (Valencia, Hiebert & Afflerbach, 1994).

In the area of English, performance assessments include teacher-student conferences (e.g., Graves, 1982, 1994), portfolio assessment (e.g., Tierney, Carter & Desai, 1991), and miscue analysis (the analysis of children's oral reading errors) (e.g., Goodman, 1996). Whether formal or informal, these assessments are compatible with literature-based approaches to the teaching of reading and process approaches to the teaching of writing.

One challenge facing teachers who administer a range of performance-based assessments in reading and writing is that the outcomes of these assessments may not be compatible with local recording and reporting requirements at the end of a course of study or at the end of a school year. Curriculum profiles allow teachers to synthesize assessment information gleaned from performance-based assessments and other classroom-based assessments to meet these requirements.

Several countries, states and districts have developed systems for profiling students' achievement in English. Among the international systems are the *Australian National Profiles* (Australian Education Council, 1994), *National Curriculum Assessment in England and Wales* (e.g., Great Britain Schools Examination and Assessment Council, 1994), and the *Victoria English Profiles* (Victoria Department of School Education, 1991; Rowe & Hill, 1996). Examples of curriculum profiles that have been developed in the United States include the *KEEP Literacy Assessment System* (Paris et al., 1991) and the *Bainbridge Island Reading/Writing Continuum* (Hill & Ruptic, 1994). Most recently, the *American Literacy Profile Scales* (Griffin, Smith & Burrill, 1995), an adaptation of the *Victoria English Profiles*, have been introduced into the United States.

The Irish Context

Among English speaking countries, Ireland is perhaps unique in that it does not have every-student national or state-level assessment at the elementary level. Instead, samples of schools are selected to participate in national survey assessments while individual schools are expected to develop and implement their own assessment policies. The recent *Report of the Primary Curriculum Review Body* (Ireland National Council for Curriculum and Assessment, [NCCA] 1990) highlighted the need for schools to adopt a more consistent approach to recording and reporting on students' achievement across all subjects, including English. The *Report* proposed that:

1. A student profile should be entered on a record card to be developed by the Department of Education,
2. The items on the profile record card should correspond to areas of the curriculum, and
3. The entries on the card should be in accordance with (a) the informal assessments made by the teacher of the student's mastery of key objectives, and (b) the results of formal tests.

In considering ways in which profile summary marks or grades might be standardized, the Review Body recommended the use of a combination of (a) standardized test results, (b) group moderation procedures (in which agreement on meaning of scores would be reached through a consensus process involving teachers), and (c) 'verbal descriptions of prototypes' corresponding to different levels of achievement within a subject.

It was in response to the *Report of the Review Body* and subsequent policy documents (e.g., Ireland NCCA, 1993; Ireland, 1995) that curriculum profiles in reading and writing developed. Before describing the development of the profiles, however, the generic components of curriculum profiles need to be described.

What are Curriculum Profiles?

Curriculum Profiles have four main elements: indicators of achievement, levels of achievement, assessment contexts, and recording and reporting frameworks.

Indicators of Achievement. Indicators of achievement are outcome statements that describe student achievement, and they are generally based on important curriculum content. Examples of indicators of achievement in English reading include:

1. *Matches known clusters of letters to clusters in unknown words* (Band B, Victoria English Profiles, Victoria Department of School Education, 1991),

2. *Uses picture and context cues, words recognized on sight and phonic cues in reading.* (Level 2, National Curriculum Assessment in England and Wales, Great Britain, Schools Examinations and Assessment Council, 1993), and

3. *Uses basic strategies for interpreting written and visual texts and maintains continuity in understanding when meaning is disrupted.* (Level 2, Australian National Profiles, Australian Education Council, 1994).

Indicators such as these are generally difficult to interpret when they stand alone. Some profiling systems provide additional support. In the *Australian National Profiles*, up to 12 pointers or instances in which an outcome may be operationalized are provided to assist with the interpretation of individual indicators. In the standard tasks strand of National Curriculum Assessment [NCA] in England and Wales[1], the meanings of statements of attainment in the core subjects, including English, are linked to (and therefore defined by) the performance of students on standard assessment tasks or tests (see below). In other systems, such as the *Victoria English Profiles,* the meanings of individual indicators are not defined precisely. Instead, teachers are expected to call upon their own knowledge of the curriculum in English to guide their interpretation of the indicators.

Levels of Achievement. Levels of achievement (also called achievement bands) are sets of indicators that have been grouped together to provide a more general description of achievement than is offered by individual indicators. Levels are usually arranged hierarchically to reflect development in the skills and knowledge that are acquired by students as they become more proficient in a subject or subject strand. For example, there are eight levels spanning Grades 1-10 (ages 6-16) in the *Australian National Profiles.* The arrangement of indicators into levels of increasing complexity enables schools and teachers to monitor a student's achievement of the curriculum at different points during his/her schooling.

Most profiling systems require the user to consider the content and processes represented by the indicators at the different levels and to identify the highest level that has been achieved by a student at a particular point in time (e.g., the end of the school year). With the exception of the standard tasks strand of NCA in England and Wales, this involves making a 'best fit' judgement based on available assessment information and knowledge about the student's achievement.

Assessment Contexts. Assessment contexts are situations in which evidence about students' achievement may be obtained. Assessment contexts in reading and writing range from teachers' observations during teaching and learning activities, to relatively unstructured performance tasks (such as conferences, projects and portfolios) to structured tasks specifically designed to generate assessment information and paper-and-pencil tests. The ways in which assessment contexts contribute to summary profile scores vary across profiling systems. For example, users of the *Victoria English Reading Profile* who wish to determine whether or not a student has achieved Band B in English, are advised to consider the student's performance in a range of relevant contexts including:

1. reading conferences,
2. shared reading,
3. retelling,
4. cloze activities,
5. parent discussions,
6. drama activities,
7. sequencing activities, and
8. writing (based on reading).

However, no specific criteria are given for linking performance on these tasks to profiles levels. In marked contrast, the standard task of NCA in England and Wales requires teachers to administer specific performance-based tasks and paper-and-pencil tests in order to assign a particular level of achivement. For example, in order to achieve Level 2 in Reading, the average level achieved by 7 year-olds, students must do the following:

1. Read and understand three classroom signs,
2. Read a passage from a book (selected by the teacher from a list of approved books), with no more than eight words told, and with meaningful phrasing and intonation,
3. In the event that oral reading errors occur, make at least one error that makes sense in context and one that includes attention to phonics,
4. Recall the content of the passage, including at least two main points,
5. Make at least one valid prediction,

6. Locate a word in a dictionary using alphabetical order, and

7. Achieve a reading accuracy grade of at least A or B.

In between these extremes are the *Australian National Profiles - English* and the teacher assessment component of NCA in England and Wales, in which the support materials made available to teachers illustrate how links between students' work samples and their performance can be made (McLean & Campagna-Wildash, 1994, Great Britain, SEAC, 1993).

Recording/Reporting Frameworks. The grades or scores achieved by students on subject profiles may be recorded and reported to other teachers and to parents in a variety of ways. Profile record cards range from the simple, where the actual (raw) levels achieved by a student are reported for each subject/subject strand, to the complex, where normative information (such as standardized profile level scores) and descriptive comments based on the profile are also included. In a comprehensive guide accompanying the *Australian National Profiles*, for example, four options for reporting to other teachers and three for reporting to parents are provided (McLean & Campagna-Wildash, 1994). Across all options, teachers and parents are alerted to the ways in which skills and competence in different aspects of English develop over time.

In general, profile ratings lend themselves to a criterion-referenced interpretation—a student's profile rating indicates the content and skills he/she has acquired, regardless of what has been achieved by other students at the same grade level. However, as indicated above, profile level scores may also be interpreted with reference to grade-level norms (e.g., Griffin, Smith and Burrill, 1995).

In summary, curriculum profiling systems have several common elements, including indicators, levels, assessment contexts and recording/reporting procedures. While there is variation in the ways in which different systems are constructed and implemented, many of the assessment contexts that profiles draw upon are compatible with process-based approaches to teaching and assessing English.

Development of Curriculum Profiles in English

The *Drumcondra English Profiles* (Ireland Educational Research Centre, 1998) were developed for use in Irish schools. The purpose of the profiles is to:

1. Allow for the continuous assessment of students in reading and writing,

2. Provide *formative* assessment information that could guide future teaching/learning activities,

3. Provide *summative* (summary) assessment information that could be used for recording purposes within schools and could be reported to parents,

4. Link teachers' ratings of students' achievement to formal and informal assessments conducted throughout the school year,

5. Provide valid assessment information that would be reliable for its purposes, and

6. Facilitate easy interpretation of assessment outcomes by teachers, parents and other educators.

One significant feature of the profiles is its focus on grade level as an organizing framework. This allows for the assessment of each student's achievement in relation to the main curriculum outcomes for the student's grade level, on an annual basis. Other systems, such as the *Australian National Profiles* and NCA in England and Wales cut across grade levels and allow for the possibility that, for example, a 7-year old and an 11-year old could achieve the same level in a subject, despite differences in age, curriculum coverage and educational experiences.

The development of the English profiles involved two main stages: (a) the identification of indicators of achievement, and (b) the scaling of indicators. Each of these stages is described briefly below. A more comprehensive description may be found in the *Drumcondra English Profiles Handbook* (Ireland Educational Research Centre, 1998).

Identification of Indicators of Achievement

A team of teachers and subject experts identified indicators of achievement in English at each of 8 different grade levels[2] in the areas of reading and writing, resulting in 16 indicator sets in all. The indicators, which were expressed in terms of processes that can be observed by teachers during ongoing teaching and assessment activities, were gleaned from research findings, current and proposed curriculum documents, and textbooks in current use. A strong attempt was made to link the indicators to a revised national curriculum in English (Ireland NCCA, 1996), which was in draft form when the indicators were being developed. In the case of the writing indicators, a decision was made to combine higher level processes (e.g., composing skills) and lower level processes (e.g., spelling) in the same indicator sets.

Scaling of Indicators

Indicators within each set (e.g., reading, first grade) were ordered in terms of their difficulty. A sample of teachers at each grade level was asked to rank the indicators for their grade levels from most difficult to least difficult. A level of agreement for each indicator set was computed using Kendall's *Co-*

efficient of Concordance (Kendall, 1952). Using stepwise deletion, any indicators on whose ranking there was substantial disagreement among teachers were dropped. The indicators were then reordered from most difficult to least difficult in line with the judgments of teachers. Table 1 provides a set of indicators for English writing in fourth grade.

The set of indicators in Table 1 represents an ordinal scale. Such a scale could be used by teachers to rate students' achievement without further modification. For example, the highest indicator achieved by a student in a particular subject strand (e.g., writing) could be interpreted as the student's summary score in that subject strand and could be used for recording and reporting purposes. However, this approach would not allow one to compare a student's achievement across different strands within a subject (e.g., reading and writing) or to monitor a student's achievement in the same subject strand from year to year. This is because a particular indicator might be more difficult to achieve in one set (e.g., reading) than in another (e.g., writing), or at one grade level (e.g., reading in first grade) than at another (e.g., reading in second grade). Therefore, it was decided to develop norms corresponding to each indicator set that would reflect the proportions of students achieving each indicator.

The development of norms necessitated asking a second sample of teachers at each grade level to (a) administer standardized tests of achievement in English to the students in their classes, and (b) rate each student on the appropriate indicator sets for his/her class level. For each indicator set, the students' profile ratings were scaled against their standardized test results. The resulting distributions were converted to standard C-scale scores which have a mean of 5, a standard deviation of 2, and a range of 0-10 (Guilford & Fruchter, 1978). In practical terms, once a teacher identifies the highest indicator achieved by a student, the value of the indicator can be translated into a scale score using a conversion table. Scale scores can then be used by the teacher in two ways: (1) to compare achievement across the strands of reading and writing, and (2) to compare performance from year to year (teachers are encouraged to take measurement error into account).

Table 1. Writing Indicators: Fourth Grade

(Final Set—Ordered by Difficulty)

When rating a student, begin at the top of the list (the indicator regarded as being the most difficult by teachers), and continue downwards until you reach the highest indicator that has been achieved by the student.

10. Makes simple global judgements about own writing which go beyond one word rejection or praise

9.* Elaborates the meanings of sentences through use of phrases and clauses

8. Returns independently to a piece of work and redrafts to improve meaning

7.* Writes a broad range of informational texts, recognizing the functions of each

6. Selects own topics and ideas for writing and writes own interpretation of 'set' topics to suit purpose and audience

5.* Writes stories with a clear beginning, middle and end which include at least one related episode and details of setting, character, plot and resolution

4. Uses knowledge of known spelling patterns, word roots and spelling rules in attempting to spell unknown words

3. Writes uniformly, legibly and fluently in cursive script with various writing implements

2. Checks spellings and meanings of words using alphabetical order (up to the third letter) in a dictionary or thesaurus

1.* Uses capital letters and a range of punctuation marks correctly in own writing

Notes:

9.* *e.g.,* They watched a film *which was not at all suitable for Mary;* One cold, misty day I decided to go on a trip walking in the Wicklow mountains.

7.* Informational texts include reports on project topics related to history, geography, civics, science or nature; book reviews, procedures and a personal log of learning.

5.* Includes stories based on own experiences, fantasy, adventure, folktales.

1.* Punctuation marks include full stops, question marks, exclamation marks, commas and quotation marks.

Implementing the Profiles in Classrooms

An assessment by teachers of the implementation of the English profiles was conducted during the 1996-97 school year. The objectives of the exercise were to

1. Determine teachers' satisfaction with different elements of the profiles,
2. Examine teachers' perceptions of the usefulness of the profiles for a variety of teaching and assessment purposes,
3. Identify any difficulties schools or teachers experience in implementing the profiles, and
4. Determine the extent to which the teachers adopted suggested support materials in implementing the profiles.

Twelve schools were selected to participate in the study. These schools were selected with regard to size (large or medium/small), gender (girls only, boys only, mixed), and status in relation to educational disadvantage. In large schools (i.e., those with more than 300 students), two teachers were randomly selected at each of four different grade levels (K1, 1st, 3rd and 5th, or K2, 2nd, 4th and 6th grades). In medium/small schools (i.e., those with 300 or fewer students), one teacher at each of four grade levels was selected. In all, 64 teachers distributed evenly over 8 grade levels in 12 different schools were selected.

The teachers (74% female, 26% male) were generally very experienced. Seventy percent indicated that they had taught for 11 years or more, while only 8% stated that they taught for fewer than 4 years. Sixty-two percent of teachers indicated that they had taught their current grade level for 3 or more years. Only 25% of the teachers had attended more than five hours of lectures, workshops or seminars on the teaching of English during the previous five years, while only 15% had attended at least one course or seminar on assessment.

Using the Profiles

Implementation of the profiles began in November 1996 and continued until May 1997. In November, participating teachers in the K2 to 6th grades were asked to rate the achievement of the pupils in reading and writing on the profiles corresponding to the grade level immediately below their current grade. This activity provided teachers an opportunity to familiarize themselves with the profiles at an early stage in the evaluation. In January, copies of the English profiles corresponding to their current grade levels were forwarded to participating teachers. The teachers were asked to reflect on the indicator sets between the months of January and May, when they would be asked to rate their students on these indicator sets. It was suggested to the teachers that they might find the indicators useful in planning teaching and learning experiences for their students during this period. The teachers were also advised that, in arriving at their end-of-school-year profile ratings, they would be invited to draw upon any sources of information about student achievement that might be relevant. The teachers were provided with illustrated notes on miscue analysis, portfolio assessment, reading logs, reading and writing conferences, and other teaching/assessment strategies that might be helpful. In addition, the teachers were provided with annotated writing samples that described links between the characteristics of students' writing at different grade levels and particular profile ratings.

School Visits

A member of the research team visited each school at least once during the months of February and March. The purpose of the visits was to discuss the implementation of the profiles and to respond to any queries that had arisen. Individual discussions with teachers raised three main issues: the interpretation of indicators on the English Profiles, the use of support materials, and more general issues related to the assessment of reading and writing.

Interpretation of Indicators. Some teachers expressed initial concern about the meaning of individual indicators and regarded them as quite demanding for students to achieve. After some discussion, however, the teachers generally agreed that children would have opportunities to demonstrate achievement of most indicators in the context of ongoing teaching and learning activities. Teachers also showed an awareness of the need for an indicator to reflect the curriculum itself and the stage of development in language acquisition implied by it. The value of discussing the meanings of indicators with teachers at other class levels was commented upon, though there was less agreement on whether this should be done on a formal or informal basis.

Support Materials. Teachers at all grade levels expressed considerable interest in the support materials. The annotated writing samples which described links between students' writing samples and their profile ratings in writing were of particular interest to the teachers, as were the descriptions of miscue analysis and reading and writing conferences.

Related Issues. While each teacher expressed different needs in relation to the profiles, there was a number of common concerns. Most notable of these was the unequivocal demand for school-based in-service on the teaching of English and on the use of appropriate assessment techniques. Several teachers also pointed to the value of the profiles in providing a framework for the teaching of reading and writing. As one teacher of students in first grade commented, 'Of all subjects English is the most difficult to teach, the most difficult to pinpoint and the most difficult to describe in terms of content.'

Outcomes

At the conclusion of the implementation study, teachers were asked to respond to an exit questionnaire. The questionnaire asked for the views of teachers about profiles themselves and their usefulness for managing and implementing the English curriculum and reporting on students' achievement.

Content of the Profiles. First, teachers were asked to evaluate the adequacy of the indicators of achievement in reading and writing for their grade level with regard to the number of indicators, the level of difficulty implied by the ordering of the indicators, the amount of detail provided by the footnotes, and the clarity of the language used.

Almost 90% of teachers indicated that the number of indicators in the reading sets was adequate, while 81% of teachers reported that the number of indicators in the writing sets was adequate. Somewhat fewer teachers – 79% in the case of the reading and 77% in the case of writing, indicated that the level of difficulty implied by the indicator sets was adequate. Over 80% of teachers expressed satisfaction with the clarity of language used in the indicators. The teachers were somewhat less satisfied with the adequacy of detail provided by the footnotes than with other aspects of the profiles, with 71% expressing satisfaction in the area of reading and 75% in writing. While these findings are generally encouraging, they point to the need to provide additional support to some teachers using the profiles for the first time.

Usefulness of the Profiles. The teachers were also asked to respond to questions about the usefulness of the profiles in a range of teaching and assessment contexts. First, the teachers were asked to consider the usefulness of the profiles for planning. Table 2 indicates that almost all of the teachers found the profiles to be either useful or very useful for yearly and termly planning. While a majority of teachers found them to be at least useful for weekly and daily planning, a significant minority did not find them useful for these purposes. This, perhaps, reflects the fact that the profiles are designed to be used once or twice a year rather than on a day-to-day basis. Hence, the indicators may not contain the level of detail that some teachers may require for short-term planning.

Table 2. Usefulness of the Profiles for Classroom Planning

	Yearly n = 61	Termly n = 62	Weekly n = 59	Daily n = 58
Very useful*	*41%	29%	18%	12%
Useful	52%	65%	52%	40%
Of little use	7%	6%	30%	48%

Percentage of teachers selecting response

Teachers reported that they found the profiles to be useful for a range of other purposes related to teaching. As indicated on Table 3, a substantial majority of teachers found them to be useful or very useful for clarifying teaching and learning goals, delivering a sequenced program of instruction, and providing feedback to children on their work.

Table 3. Usefulness of the Profiles for Aspects of Classroom Teaching

	Day-to-day Teaching	Clarifying teaching and learning goals	Giving a sequenced programme of work	Providing feedback to children on their work
	n = 59	*n = 62*	*n = 60*	*n = 62*
Very useful	˙19%	40%	35%	24%
Useful	56%	53%	55%	44%
Of little use	25%	7%	10%	32%

˙*Percentage of teachers selecting response*

Since curriculum profiles are designed to provide teachers with a tool for recording and reporting their students' achievement, we were particularly interested in how useful the teachers would find the profiles for these purposes. As indicated in Table 4, teachers found the profiles to be particularly useful for maintaining their own records, with 45% indicating that they were very useful for this purpose. The profiles were perceived as being somewhat less useful in relation to recording progress on the school record card—perhaps because record cards were not in use in all schools in the study. Although teachers were not overly satisfied with the usefulness of the profiles for communicating progress to parents, it should be noted that parents would not have been familiar with the profiles as, on this occasion they were not involved in the implementation process.

Table 4. Usefulness of the Profiles for Recording and Reporting

	Maintaining own records	Recording progress on school record card	Communicating progress to parents orally	Reporting progress to parents on written report card
	n = 62	*n = 62*	*n = 62*	*n = 61*
Very useful	˙45%	36%	26%	31%
Useful	44%	48%	60%	53%
Of little use	11%	16%	14%	16%

˙*Percentage of teachers selecting response*

Effectiveness of the Profiles. Teachers were asked to draw comparisons between the effectiveness of the English profiles and two other assessment tools, standardized tests and checklists. Table 5 indicates percentages of teachers who perceived each tool to be most effective for a range of purposes related to teaching and assessment. Standardized tests were regarded as being more effective than either checklists or the English profiles in terms of their relevance to classroom learning, the ease with which students' achievement could be communicated to other teachers, and the extent to which the risk of assessment error could be reduced. Teachers' perceptions of the usefulness of the profiles for communicating students' achievement to other teachers may have been affected by the fact that only selected teachers in participating schools were involved in implementing the profiles. If the profiles had been implemented on a school-wide basis (i.e., at all grade levels) in at least some schools, teachers might have identified them as being more effective for communicating with one another about the achievement of students.

The English profiles were deemed to be more effective then either standardized tests or checklists for allowing the progress of students with different learning abilities to be recognized, reducing students' anxiety over assessment, and fitting to the school curriculum.

Table 5. Comparisons between the English Profiles and Other Assessment Tools for Various Purposes

	N	Standardized Tests *Most Effective*	Checklists *Most Effective*	English Profiles *Most Effective*
Ease of communicating a student's achievement to other teachers	60	*58%	15%	27%
Allowing progress of students with different learning abilities to be recognized	60	30%	10%	60%
Reducing the student's anxiety over assessment	58	9%	22%	69%
Reducing the risk of assessment error	58	46%	21%	33%
Fit to the school curriculum	59	34%	17%	49%

*Percentage of teachers selecting response

Finally, we compared the responses to teachers at different grade ranges (K1-K2, 1st-2nd, 3rd-4th, 5th-6th) to the teaching and assessment purposes found in Table 5. Teachers of students in kindergarten reported that they found the profiles to be more effective than either standardized tests or checklists in terms of their relevance to classroom learning and the ease with which assessment information could be reported to other teachers. Teachers at this level also indicated that, of the three assessment tools mentioned, profiles were most closely fitted to the school curriculum. In contrast, teachers of students in the fifth and sixth grades regarded the profiles as being less relevant to classroom learning, and somewhat less congruent with the school curriculum. This may reflect the fact that teachers at these levels are often concerned with preparing students for the transition to second-level schooling. In Ireland, this may involve preparing students for formal 'entrance' examinations that are more similar to standardized tests than to performance-based assessments.

Conclusions

A substantial majority of teachers indicated that they found the profiles to be useful for a range of formative and summative assessment purposes. The formative purposes for which the profiles were deemed to be most useful included clarifying teaching and learning goals, delivering a sequenced program of instruction, and recording the progress of students. Among the summative assessment purposes supported by the profiles were maintaining assessment records, recording progress on the school record card, and reporting students' progress to parents on written report cards. The profiles were found by teachers to be more effective than either standardized tests or checklists for reducing students' anxiety about assessments and allowing the progress of students with different learning abilities to be recognized.

The majority of teachers who evaluated the implementation of the profiles in their classrooms had not participated in inservice courses on the teaching or assessment of English in the five years preceding their evaluation of the profiles. This may explain both the enthusiasm of teachers for the support materials with which they were provided, and, conversely, the perception among some teachers that standardized tests were more effective than either the profiles or checklists for purposes such as communicating a student's achievement to other teachers. It is clear that the effective implementation of the profiles across greater numbers of teachers will need to take into account (a) the existing situation in many schools, in which standardized testing is the most common form of assessment, particularly at the middle-school grade levels; (b) teachers' understanding of the processes underlying reading and writing, and the confidence of teachers in using various strategies to assess those processes; and (c) the shared understanding of the profiles achieved by teachers.

The profiles represent a manageable approach to recording students' achievement on key achievement outcomes in reading and writing. The strong interest of teachers in alternative assessment procedures and their overall positive response to the profiles themselves suggest that the profiles can be used successfully by teachers to synthesize authentic assessment information.

Notes

[1] National Currriculum Assessment in England and Wales has two strands. One, the standard tasks strand, consists of performance tasks and paper-and-pencil tests, which teachers are required to administer to their students at ages 7, 11 and 14. These assessments are criterion-referenced, and point to the highest level (on an eight-level scale) that a student has achieved. The second assessment strand, teacher assessments, requires teachers to make their own (more informal) assessments of their students. Only results generated by the standard tasks are used for accountability purposes (i.e., comparisons between schools), whereas the outcomes of standard tasks and teacher assessments are recorded at the school level and are reported to parents.

[2] Irish children generally begin elementary school at age four and move through Kindergarten 1 (K1), Kindergarten 2 (K2), and Grades 1 to 6 before progressing to second-level schooling at about age 12.

References

Australian Education Council. (1994). *English — A curriculum profile for Australian schools.* Carlton: Victoria Curriculum Corporation.

Calfee, R., & Hiebert, E. (1991). Classroom assessment of reading. In R. Barr, M. Kamil, P. Mosenthal and P. D. Pearson (Eds.), *Handbook of reading research* (Vol. 2, pp. 281-309). White Plains, NY: Longman.

Darling-Hammond, L. (1994). Performance based assessment and educational equity. *Harvard Educational Review, 64,* 5-30.

Education Department of Western Australia. (1994). *First Steps: Reading developmental continuum.* Melbourne: Longman.

Gipps, C. V., & Murphy, P. (1994). *A fair test? Assessment, achievement and equality.* Buckingham: Open University Press.

Goodman, Y. M. (1996). Revaluing readers while readers revalue themselves: Retrospective miscue analysis. *Reading Teacher, 49,* 600-609.

Graves, D. (1982). *Writing: Teachers and children at work.* Portsmouth, NH: Heinemann.

Graves, D. (1994). *A fresh look at writing.* Portsmouth, NH: Heinemann.

Great Britain Schools Examinations and Assessment Council. [SEAC]. (1993). *Assessment handbook: English (Key Stage 1)*. London: Author.

Great Britain School Curriculum and Assessment Authority (1994). *English in the national curriculum*. London: Author.

Griffin, P. E., Smith, P., & Burrill, L. E. (1995). *The American literacy profile scales: A framework for authentic assessment*. New Hampshire: Heinemann.

Guilford, J. P., & Fruchter, B. (1978). *Fundamental statistics in psychology and education* (6th ed.). Tokyo: McGraw-Hill Kogakusha.

Hill, B. C., & Ruptic, C. (1994). *Practical aspects of authentic assessment: Putting the pieces together*. Norwood, MA: Christopher-Gordon Publications.

Ireland. (1995). *Government white paper on education: Charting our education future*. Dublin: Stationery Office.

Ireland Educational Research Centre. (1998). *Drumcondra English profiles handbook*. Dublin: Author.

Ireland National Council for Curriculum and Assessment. (1990). *Report of the Review Body on the primary curriculum*. Dublin: Stationary Office.

Ireland National Council for Curriculum and Assessment. (1993). *A programme for reform: Curriculum and assessment policy towards the new century*. Dublin: Stationary Office.

Ireland National Council for Curriculum and Assessment. (1996). *Curriculum for primary schools: English—Draft Edition (June)*. Dublin: Author.

Kendal, M. D. (1952). *The advanced theory of statistics* (Vol.1) (5th ed.). London: Charles Griffin.

McLean, K., & Campagna-Wildash, H. (1994). *Using the English profile*. Victoria, Australia: Curriculum Corporation.

O'Leary, M., Shiel, G. (1994). Curriculum profiling in Australia and the United Kingdom: Some implications for performance-based assessment in the United States. *Educational Assessment, 4*, 203-235.

Paris, S. G., Calfee, R.C., Filby, N., Hiebert, E. H., Pearson, P. D., Valencia, S. W., Wolf, K. P., & Hansen, J. (1991). A framework for authentic literacy assessment. *Reading Teacher, 46*, 88-99.

Rowe, K. J., & Hill, P. W. (1996). Assessing, recording and reporting students' progress: the case for 'subject profiles'. *Assessment in Education, 3*, 309-351.

Tierney, R., Carter, M., & Desai, L. (1991). *Portfolio assessment in the reading-writing classroom*. Norwood, MA: Christopher Gordon.

Valencia, S. W., Hiebert, E. H., & Afflerbach, P. P. (1994). Realizing the possibilities of authentic assessment: Current trends and future issues. In S. W. Valencia, E. H. Hiebert, & P. A. Afflerbach (Eds.), *Authentic reading assessment: Practices and possibilities* (pp. 286-290). Newark, DE: International Reading Association.

Victoria Department of School Education. (1991). *English profiles handbook: Assessing and reporting students' progress in English*. Victoria, Australia: Author.

Assessing Oracy and Literacy in Bilingual Students: Getting the Whole Picture

Linda Lewis-White

Eastern Michigan University

Abstract

In this descriptive study, formal and informal measures of language and literacy proficiency are analyzed and compared in order to evaluate and describe the language competencies of four bilingual students. The study also describes and compares the use of that information in making instructional program placement decisions.

Introduction

Educational policy makers have been faced with the problem of identifying and assessing language minority students since the passage of the federal Bilingual Education Act in 1968. According to Tinajero (1985) most states adopted a three-step process which included (a) a home language survey, (b) an oral language proficiency test in English, and (c) assessment of language development in the home language to identify eligible students. In addition to these, a standardized norm-referenced test, such as the *Iowa Test of Basic Skills* or the *Comprehensive Test of Basic Skills*, was included for students in the second grade and above in order to (a) determine eligibility (Haney, 1985); (b) determine which students should exit (Bennett, 1987); and (c) avoid placement in and exit from bilingual programs based solely upon assessment of what Tinajero (1985) calls the "surface proficiency of the language" (p. 70).

Two assumptions underlie the development of such a screening process for language minority students. First, oral language development precedes written language development and that language is linear in nature; what Harste, Woodward and Burke (1984) call the Oral Language Supremacy Assumption. Such a view polarizes language, oral and written, to the extent that language instruction moves from concept development in oral language to reading and then writing instruction. The second assumption is that the current standardized tests can measure "the complex cognitive processes of language, reading, (and) writing...through simplistic means" (Flores, Cousin, Díaz, 1991, p.372).

Bruck, Shultz and Rodriguez-Brown (1979) state that product data cannot be accurately interpreted without process data. Given the complexity of language acquisition and literacy development, it would be unreasonable to allow these singularly product oriented assessments to stand as representatives of the richness of language use among bilingual students. It seems more appropriate to find more holistic measures to use in assessing language proficiency and literacy development. Since teachers see the "whole" language performance of their students, their observations over a period of time are essential in interpreting test data and in making instructional program placement decisions.

Teachers observe students day in and day out and possess the most intimate knowledge of their students' acquisition of language and literacy skills. Such knowledge is often considered to be subjective and therefore not entirely credible. But, what if the teachers' observations were "formalized" through the use of anecdotal records and reading and writing portfolios? Would this collection of student behaviors and work samples be objective in describing a student's academic linguistic abilities? Would the data gathered from classroom-based reading and writing activities give a more accurate description of a student's second language development thereby enabling those involved in instructional program placement to make better choices for the student? Ultimately, these are the questions this research project sought to answer.

Theoretical Framework

Among language and reading educators, there is a widespread interest in how students construct meaning (Goodman, 1967; Rosenblatt, 1978; Valencia and Pearson, 1987). More and more, language is seen as a whole in which listening, speaking, reading and writing are separate but interdependent subcomponents of one system (Halliday, 1978; Edelsky, Altewerger, and Flores, 1991). Reading and writing are language processes which are learned by doing (Wilson, 1985). As such, it is difficult to break them down into testable subcomponents, the sum of which equals the whole.

Reading achievement tests tend to evaluate reading performance through a variety of subtests, such as "vocabulary identification, sight-word reading, the matching of pictures with simple sentences, the comprehension of simple passages, and literal recall" (Garcia, 1992, p.4). Writing achievement tests evaluate student ability in writing in a similar manner with subtests in spelling, grammar, sentence structure and punctuation. Such measures provide little insight into reading and writing as processes and do not reveal how students are utilizing strategies in order to make sense of text, or acknowledge the role of prior knowledge in comprehension (Valencia and Pearson, 1987). Nor do they recognize the recursive natures of reading and writing. In addition to what seems an incongruence between current language instruction theories and practice and traditional assessment (Chittenden, 1991; Gottlieb, 1995; McNamara, 1995), traditional assessment practices present other problems for the language minority student.

Traditional assessments have a three-quarter century history of racism and discrimination. They have been used to blame students' diversity for their lack of academic achievement, direct instructional placement, determine who attends college, and decide who is eligible for special programs (Garcia and Pearson, 1991). Language minority students' experiences with special programs such as English as a Second Language and bilingual education are based largely on the reading and language scores gathered from traditional assessment instruments. Scores for entry and exit from special language programs are set based on the assumption that the assessment instruments used give valid and reliable data. However, many of the tests contain biases which work against the language minority student, and many were intended for program evaluation (Norris, 1990) rather than placement decisions. Thus, the use of these scores alone in entry and exit decisions is questionable.

Traditional assessment instruments were selected because they were well-developed, fairly easy to administer, available and cheap (Madaus, 1985). Little consideration was given to the linguistic differences between monolingual and bilingual students which would adversely affect the reliability of the test results for language minority students. Semantic content of key vocabulary (Clarke, 1979, Cziko, 1978; Perkins, 1983), knowledge of test procedures (Tyler and White, 1979), and differential perception of questions and answers (Au, 1981; Heath, 1982) have been questioned as factors affecting the test performance of language minority students. Also, the prescribed time limits for such tests may discriminate against bilingual students. Research by Chamot (1980) and Eaton (1980) demonstrated that the second-language learner needs more time on timed tests because s/he takes longer to process information in either L1 (primary language) or L2 (secondary language), and they read more slowly in their second language. Lennon (1970) writes, "Rate is only meaningful as it defines the rapidity with which the reader covers the material at a particular level of comprehension" (p.31). In a discussion of what aspects of text influence recall, Johnson (1983) suggests that density of information and quantity of information slow the reading process. For the second language learner, the amount of information to process is doubled in any reading tasks and thus the rate of reading is slowed. To compare the reading rate of bilingual students to that of monolingual students produces a bias against the bilingual student. When reading rate is calculated as part of a comprehension score, the implication is that bilingual students are poor readers, when in reality they may read just as well as their monolingual peers.

Most language proficiency assessments measure phonology, lexicon, semantics and syntax and are based on "the assumption that language can be separated into various components" (p.34) which can be assessed in isolation (Ortiz and Polyzoi, 1988), (i.e., context-reduced communication). In a survey of 46 language proficiency tests, DeAvila and Duncan (1976) found that 43 measured vocabulary, 34 assessed oral syntax comprehension and 9 assessed functional use of language. The focus of the tests is on the structural aspect of language, although research indicates that tests of phonology and grammar are not accurate predictors of communicative competence (Savignon, 1972; Tucker, 1974; Upshur and Palmer, 1974).

Cummins (1981, 1984), Troike (1982), and Tinajero (1985) warn against an over reliance on language proficiency test scores for placement, transfer, and exit of students from programs without including reading and writing measures. At best, language proficiency assessments are descriptors of surface language proficiency. Rarely are they indicators of a student's underlying language proficiency or his/her ability to read and/or write. When instructional placement decisions are based solely upon language proficiency scores, the consequences for the student can be devastating. Students who are exited from second language programs based on language proficiency scores alone often meet failure in the general education program. It is then assumed that because the students demonstrate "language proficiency" in face-to-face communication that poor academic performance is not attributable to language but to deficient cognitive abilities. However, the more likely explanation for poor academic performance may be the lack of literacy development in L1 and L2 "necessary to learn information from text" (Garcia, 1992, p. 3).

Just as listening, speaking, reading and writing are interactive, so too must the instruments used for their assessment. Partridge (1992) suggests that language assessment should be an intermediary between real-world language tasks and behaviors and theoretical instructional practice. Short (1993) argues that because assessment plays a gatekeeping role in second language programs it should be commensurate with academic demands students will encounter, and it should correspond to instruction.

According to Chittenden (1991) assessment must be open-ended, cumulative and based on theory that matches the instructional practices in the classroom. Portfolios offer such an assessment schemata because they "implement assessment practices that (a) capitalize on the actual work of the classroom, (b) enhance teacher and student involvement in evaluation, and (c) meet some of the accountability concerns of the district" (Chittenden, 1991, p. 23).

Valencia (1990) writes that in order for assessment to be sound, it must be authentic, continuous, multifaceted, multidimensional, and collaborative. In order for assessment to be authentic the task must be meaningful and purposeful to the student. Assessment is continuous when it is formative in nature. Assessment is multifaceted and multidimensional when it is composed of a variety of tasks which are evaluated on many levels. Good assessment provides opportunities for teacher and student to reflect upon learning (Valencia, 1990). When teacher and students conference about things important to them, then the learning has the potential to extend into the real world (Tierney, et al., 1991).

Such an instrument would have the potential to be as diverse as the student population it is meant to assess. One such instrument is the portfolio, a systematic, organized collection of student work, chosen by both the teacher and student as evidence of growth in knowledge, skills and abilities in a subject area.

In addition to portfolios, anecdotal records, which record a teacher's observations of students' everyday use of reading and writing, have become a widely accepted tool for the assessment of literacy in the classroom (Bird, 1989; Galindo, 1989; Y. Goodman, 1985; Morrissey, 1989). Y. Goodman (1985) writes that teachers can gain greater insight into children's language development with such assessment. These records offer an opportunity to observe the dual language abilities of the students and to develop an accurate view of the child's total language knowledge.

Portfolios and anecdotal records have emerged as instruments for recording and interpreting student development in language and literacy (Bird, 1989; Camp, 1993; Chittenden, 1991; Glazer and Brown, 1993; Gottlieb, 1995; Krest, 1990; Tierney et al., 1991, Valencia, 1990). In contrast to traditional assessment, portfolios represent the multiple settings and purposes for reading and writing, allow for linguistic and cultural diversity, provide opportunities for collaborative evaluation, link learning to teaching and assessment, and give a more accurate picture of student knowledge and ability (Allaei and Connor, 1991; Short, 1993; Tierney, et al., 1991; Valencia, 1990). Moss, et al. (1992) suggest that the information provided in portfolios is richer and reflects the processes of thinking and revising.

According to Huerta-Macías (1995) these alternative assessments "consist(s) of valid and reliable procedures that avoid many of the problems inherent in traditional testing including norming, linguistic, and cultural biases" (p. 10). Gottlieb (1995) states that validity and reliability are ensured by the sampling of authentic classroom tasks that are aligned with the curriculum. Miller and Legg (1993) write that such a multi-faceted approach to information gathering is effective in diagnostic situations.

Writing on alternative assessment, Worthen (1993) notes that portfolios and anecdotal records date back to Socrates, and elementary teachers have been keeping such records for some time. If they have been used for a long time as evaluation tools in a variety of disciplines, is it not reasonable to use them in the area of language and literacy development? (Tierney, et al., 1991). Like the fine arts, language and literacy are process and product driven, and they are developmental in nature.

As assessment tools, portfolios and anecdotal records offer flexibility in the assessment schedule and in the types of information used for making academic decisions. In addition, Hiebert and Calfee (1989) write that "assessments based on observations and performance samples are consistent and repeatable, and they provide insights often lacking in the reports of standardized test results" (p. 52).

Design of the Study
Research Questions

Through the description, comparison, evaluation, and analysis of the results of oral language proficiency assessments and standardized test scores with holistic assessment measures, the following questions were explored:
1. What do authentic assessments tell us about a bilingual student's English language proficiency?
2. What do traditional assessments of reading and language tell us about a bilingual student's language proficiency?
3. What is the overall picture of a bilingual student's English language proficiency based on traditional language assessment compared to the overall picture of a bilingual student's English language proficiency based on real-time language assessment?

Subjects

The subjects for this study were four language minority students in a bilingual third-grade class in an urban, public school. The students were randomly selected from a field of seven boys and seven girls, whose oral language proficiency scores on the IDEA-Oral Language Proficiency Test in the spring were LES (limited English speaker) or FES (fluent English speaker). Because the study focused on the use of authentic assessment as data for making decisions about program placement, only students with the proficiency levels of LES or FES, as designated by the IDEA-Oral Language Proficiency Test, were included. Students with oral language proficiency scores of NES (non-English speaker) were excluded from the selection pool because they were not eligible for transition to an English as a Second Language Program or exit from the bilingual program based on state guidelines for bilingual education. However, anecdotal records and portfolios were kept for all students in the classroom.

Data Collection and Analysis

Data was collected in the form of portfolio artifacts and traditional assessments over the course of one academic year.

Portfolio

The teacher and students collected samples of student work to be included in a portfolio. Each student portfolio included: an audiotape of student's oral reading, oral retellings, reading logs, anecdotal records from reading conferences, interactive journal entries, and compositions. Each of these items was selected because of the integration of language knowledge and abilities necessary to produce the item.

Audiotape of Students' Readings

In October, January, and April each subject taped a book that s/he chose to read. Each subject was instructed to choose a book, written in English, that s/he could read independently and that would demonstrate her/his best reading behaviors. Throughout the year, the students and teacher discussed what behaviors comprised good oral reading. As a group, the students and teacher agreed that good oral reading is fluent, expressive, and has few miscues which affect the meaning of the text. The group also agreed that it is important to pay attention to punctuation, to pronounce English like English, and to match the speed or rate at which the text is read to the text.

Each audiotape was analyzed by two researchers using an Oral Reading Rubric (Lewis-White, 1994) (see Appendix A) with an interrater reliability of 92 percent using this rubric. The researchers then negotiated the scoring of the one discrepancy. The criteria for the rubric was based on the teacher/student discussion of what behaviors comprise good oral reading. The rubric was also based on (a) a definition of reading as a language process (Wilson, 1985) for the reconstruction of meaning (Smith, et al., 1972), (b) the characteristics of good oral reading (Karlin, 1975), and (c) the nature of miscues (Y. Goodman, et al., 1987). The rubrics were used to describe language and literacy development over the course of the study.

Oral Retellings

In October, January, and April each subject was asked to read *The Snowy Day* by Ezra Jack Keats, *The Giving Tree* by Shel Silverstein, and *The Paper Bag Princess* by Robert Munsch, respectively. Each story was read first in English, then in Spanish. After reading the story, the students were instructed to tell the story to the teacher in their own words. The retellings were audiotaped and later transcribed for analysis.

Each retelling was analyzed by two researchers using Feathers' Holistic Scoring: Retelling Evaluation (Feathers, 1989) (see Appendix B) with an interrater reliability of 98 percent. The evaluation of each retelling was used to describe the subjects' oral language and literacy proficiencies.

Reading Logs

From October to April, students were asked to keep a record of all the books they read during the year. In addition to the list of books, they were told to keep a log in which they discussed their thoughts and reactions to the books they read. Each subject wrote in his/her reading log twice a week, with one entry being shared during the reading conferences. At the end of each month, each student selected his/her favorite entry to be included in the portfolio during the reading conference. Students were given no other criteria upon which to base their choice.

The reading logs were analyzed using the Book Talk section from the Reading Conference Inventory (Lewis-White, 1994) (See Appendix C). The analysis of the reading logs was used to describe each subject's literacy proficiency.

Anecdotal Records

Each week, the students met with the teacher in groups of four for reading conferences. They brought to the conference their reading log and the book that they wished to share with the conference group. During the conference each member of the group, including the teacher, introduced his/her book, read the entry in the reading log, and read a favorite passage from the book. Group members then asked questions and made recommendations for further reading. During the conferences, the teacher used the Reading Conference Inventory (see Appendix C) to annotate development in speaking, reading aloud, and book talk. In addition to this, she made anecdotal notes about the discussions the students had and the comments they made.

The Reading Inventory Checklist is divided into three sections: (a) Speaking, (b) Reads Shared Selection, and (c) Book Talk. The scores on these three sections, along with the anecdotal records from the conference, were used to describe the oral language proficiency and the literacy development of each subject.

Interactive Journals

The students wrote in their journals on a daily basis, and the teacher wrote back in each journal about twice a week. Students had a list of journal topic ideas from which to choose when they couldn't think of anything to say. Students were instructed to use everything they knew about good writing as they wrote in their journals, although they knew that the journals were not to be graded for report cards.

The journals were analyzed using the Journals: Written Language Inventory (Lewis-White, 1994) (see Appendix D), which was adapted for the second-language student from the Written Language Inventory (Batzle, 1992). The inventory is divided into four sections: (a) Writing Process, (b) Punctuation/Capitalization, (c) Spelling, and (d) Grammar. The scores on these three sections, along with the anecdotal records will be used to describe the oral language proficiency and the literacy development of each subject.

Compositions

Throughout the year, the students and teacher engaged in a workshop for writing. Each day they wrote either on personal topics or assigned topics. Discussions centered on writing compositions that communicated their ideas to others, using words effectively, and developing the topic. The teacher led the students to discover how the mechanics of writing aided the reader in understanding what the writer wanted to say.

In October, January, and April, each subject selected a composition that represented his/her best written work. The compositions were analyzed using the Writing Rubric (Lewis-White, 1994) (see Appendix E) which was adapted from the TAAS Scoring Rubric (Sampson, Allen, & Sampson, 1991) and the Idea Writing Test Rubric (Amori, Dalton, & Tighe, 1992). Each composition was analyzed by two researchers with an inter-rater reliability of 93 percent.

The rubric ranges from 0 (the lowest score) to 4 (the highest score). The rubric descriptors define a range of observable traits in a composition which, when present, constitute a well-written piece of work. The descriptors include topic development, sentence variation, beginning, ending, elaboration, transitions, cohesion, vocabulary, and writing conventions.

The rubrics are used to describe the language and literacy development of the students over the course of the study.

Traditional Assessment Instruments

The students were given the pre-Texas Assessment of Academic Skills (pre-TAAS), the Spanish Assessment of Basic Education (SABE), the Iowa Test of Basic Skills (ITBS), the IPT1-Reading & Writing Test, and the IDEA-Oral Language Proficiency Test (IDEA-OLPT) in accordance with state and local guidelines. The pre-TAAS was administered in January over a two-day period. The SABE and ITBS were administered in April, each over a two-day period two weeks apart. The IPT1-Reading & Writing Tests was administered in mid-May over a two-day period. The IDEA-OLPT was administered throughout the months of April and May. The state criteria for exit from the bilingual program using these instruments is a score of FES (fluent English speaker) on an oral language proficiency test and 40th percentile or above in the reading comprehension and language sections of a standardized norm-referenced test.

The data from the student portfolios and the traditional assessment instruments was used to write oracy and literacy profiles on each of the four subjects.

Results of the Study

Alberto, Benito, Carmen, and Dulce (pseudonyms) were all Hispanic students who were placed in either an English as a Second Language or a bilingual program upon initial entry into school kindergarten or first grade. The students were placed in these programs based upon the reports their parents made regarding language(s) spoken in the home and their initial scores on the IDEA Oral Language Proficiency Test. By first grade, all four students were participating in a bilingual classroom. Academic records for the four subjects indicated that they were average students. During the course of the study, they were in a third grade bilingual classroom.

The results of the traditional assessments (Table 1) indicated that all subjects were fluent speakers of English but were unable to read or write at a competency level high enough for them to exit the bilingual program (Table 2). However, the data from the portfolios provided very different views of the student's competencies in oral and written language (Table 3, Table 4, and Table 5).

Table 1. Scores for the IDEA-Oral Language Proficiency Test

	Oral Language Proficiency Score
Alberto	Fluent English Speaker
Benito	Fluent English Speaker
Carmen	Fluent English Speaker
Dulce	Fluent English Speaker

Table 2. Scores from Traditional Assessments

	SABE %ile Rank	ITBS RDNG %ile Rank	ITBS WRTNG %ile Rank	IPT:1 RDNG %ile %ile	PRE-TAAS RDNG % Cor.	IPT:1 WRTNG
Alberto	12	4	13	16	31	LMT
Benito	99	25	37	68	65	COMP
Carmen	73	4	25	30	85	COMP
Dulce	86	1	6	19	54	LMT

Table 3. Oral Language: Comparison of the Level of Proficiency Indicated by Traditional Assessment and the Level of Proficiency Indicated by Portfolio Assessment and Anecdotal Records

	IDEA-OLPT	Portfolio/Anecdotal
Alberto	Fluent English	Fluent English
Benito	Fluent English	Fluent English
Carmen	Fluent English	Fluent English
Dulce	Fluent English	Limited English

Table 4. Reading: Comparison of the Level of Proficiency Indicated by Traditional Assessment and the Level of Proficiency Indicated by Portfolio Assessment and Anecdotal Records

	ITBS	IPT:1	TAAS	Portfolio/ Anecdotal
Alberto	Non-reader	Non-reader	Limited reader	Competent reader
Benito	Limited reader	Limited reader	Limited reader	Competent reader
Carmen	Non-reader	Limited reader	Competent reader	Competent reader
Dulce	Non-reader	Non-reader	Limited reader	Limited reader

Table 5. Writing: Comparison of the Level of Proficiency Indicated by Traditional Assessment and the Level of Proficiency Indicated by Portfolio Assessment and Anecdotal Records

	ITBS Writing	IPT:1 Writing	Portfolio/ Anecdotal
Alberto	Non-English Writer	Limited English Writer	Limited English Writer
Benito	Limited English Writer	Competent English Writer	Competent English Writer
Carmen	Limited English Writer	Competent English Writer	Competent English Writer
Dulce	Non-English Writer	Limited English Writer	Limited English Writer

Case Summary for Alberto

At the beginning of the school year, Alberto had no difficulties with the surface features of English. During reading conferences, he spoke with fluency at the appropriate rate and tone for the conversation. He had little difficulty with pronunciation or grammar. His reading was disfluent and the miscues he had were mostly semantic, due to an over reliance on decoding strategies. He had problems retelling stories and in using academic language to discuss the books he read. He did not initiate the discussion, nor did he add to the conversations initiated by other students. He was unable to communicate his interpretation of a story or how a story related to his own life experiences. When he did share his ideas and opinions as responses to teacher-directed questions, he was unable to give reasons to support those ideas and opinions.

In his writing, Alberto had little difficulty with the surface features of written English from the beginning of the school year. He used his writing to share personal information with the teacher and was aware that writing was a way to communicate with other people in another place and time. However, he did have difficulty expressing himself in writing. His topics were minimally developed and lacked cohesion. His compositions lacked supporting details and had few descriptive words.

By the end of the year, Alberto was involved in reading conferences, discussing his own books as well as the books that others read. He recommended books to others based upon his observations of their reading interests. He employed multiple sources of information to deepen his own understanding and shared his reasoning with others. During a reading conference he shared *The Gull that Lost the Sea.* In his discussion of the book, he stated that he chose the book because of the class unit on the sea. He related the book to the information in science about sea birds and discussed how gulls traveled on "upper wind currents" after hurricanes.

He discussed author style, debated about the implied or hidden meaning in books, and compared the ways in which different authors treated a subject. He was able to manipulate the text structure of a book to relate the story in detail while at the same time making the story his own. His language was fluid and precise. He began to internalize stories, and his choice of words when relating them indicated that he was interpreting the story for his listener. His oral reading continued to be disfluent.

By the end of the year, Alberto had made progress in his writing, but he continued to have difficulty with written academic language when a topic was imposed upon him. His writing was more structured and elaborate than it had been in the beginning. He employed a richer vocabulary.

The portfolio assessment and anecdotal data indicated that Alberto had both the personal and academic proficiencies to be considered a proficient speaker and reader of English. While he controlled the surface structure in English, and while the deep surface proficiencies were developing, he could not yet be said to be a proficient writer of English.

This is in opposition to the traditional assessment data which indicated that Alberto was a non- to limited-English reader. He was a limited-English writer. He was a fluent English speaker.

Case Study Summary for Benito

At the beginning of the school year, Benito had a few difficulties with some of the surface features of English. He had pronunciation errors in words that began with s /s/ and with words that contained th, /ð/ and /θ/. His speech contained numerous grammar errors, the most frequent being verb tense agreement and pronoun usage (gender and possessive pronouns). In spite of these problems, he spoke with fluency at an appropriate rate and tone for conversation. However, he read in a monotone. His reading was disfluent, with numerous Spanish pronunciations for English words. The miscues he made were both syntactic and semantic; he corrected them as he read.

The content of his discussions in the reading conferences indicated that Benito was able to use academic language from early on in the school year. He was able to use the community of learners to affectively enable his own learning. When reading *Hole in the Dike*, he used his peers in the reading conference group to help figure out why there were dikes. He was aware of his own lack of comprehension, due to lack of information about a topic, and he used multiple sources in order to construct meaning.

In his writing, Benito had control of most of the surface features of English from the beginning. These included the use of punctuation and capitalization. He had some subject/predicate agreement errors early in the year, but by mid-year these errors no longer occurred. His early writing had adequate structure, but lacked elaboration and personal voice. The topics were underdeveloped, and the writing was stilted. He wrote anything to fill a page without a plan of what he wanted to communicate.

By the end of the year, Benito continued to have pronunciation errors in words that began with s /s/. His reading was more fluent but continued to have some Spanish pronunciation of English words. He had literary discussions with the members of his group, discussing the books they had read and comparing them. His reading continued to be uneven, as he stopped to correct miscues when they affected the meaning of the text. He was actively engaged in the construction of meaning, knowing the limitations of his own understanding of text and searching out answers to questions among the community of learners.

Benito's writing demonstrated control of the conventions of written English. His compositions were more structured and better organized. He began to use complex sentence structures, such as ". . . they say that I say that . . . ," in his writing which also became more detailed. His journal entries became more personal with greater voice than had been seen in his earlier entries. In one entry, he communicates his frustration at being sent to OCS (On Campus Suspension) for fighting. While Benito needed to develop more as a writer, his stories showed potential to be a skilled storyteller. He had developed into a competent writer.

The portfolio assessments and anecdotal notes indicated that Benito had the personal and academic proficiencies in oral and written language to be considered a speaker, reader, and writer of English. He controlled the surface and deep structures of English and was able to manipulate them in order to learn from his own interactions within the language community.

This is in opposition to the traditional assessment data, which suggested that Benito was a limited- to competent-English reader and writer, and a fluent English speaker.

Case Study Summary for Carmen

At the beginning of the school year, Carmen had difficulty speaking loudly enough for others to hear her. She spoke at an appropriate tone and rate for conversation and had little difficulty with the pronunciation and grammar of spoken English. She had a few problems with verb tense agreement. She relied on the teacher's questions to discuss her books with the reading conference group. From the beginning of the year, Carmen was a fluent reader. The miscues she made were both syntactic and semantic. She was able to correct the miscues as she read. She was able to discuss the story elements of her books but was unable to extend or support her ideas.

In her writing, Carmen controlled most of the surface features of English from the beginning, including punctuation, capitalization, sentence structure and grammar. She was able to manipulate written expression in order to summarize materials of her own choosing. She had difficulty focusing on a topic, adding extraneous details which made no sense in the context of her writing. Her compositions had adequate structure but contained gaps which interrupted the flow of the writing. They lacked cohesion, detail and elaboration.

By the end of the year, Carmen was able to see relationships between what she read and what she experienced on a day-to-day basis. She demonstrated an awareness of story props which are carried throughout a story to assist in the telling of the story. She began to be critical of text, making judgements about what was or was not well-written. Her spoken and written vocabulary was expanded through the literature that she read. She exhibited an interest in the deep structure of the books she and others read indicating that she was aware of the dual constructions of meaning within a story. She was engaged in the construction of meaning on both the surface structure of the text and the deep structure. Her reading log entry for *The Legend of the Indian Paintbrush* begins, "Little Gopher follows his destiny as revealed in a dream vision of becoming an artist for his people and eventually is able to bring the colors of the sunset down to the earth. . . ."

By the end of the year, Carmen began to use story structure in her writing. The topics were well developed with good story structure. Her personal voice was evident, and she began to take risks with her writing. Her writing was detailed with smooth transitions between events. She manipulated sentence length to set the tone of her story. In one story she titled "Scared of the Night," she established a repetitive pattern to move the story.

She wrote, ". . . When I got in bed I thought I heard somebody say something . . . I started to go to sleep and I thought I heard somebody say something . . . I was almost asleep when I thought I heard somebody . . ." say something. . . .

The portfolio assessment and anecdotal data indicated that Carmen had the personal and academic proficiencies in oral and written language to be considered a speaker, reader, and writer of English. She controlled the surface and deep structures of English and was able to manipulate them in order to learn from her own interactions within the language community.

This is in opposition to the traditional assessment data, which suggested that Carmen was a non- to limited- English reader and a limited- to competent-English writer. She was a fluent English speaker.

Case Study Summary for Dulce

At the beginning of the school year, Dulce had both speech and reading fluency problems. She often paused in mid-sentence to search for an English word during conversations. She spoke at an appropriate tone and volume for conversation and had little difficulty with the pronunciation and grammar of spoken English. She had some surface feature problems with verb tense agreement and occasionally used Spanish syntax in spoken English.

She relied on the teacher to bring her into the discussion, but once she entered the conversation she had no problems interacting in the group. She talked easily about the books she read, often pointing out the print in the text and illustrations and commenting on it. She had an unusual insight into the underlying lessons in the books she read. After reading *Helga's Dowry*, she said she had learned that when she grows up she should marry someone for what is inside them not what they have.

Her reading was disfluent. She read English text with Spanish intonation patterns. She had numerous semantic miscues which were caused by an overreliance on decoding strategies and use of the Spanish sound system.

Dulce controlled the conventions of written English from the beginning. However, her writing contained Spanish syntax patterns, and many of her invented spellings reflected L2 pronunciation errors. She had problems with verb tense and subject/predicate agreement in English. Her writing was generally unfocused, without a central theme or topic. Her compositions lacked structure and were filled with extraneous information. She had difficulty manipulating written language in order to discuss the books that she had read and with stating an opinion and supporting it.

By the end of the year, Dulce interacted with the other members of her group by asking questions about the books they were sharing and about the authors. Her speech continued to be disfluent, with pauses as if she were searching for words. There was still evidence of Spanish syntax in her spoken English. Her disfluency in speaking may have been an indication that she was not yet processing information about what she read in English, but rather translating between the two languages.

She read with some fluency, and her intonation as she read was like English. She read with expression, paying attention to the punctuation marks. Her miscues continued to be semantic and over-reliant on decoding, although the Spanish pronunciation of English words was no longer present. She continued to be interested in the way in which the text was arranged in a book, often commenting on text type and/or placement.

By the end of the year, Dulce's compositions were well-written and cohesive. They had elaboration, were detailed, and contained a rich vocabulary. Her personal voice was evident, and she began to take risks with her writing. The continued appearance of Spanish syntax in her writing may indicate that she was constructing meaning in Spanish and then translating as she wrote. Such behavior could suggest that while the student may appear to be proficient in English, in reality the student is still Spanish dominant.

The portfolio assessments and anecdotal notes indicated that Dulce had the personal proficiencies (BICs) in oral language, but she did not have the academic oral and written proficiencies to be considered a fluent speaker, reader, and writer of English. While she controls most of the surface features of English, there is sufficient evidence from the continued used of Spanish syntax in her spoken and written language to suggest that she may still be Spanish dominant.

This is in opposition to the traditional assessment data, which suggested that Dulce was a non- to limited-English reader and writer. She was a fluent English speaker.

Discussion

From the data it is apparent that the information gathered through the use of authentic assessments (portfolios and anecdotal notes) is very different from the information gathered through the use of traditional assessment tools. What happened and why?

The authentic assessments indicated that the students were functioning above what the traditional assessment indicated (see Table 3, Table 4, and Table 5). The descriptions of the students' language and literacy proficiencies were fuller and more detailed because they were ongoing. They looked at natural language, and they consisted of information gathered from dynamic, multi-dimensional, integrated process evaluation instruments. They were designed by the teacher for a specific group of students. Each part of the portfolio evaluated inter-related language processes in the context of the language community. The teacher and students investigated language in a natural environment that used language as a medium for learning rather than a subject to be learned. The evaluations involved the interaction of language users with other language users, whether it was speaking, reading, or writing.

The most striking example of this can be seen in Carmen. Low scores on both the ITBS and IPT1: Reading Test would seem to indicate that she is a non-reader. However, the description of her language and literacy proficiencies based on the portfolio assessments and anecdotal notes indicated that not only is she a reader but that she reads material on or above grade level with fluency and comprehension. The description of her language and literacy proficiencies is based on multiple sources which were collected over a period of seven months. These assessments indicated a richness of vocabulary and a depth of comprehension that could not be seen in the data from the traditional assessments. Even her writing provided clues to her literacy proficiencies. Students who are non-readers don't write stories like "Scared of the Night."

While the difference between authentic assessment and traditional assessment was most marked for Carmen, it was also true for the other students in the study. An evaluation of their portfolios and the anecdotal notes indicated that they were functioning above the levels indicated by the traditional assessments.

The portfolio assessments and anecdotal notes were ongoing and caught subtle changes in the students' language and literacy proficiencies. For example, anecdotal notes for Alberto from the reading conference trace the development of pronoun usage from October through January when Alberto appears to have gained control of them in his spoken language.

The teacher was able to track the development of both surface (BICS) and deep (CALPs) structure language use in the students. She was able to monitor the interplay of both languages in the construction of meaning. She was also able to determine language dominance in the students based on what they did on a day-to-day basis in the classroom. This was especially true for Dulce. On the surface, it appeared that she was a fluent English speaker. Only because it was documented through the portfolio and anecdotal notes, was the teacher able to see evidence that Dulce was probably Spanish dominant, although the traditional language proficiency assessment instrument indicated that she was a fluent English speaker. The traditional assessments gave no information about language dominance for any of the students; they just indicated that they were fluent English speakers. For language minority students, language dominance may be a more important issue than language fluency when making instructional placement decisions.

Language and literacy development are continuous growth processes. The use of authentic assessment enabled the teacher to gather primary source evidence of language growth on her students over a seven month period. They gave the teacher the information that enabled her to structure opportunities that enhanced the students' language acquisition and moved them along the language development continuum. The information she gathered was very specific about the strengths and weaknesses of each student.

Because authentic assessments are ongoing, fluid instruments, they are able to evaluate a student's language and literacy development using natural, non-threatening language opportunities. Traditional assessments, on the other hand, are static and intrusive. To accommodate the testing schedule for the various traditional assessments, the normal routines of the classroom are disrupted.

For the most part, the traditional assessments indicated that the students were functioning at a lower level in reading and writing than the authentic assessments indicated. Researchers have described reasons for this. Clarke (1979), Cziko (1978), and Perkins (1983) cited semantic content of key vocabulary. Knowledge of test procedures was cited by Tyler and White (1979). Au (1981) and Heath (1982) cited differential perception of questions and answers. Chamot (1980) and Eaton (1980) both cite prescribed time limits in the tests as being a factor in the low test scores for second language students.

In addition to these factors, traditional assessments evaluate language (reading and writing) in context-reduced situations which make the construction of meaning more difficult for L2 students. Reading tasks on the comprehension assessments are sometimes composed of stories that have no resemblance to the books that students read in the language rich classroom. Little or no attempt may be made to assist students in bringing their prior knowledge into the reading act.

On traditional assessments, language is generally assessed through mechanics, spelling, and usage outside of the natural context of written communication. However, authentic assessments document the use of mechanics, spelling, and usage within the context of natural language usage. The teacher is able to track a student's development from no evidence of a particular "skill" through experimenting with the "skill" to control of the "skill."

Writing tasks can be equally questionable. They offer little in the way of stimulus for the students, often assuming that the student has had sufficient experiences to write on the topic. Many prompts which use pictures have little resemblance to the rich, detailed illustrations that students in a natural language environment are used to. Without the student's personal voice, the compositions written for the test rarely achieve the richness or depth of those found in student portfolios. Traditional assessment tools are static, one-dimensional instruments which yield up their information about students in numbers which teachers, for the most part, do not comprehend.

Traditional assessment scores do not give the teacher insight into what a student was thinking as s/he marked a particular answer. The teacher does not know if the student guessed, made an error in his logic, or had a personal insight which made a "wrong" answer choice better than a "right" answer.

For the teacher, the fact that a student answered a question "wrong" is not the most important piece of information. The teacher needs to know why the student answered the question "wrong". Traditional assessment scores do not provide that information. They rarely provide the teacher information about the types of questions the students answered wrong in a format that the teacher can read and understand.

Based on the information provided by some traditional assessment scores, the teacher has no idea where the strengths and/or weaknesses are for any particular student. The teacher is asked to put his/her faith in the test as an accurate measure of the students' language and literacy proficiencies. So, armed with only traditional assessment scores, the teacher may be taking a shot in the dark when making instructional decisions for a student.

Implications of the Study

Due to the small number of subjects in this study and the subjectivity of design and interpretation inherent in authentic assessment instruments, it is difficult to generalize the results of this study to the whole population. Additionally, the results of this study do not offer conclusive proof that authentic assessments are more valid or reliable measures of a student's language and literacy proficiencies. However, they do lend support to the body of educators who have claimed for two decades that traditional assessments do not adequately or fairly measure the language proficiencies or the academic achievements of language minority students.

Even if traditional assessment instruments do make it easier to determine who qualifies for a special language program, teachers are still left with the problem of assessing student needs more accurately for better instruction. Teachers can assess students for program placement and instructional decisions through portfolios and authentic assessments in the context of the language community.

The authentic assessments are relatively inexpensive, are fairly easy to organize and keep, do not take time away from instructions, are an integral part of the language centered classroom, and are capable of providing the information necessary to make instructional decisions for language minority students.

Teachers who keep reading and writing portfolios have a wealth of information about their students at their fingertips. Huerta-Macías (1995) maintains that due to the nature of alternative assessments, they are in and of themselves valid and reliable. To not use the information in the portfolio for instructional placement decisions is to discredit the actual language learning that takes place in the classroom.

Summary

The numbers of non-English speaking children who initially fail in learning to read and thereby fail in the schooling process is staggering. Low reading test performance (Applebee, Langer, & Mullis, 1987) and the subsequent decontextualization of language experiences (Edelsky, 1989) have been cited as factors in this ever-growing problem among language minority students.

If educators are to stem the tide of academic failures among second language learners, then they must be able to accurately assess the learners' strengths and weaknesses as they engage in the language process. Traditional assessment tools alone may not be up to this task.

Educators must embrace a broader view of evaluation. The assessment instruments must be appropriate for the purposes for which they are being used, be integrated with curriculum and instruction based upon the student's actual work, and consider elements and characteristics of second language acquisition. Further, instructional placement should be based upon more than a single assessment instrument. A teacher's observations and the portfolio of authentic assessments (actual student work sample) must be considered along with the results of traditional assessments in any instructional placement decision.

References

Allasi, S. K., & Connor, U. (1991). Using performance assessment instruments with ESL student writers. In Hamp-Lyons, L. (Ed.), *Assessing second language writing in academic contexts* (pp.227-240). Norwood, NJ: Ablex Publishing Corp.

Amori, B. A., Dalton, E. F., and Tighe, P. L. (1992). *IPT 1: Reading and writing grades 2-3, Examiner's manual.* Brea, CA: Ballard and Tighe.

Applebee, A. N., Langer, J. A. and Mullis, I. V. S. (1987). *The nation's report card: Learning to be literate: Reading.* Princeton, NJ: Educational Testing Service.

Au, K. H. (1981). Participation structures in a reading lesson with Hawaiian children: Analysis of a culturally appropriate instructional event. *Anthropology and Education Quarterly*, 11, 91-115.

Batzle, J. (1992). *Portfolio assessment and evaluation.* Cypress, CA: Creative Teaching Press.

Bennett, W. J. (1987). *The condition of bilingual education in the nation 1986. (A report from the Secretary of Education to the President and Congress).* Washington, DC: United States Department of Education.

Bird, L. B. (1989). The art of teaching: Evaluation and revision. In K. Goodman, Y. Goodman, and W. Hood (Eds.), *The whole language evaluation book.* Portsmouth, NH; Heinemann, 15-24.

Bruck, M., Shultz, J. and Rodriguez-Brown, F. V. (1979). Assessing language use in bilingual classrooms: An ethnographic analysis. In A. D. Cohen, M. Bruck, F. V. Rodriguez-Brown (Eds.), *Bilingual education series: 6 evaluating evaluation.* Arlington, VA: Center for Applied Linguistics, 40-56.

Camp, R. (1993). The place of portfolios in our changing views of writing assessment. In R. S. Bennett & W. C. Ward (Eds.), *Construction versus choice in cognitive measurement: Issues in constructed response, performance testing and portfolio assessment* (pp. 183-212). Hillsdale, NJ: Lawrence Erlbaum Assoc., Publishers

Chamot, A. U. (1980). Recent research on second-language reading. *NABE Forum*, November, 3-4.

Chittenden, E. (1991). Authentic assessment, evaluation, and documentation. In V. Perrone (Ed.), *Expanding student assessment.* Alexander, VA: ASCD; 22-31.

Clarke, M. A. (1979). Reading in Spanish and English: evidence from adult ESL students. In S. Hudelson (Ed.), *Learning to read in different languages.* Washington,DC: Center for Applied Linguistics, 69-92.

Cummins, J. (1981). The role of primary language development in promoting educational success for language minority students. In *Schooling and language minority students: A theoretical framework.* Los Angeles, CA: California State Department of Education, National Dissemination and Assessment Center, 3-49.

Cummins, J. (1984). *Bilingualism and special education issues: The text or the reader's own projections?* A reply to Edelsky et al. *Applied linguistics. 4,* 1, 23-31.

Cziko, G. (1978). Differences in first- and second-language reading: The use of syntactic, semantic, and discourse constraints. *Canadian Modern Language Review,* 34, 471-489.

DeAvila, E. and Duncan, S. (1976). *A few thoughts about language assessment: The Lau decision reconsidered.* Unpublished manuscript.

Eaton, A.J. (1980). A psycholinguistic analysis of the oral reading miscues of selected field-dependent and field-independent native Spanish-speaking Mexican-American first grade children. In *Outstanding dissertations in bilingual education.,* 71-86.

Edelsky, C. (1989). *Writing is a bilingual program: Habia una vez.* Norwood,NJ: ABLEX.

Edelsky, C., Altwerger, B., and Flores, B. (1991). *Whole language: What's the difference?.* Portsmouth, NH: Heinemann.

Feathers, K. (1989). Assessing retellings: A comparison of methods- using a holistic approach to analyze retellings. NRC, Nov. 28-Dec.2, Austin, TX.

Flores, B., Cousins, P.T., and Díaz, E. (1991). Transforming deficit myths about learning language and culture. *Language Arts, 68,* 369-79.

Galindo, R. (1989). "Asi no se pone, si" (That's not how you write, "si"). In K. Goodman, Y. Goodman, and W. Hood (Eds.), *The whole language evaluation book.* Portsmouth, NH; Heinemann, 55-68.

Garcia, G. E. and Pearson, P. D. (1991). *Literacy assessment in a diverse society.* Champaign, IL: Center for the Study of Reading.

Garcia, G. E. (1992). *The literacy assessment of second-language learners.* Urbana-Champagne: University of Illinois, Center for the Study of Reading.

Glazer, S. M. and Brown, C. S. (1993). *Portfolios and beyond: Collaborative assessment in reading and writing.* Norwood, MA: Christopher-Gordon Publishers.

Goodman, K. (1967). Reading: A psycholinguistic guessing game. Ontario: Scholastic.

Goodman, Y. (1985). Kidwatching. In A. Jaggar and M. T. Smith-Burke (Eds.), *Observing the language learner.* Newark, DE: IRA.

Goodman, Y., Watson, D., and Burke, C. (1987). *Reading Miscue Inventory: Alternative procedures.* New York: Owens.

Gottlieb, M. (1995). Nurturing student learning through portfolios. *TESOL Journal, 5*(1), 12-14.

Halliday, M. A. K. (1978). *Language as a social semiotic: The social interpretation of language and meaning.* Baltimore, MD: University Park Press.

Haney, W. (1985). Making testing more educational. *Educational Leadership, 43*(2), 4-13.

Harste, J., Woodward, V. and Burke, C. (1984). *Language stories and literacy lessons.* Portsmouth, NH: Heinemann

Heath, S. B. (1982). Questioning at home and at school: A comparative study. In

G. Spindler (Ed.), *Doing the ethnography of schooling: Educational anthropology in action.* New York: Holt, Rinehart, & Winston.

Hiebert, E. H. and Calfee, R. C. (1989). Advancing academic literacy through teachers' assessments. *Educational Leadership, 46*(7), 50-54.

Huerta-Macías, A. (1995). Alternative assessment: Responses to commonly asked questions. *TESOL Journal, 5*(2). 8-11.

Johnson, P. H. (1983). *Reading comprehension assessment: A cognitive basis.* Newark,DL: International Reading Association.

Karlin, R. (1975). *Teaching elementary reading (2nd ed.)* New York: Harcourt Brace Jovanovich.

Krest, M. (1990). Adapting the portfolio to my student needs. *English Journal,* 79 (2), 29-34.

Lennon, R. (1970). What can be measured?. In R. Farr (Ed.), *Measurement and evaluation of reading.* New York: Harcourt, Brace, & World, 18-34.

Lewis-White, L. (1994). *Assessing oracy and literacy in bilingual students: Getting the whole picture.* Unpublished doctoral dissertation. East Texas State University, Commerce, TX.

McLaughlin, B. (1982). *Children's second language learning.* Washington, DC: Center for Applied Linguistics.

McNamara, T. F. (1995). Modeling performance: Opening Pandora'sbox. *Applied Linguistics, 16*(2), 159-179.

Madaus, G. F. (1985). What do test score "really" mean in educational policy? In J. D. Beard and S. E. McNabb (Eds.), *Testing in the English language arts: Uses and abuses.* Rochester, MI: Michigan Council of Teachers of English, 1-11.

Mehrens, W. A. (1992). Using performance assessment for accountability purposes. *Educational measurement: Issues and Practice, 11*(1). 3-9, 20.

Miller, M. D., & Legg, S. M. (1993). Alternative assessment in a high-stakes environment. *Educational Measurement: Issues and Practice, 12,* 9-15.

Morrissey, M. (1989). When "shut up" is a sign of growth. In K. Goodman, Y. Goodman, and W. Woods (Eds.) *The whole language evaluation book* (pp. 85-97). Portsmouth, NH; Heinemann.

Moss, P. A., Beck, J. S., Ebbs, C., Matson, B., Muchmore, J., Steele, D., Taylor, C., & Herter, R. (1992). Portfolios, accountability and an interpretive approach to validity. *Educational Measurement: Issues and Practice, 11*(3), 12-21.

Norris, N. (1990). *Understanding educational evaluation.* New York: St. Martin Press.

Ortiz, A. A. and Polyzoi, E. (1988). Language assessment of Hispanic learning disabled and speech and language handicapped students: Research in progress. In *Schools and the culturally diverse exceptional student: Promising practices and future directions,* sec EC210633. Paper presented at the Ethnic and Multicultural Symposia, Dallas, TX 1986.

Paltridge, B. (1992). EAP placement testing: An integrated approach. *English for Specific Purposes, 11,* 243-268.

Perkins, K. (1983). Semantic constructivity in ESL reading and composition. *TESOL Quarterly,* 17, 19-27.

Rosenblatt, L. (1978). *The reader, the test, the poem: The transactional theory of the literary work.* Carbondale, IL: Southern Illinois University Press.

Sampson, M. R., Allen, R. V., and Sampson, M. B. (1990). *Pathways to literacy: A meaning-centered perspective.* Ft. Worth, TX: Holt, Rinehart, and Winston.

Savignon, S. (1972) *Communicative competence: An experiment in foreign language teaching*. Philadelphia: Center for Curriculum Development.

Short, D. J. (1993). Assessing integrated language and content instruction. *TESOL Quarterly, 27*(4), 627-656.

Smith, E. B., Goodman, K., and Meredith, R. (1972). *Language and thinking in the elementary school*. New York: Holt, Rinehart and Winston.

Tierney, R.J., Carter, M.A., and Desai, L.E. (1991). *Portfolio assessment in the reading writing classroom*. Norwood, MA: Christopher-Gordon Publishers.

Tinajero, J.V. (1985). Trends and issues in the use and misuse of oral language proficiency testing for bilingual program planning. In J. . Beard and S. E. McNabb (Eds.), *Testing in the English language arts: Uses and abuses*. Rochester, MI: Michigan Council of Teachers of English, 61-73.

Troike, R.C. (1982). Zeno's paradox and language assessment. In S.S. Seidner (Ed.), *Issues of language assessment: Foundations and research*. Springfield, IL: Illinois State Board of Education, 3-5.

Tucker, G. (1974). The assessment of bilingual and bicultural factors of communication. In S. Carey (Ed.), *Bilingualism, biculturalism and education*. Edmonton, Canada: University of Alberta Press.

Tyler, R. W. and White, S. H. (1979). Chairmen's report. In *National institute of education, testing, teaching, and learning: Report of a conference on research on testing*. Washington, DC: Government Printing Office, 3-32.

Upshur, J. and Palmer, A. (1974). Measures of accuracy: Communicative and social judgements for two classes of foreign language speakers. In A. Verdoodt (Ed.), *AILA Proceedings, Copenhagen 1972:* Vol 3: *Applied Sociolinguistics*. Heidelberg: Julius Gross Verlag.

Valencia, S. and Pearson, P. D. (1987). Reading assessment: Time for a change. *Reading Teacher, 40*, 726-32.

Valencia, S. (1990). A portfolio approach to classroom reading assessment. *Reading Teacher, 43*, 338-40.

Wilson, M. (1985). Testing and literacy: A contradiction in terms? In J. D. Beard and S. E. McNabb (Eds.), *Testing in the English language arts: uses and abuses*. Rochester, MI: Michigan Council of Teachers of English, 12-16.

Worthen, B. R. (1993). Critical issues that will determine the future of alternative assessment. *Phi Delta Kappan. 74*(6), 444-54.

Appendix A. Oral Reading Rubric

Student _____ Date _____

Age/Grade _____ Score _____

Selection _____

Relative Difficulty of Selection

| Low | Low Average | Average | High Average | High |

Rubric Descriptors

Score of 0
Reads without fluency
Reads without intonation
Reads without expression
Reads without attention
  to punctuation marks
Reads with over reliance
  one decoding skills
Reads with frequent miscues
  which affect meaning and
  interfere with aural
  comprehension(Miscues
  are not corrected.)

Score of 1
Reads without fluency
Reads without intonation
Reads without expression
Reads with some attention
  to punctuation marks
Reads with some reliance
  on decoding skills
Reads with frequent miscues
  which affect meaning and
  interfere with aural
  comprehension (Some
  miscues are corrected.)

Score of 2
Reads with some fluency
Reads with some intonation
Reads with some expression
Reads with some attention
  to punctuation marks
Reads at an uneven rate
Reads with some miscues
  which affect meaning and
  interfere with aural
  comprehension but are
  corrected

Score of 3
Reads with fluency
Reads with intonation
Reads with expression
Reads with attention to
  punctuation marks
Reads at an even rate
Reads with few miscues
  which affect meaning and
  interfere with aural
  comprehension but are
  corrected

Score of 4
Reads with fluency
Reads with appropriate
  intonation for the text
Reads with appropriate
  expression for the text
Reads with attention to punctuation marks
Reads at an appropriate rate for text
Reads with few miscues
  (Miscues do not affect meaning or
  interfere with aural comprehension)

Appendix B. Feather's Holistic Scoring: Retelling Evaluation

Student _____ Grade _____

Date	Text Title
1.	
2.	
3.	
4.	

Evaluation

Text #	1	2	3	4
Major Events				
Explication				
Completeness				
Topic/Theme				
Voice				
Coherence				
Text Structure				
Lit. Aware				

Key: 0=Non-Existent   4=Complete

Appendix C. Reading Conference Inventory

Student _____ Grade _____

Date							
Speaking							
Uses appropriate volume							
Speaks fluently							
Uses appropriate tone							
Uses clear pronunciation							
Uses correct grammar							
Initiates discussion							
Reads shared selection							
Uses appropriate volume							
Reads with fluency							
Reads with expression							
Book talk							
Discusses setting							
Discusses characters							
Discusses events/problem							
Relates book to own experiences							
Asks questions of others							
Supports ideas/opinions							

Anecdotal Notes:

Key: N=No evidence   D=Developing   C=Controlling

Appendix D. Journals: Written Language Inventory

Student _____ Grade _____

Date							
Writing Process							
Personal voice is present in entries							
Develops topic beyond list							
Takes risks in writing							
Punctuation/Capitalization							
Uses periods, question marks and							
exclamation marks							
Uses commas							
Uses quotations							
Uses capitals to begin sentences							
Uses capitals for proper nouns							
Spelling							
Takes risks in spelling							
Conventional spelling of high							
frequency words							
Approximations reflect L2 pronunciations							
Uses incorrect vowel but in correct							
place							
Grammar							
Uses complete sentences							
Uses compound sentences							
Uses complex sentences							
Varies sentence beginnings							
Uses verb tense agreement							
Uses subject/predicate agreement							
Entry Topics/Anecdotal Notes							

Key: N= No evidence D=Developing C= Controlling
Batzle, 1992

Appendix E. Writing Rubric

Student _____ Score _____

Age/Grade _____ Draft or Published

Title _____

Rubric Descriptors

Score of 0
  Is unintelligible

Score of 1
  Inadequately develops topic
  Contains few complete sentences
  Lacks structure
    organization
    support
    elaboration
  Vocabulary unacceptable for
    student's proficiency level
  Lack of writing conventions;
    interferes with understanding
    conventions

Score of 2
  Minimally develops topic
  Complete sentences
  Adequate structure however
    composition contains gaps
    or wanders
  Lacks elaboration/details
  Vocabulary is partially
    acceptable for student's
    proficiency level
  Developing control of writing

Score of 3
  Somewhat developed topic
  Variety of sentences
  Structure suggests use of plan
    in writing
  Elaboration
  Transitions
  Rich vocabulary
  Controls writing conventions

Score of 4
  Well developed topic
  Variety of sentences
  Strong beginning and ending
  Rich elaboration
  Strong transitions
  Cohesive (no gaps)
  Rich vocabulary
  Controls writing conventions

PROFESSIONAL DEVELOPMENT AND LITERACY

Mentoring Teachers in Professional Development School Learn from Student Interns

Susan Davis Lenski

Illinois State University

Abstract

This article reports the results of a study investigating the impact of student interns in a Professional Development School (PDS) on the knowledge and use of reading strategies of mentoring teachers. Before student interns taught reading strategies in classrooms, mentoring teachers were asked to rate their familiarity with the strategies. After the student interns taught the strategies, the teachers rated how likely they were to use the strategy themselves. A paired t-test was calculated, and descriptive data in the form of interviews and written responses were collected. The results indicated that mentoring teachers in a PDS were influenced by the knowledge brought to their classrooms by their student interns.

One of the central premises underlying the Professional Development School (PDS) movement is that theory and practice can inform each other in reciprocal ways. Traditionally, the knowledge that preservice teachers have brought to teaching experiences has been divided into distinctly separate ways of knowing. University professors bring knowledge from research; mentoring teachers bring knowledge about practice; and preservice teachers bring knowledge from their own experiences in school. The traditional organization of the preservice teacher's education has reflected this belief. Students entering the field of education have taken general studies for their first two years in college, have moved on to classes in pedagogy, and then have tried their ideas in the classroom during student teaching under the supervision of a classroom teacher. One of the goals of the PDS is to break the traditional mode of separate knowledges.

According to the social constructivist view of learning, the implicit and explicit teaching of pedagogy is grounded in the social context of schools and the practice of teaching. Preservice teachers draw on prior knowledge, experience, and current interactions as they learn about teaching. Research on teacher education over the past decade indicates that student teachers tend to experience conflict between their initial ideas of teaching and learning and their experience in practice. The conflict pushes the students to adapt their current knowledge structures into new knowledge (Jones & Vesilind, 1996). Therefore, as preservice teachers use their knowledge drawn from various sources, they construct knowledge about teaching through their social interactions as teachers and as students (Oldfather, Bonds, & Bray, 1994).

If what student interns learn is shaped by their classroom experiences, it is extremely important that student interns be placed in exemplary classrooms. Many educators interested in school reform believe that for changes in school to take place, initiatives must be shaped by practitioners and guided by craft wisdom (Hardy, 1993). This places a heavy responsibility on mentoring teachers. In order for student interns to learn how to become effective teachers who can teach to the current high literacy demands, they must have mentoring teachers who are "infinitely skilled teachers" (Darling-Hammond, 1994). Ideally, student interns should have classroom experiences where they encounter state-of-the art practice (Holmes, 1990). If preservice teachers learn how to teach in school settings where they experience current educational practice, there is a greater likelihood that they will use their knowledge from their experience as they enter the teaching profession.

Professional Development Schools are an ideal venue for change to occur, both in how preservice teachers learn to become teachers and in changing current classroom practice. One of the goals in the PDS movement is for the simultaneous renewal of both schooling and the education of educators by the "bumping together" of university and school cultures (Goodlad, 1993). "PDSs are a special case of school restructuring: as they simultaneously restructure schools and teacher education programs, they redefine teaching and learning for all members of the professions and the school community" (Darling-Hammond, 1994, p. 1). No evidence yet exists, however, that school-university collaborations can bring about school improvement (Smith, 1992).

If the goals of exemplary schools for student interns and school reform are to be met, there should be a concerted effort on the part of the participants to make changes both in schools and in teacher education. One of the many ways to achieve these goals is to provide a venue for increasing the knowledge base of teachers and to make school a better place for teachers to work and to learn (Holmes, 1986). The change that can be made in schools should not be imposed either from the university or from those who hold power in the schools. Since education is located in neither the university nor the school but in the collaborative synergy of the two (Cochran-Smith, 1991), all of the participants in a PDS must respect each other's knowledge and be willing to share that knowledge.

Classroom teachers have a great deal of necessary knowledge from which student interns can learn, not all of which is craft knowledge. But classroom teachers are also learners. In a description of a PDS in Maine, Miller and Silvernail (1994) reported that the knowledge student interns brought to the classroom had an influence on their mentoring teachers. "Perhaps the most powerful professional development experience at work in Wells was the relatively unplanned, the professional development and refinement of educational practices that flows from the mere presence of interns in the schools" (Miller & Silvernail, 1994, p. 41). Teachers can be receptive to new learning by student interns. In fact, when given the opportunity, teachers in a demonstration school pursued teaching practices not previously contained in their teaching repertoire (Hardy, 1993).

In order to work toward the dual goals of providing classroom teachers with new information about teaching reading strategies and in working with student interns, this project was developed.

Teachers Learning From Interns Project

From the onset, the Illinois State University/Wheeling PDS had four goals: (1) to provide more authentic pre-service teacher preparation, (2) to assist in the professional development of classroom teachers, (3) to conduct research focused on teaching and learning, and (4) to provide recency of experience for university faculty. Illinois State University is a large multipurpose university originally established as a normal school in 1857. Approximately 1,100 students graduate from teacher education programs each year. Community Consolidated School District #21 is a K-8 public school district headquartered in Wheeling, Illinois. Located in the Chicago suburbs, it is a culturally and economically diverse school district. Students in the district attend one of eight elementary schools or three middle schools. The partners are separated geographically by an automobile drive of three hours.

In planning meetings before the PDS was established, a steering committee of school district administrators, teachers, and university personnel met to discuss the four goals. The second goal, the professional development of teachers, was of primary interest to the district participants. They believed that the teachers of their district were interested in learning about recent innovations in education, but because of a variety of factors, the district participants felt their current professional development staff was unable to keep up with the demands of the teachers. The district's goal, to be first in the world in achievement, was an ambitious one; they were committed to use every resource available to meet their goal.

The steering committee met several times to plan ways to inservice the staff on changes in their schools. Several traditional plans were developed: holding graduate classes, providing staff inservice, and delivering advanced degrees from the university, but the steering committee felt that the use of the student interns to influence classroom practice should also be explored.

The steering committee developed a collaborative plan. The university instructor of the reading methods class and the district personnel who taught the university course on language arts methods met to discuss ways the student interns could be used to provide information about reading strategies. They developed a list of proposed strategies. After the list was prepared, the mentoring teachers were invited to attend a two-day workshop where they would discuss the PDS program and have an opportunity to have input in the content of the university courses. Thirty-four mentoring teachers attended this meeting. At the meeting, the list of reading strategies was presented, and the teachers had the opportunity to add their own ideas to the list.

After the list was revised, the university and district instructors met with the mentoring teachers in each school to discuss their role in respect to the teaching of reading strategies. The mentoring teachers agreed to become flexible about allowing students to use new content and methods in their classrooms. During these experiences, the mentoring teachers would assume a new role. The mentoring teachers would become the reflective link between theory and practice. They would learn the new strategies from the student interns, assist the preservice teacher in finding how new strategies could fit in the existing classroom routines, and give the preservice teachers feedback on each teaching experience. The preservice teachers would then come back to the university classroom to discuss with the university and district instructors the experiences they had in the schools.

Purpose

The purpose of this study was to determine whether student interns had an influence on the literacy teaching of their mentoring teachers. The administrators in the district strongly believed that the interns infused new learning and energy into the fabric of the district in subtle ways. This study was conducted to determine whether the belief that interns influenced classroom teachers could be substantiated. Data for this study, therefore, were collected to determine whether the students were having an impact on their mentoring teachers' knowledge of reading strategies with the belief that this was the first step toward identifying the changes interns brought to the schools.

Methods

The methods used in this study were both quantitative and qualitative. Mentoring teachers were given a rating scale used as a pre- and post-test and analyzed by a paired t-test. Mentoring teachers and student interns were also asked to write their opinions about the reading strategies implemented in the classrooms, and mentoring teachers were interviewed. The qualitative data were transcribed and analyzed to find data supporting and enriching the quantitative data.

Participants

Thirty-nine undergraduate students in their senior year and their mentoring teachers were the subjects of this study. The undergraduates were enrolled in a large Midwestern University and had volunteered to be placed in a year-long Professional Development School (PDS) program in an urban area three hours from the university campus. The student interns in the program relocated to the Chicago area during their last year of schooling. The students in the PDS took eight semester hours of literacy-related courses and eight semester hours of science and social studies methods during their fall semester. Previous to that time, none of the students had taken any methods coursework.

Each of the student interns was placed in a school with one or more mentoring teachers during the fall. The student interns attended university classes in the district two full days during the week, were placed in schools for two days, and had one day to complete assignments for the university courses and/or projects for their mentoring teachers.

The student interns were assigned to different mentoring teachers on different teams. The mentoring teachers had volunteered to take a student intern for either Phase 1 (the first six weeks) and student teaching, Phase 2 (the second six weeks), or Phase 3 (the third six weeks of school). A total number of 46 mentoring teachers ranging from kindergarten through eighth grade took part in this study.

Procedure

The student interns were given a list of 12 lessons to teach in the classroom. Eight of the lessons were modeled by the university instructor using a chain of specific reading strategies (Anticipation Guide, DR-TA, Story Pyramid), and five lessons were designed by the students using what they had learned in the methods classes. For each lesson the following procedure was used. The students were asked to describe the strategies they would be using, to discuss their reasons for using these strategies, and to outline the procedures for classroom instruction. In a meeting prior to teaching the lesson, the student interns met with the mentoring teacher to discuss the lesson. At this time the mentoring teachers were asked to rate from 1 to 5 their familiarity with the strategy. The ratings were from "not at all familiar" to "already use the strategy in the classroom." After the student interns taught the lesson, the mentoring teachers were asked to rate from 1 to 5 whether or not they would consider using the strategy in their own teaching. The ratings went from "no" to "definitely." Mentoring teachers were then interviewed to determine how they felt about the strategies the student interns were presenting.

Thirty-nine student interns participated in the study, completing an average of 12 lessons. Mean scores were calculated to find the extent of the

Figure 1. Mean Scores of Teacher Ratings of Strategies

Strategies	*Number*	*Prior Knowledge* (mean score)	*SD*	*Intent to Use* (mean score)	*SD*
Read aloud, DR-TA, Think-Pair-Share	39	4.38	.74	5.0	.0
Predict-O-Gram, DR-TA, Think-Pair-Share, Story Pyramid	39	4.02	1.1	4.89	.38
Book Talk	39	3.87	1.0	4.69	.56
Story Impression, Story Frame	39	3.87	1.38	4.84	.58
Anticipation Guide, Discussion Web	39	4.07	1.01	4.74	.59
Preview vocab. in context	39	4.20	.89	4.94	.22
List-Group-Label, four-square	37	3.69	1.45	4.51	.94
Decoding #1 (student choice)	35	4.20	.83	4.74	.9
Comprehension #1 (student choice)	38	4.30	.89	4.79	.52
Vocabulary (student choice)	38	4.33	.83	4.61	.87
Decoding #2 (student choice)	36	4.4	.96	4.84	.43
Comprehension #2 (student choice)	39	4.25	.51	4.86	.58

prior knowledge the mentoring teachers had for each lesson. The means ranged from 3.69 to 4.38. Means were also calculated to determine the willingness of the mentoring teachers to use the strategies presented. The range of means was from 4.51 to 5.0. A paired t-test was calculated for each of the scores of the lessons. (See Table 1 for pre- and post-scores.)

Because a self-report score does not give a complete picture of changes that occur to specific participants, additional data were collected. Four schools, three elementary schools and one middle school were randomly selected to meet with the university and district instructors for group interviews. Each of the groups of teachers was interviewed twice during the semester about the reading lessons the student interns were teaching. Mentoring teachers were asked in what ways they had benefited from the lessons taught by the students. Notes were taken of the interviews by the university instructor and the two district instructors. For more specific data, teachers were asked to give a response to each of the reading lessons taught by the students. These data were collected by the university instructor. Student interns were also asked to respond to each reading lesson they taught. These data were also collected by the university instructor.

Four times during the semester, the university instructor and the two district instructors met to read the qualitative data and to discuss their individual interpretations. With each reading, the investigators looked for thematic premises consistent with the constant comparative method (Glaser & Strauss, 1967). A nonparticipant graduate assistant also read and reviewed the data for additional insight. In each case the data were read looking for themes to try to answer the question, "What's going on here?" (Wolcott, 1988).

Results and Discussion

The quantitative data indicated that teachers' knowledge of some reading strategies did increase. The mean scores of the lessons taught by the students indicated some change, three of them significant: book talks ($t = 3.84$, $p < .05$), story impressions/story frames ($t = 5.15$, $p < .05$), and list-group-label ($t = 3.54$, $p < .05$). Teachers reported in their response to their lessons, however, that since student interns were teaching groups of strategies, at times one strategy was familiar, and one was new. Therefore, some teachers reported that they were familiar with the strategy if they knew at least one of them.

The qualitative data were more informative. During the interviews, teachers discussed the strategies that were new to them and talked about ways they had implemented the strategies modeled by the students. The themes of the data relating to mentoring teachers grouped around five central ideas.

1. Teachers Embraced New Ideas.

The mean scores of the teachers' responses to the teaching of the interns indicated that many of them learned new strategies from the student interns. Individual teaching responses indicated that teachers were enthusiastic about the teaching ideas they received from watching their student interns teach. They expressed their enthusiasm by their interest in the ideas for their own teaching repertoire as exemplified by this teacher's comment. "I wasn't aware of this strategy (Anticipation Guide), but I was aware of the concept of asking students questions before reading. I really like this strategy and I intend to use it in the future." Teachers also expressed interest in ways the students in their classroom were becoming engaged in reading. "When the student intern teaches one of those reading lessons, it's exciting for my students. They learn so much from these lessons."

2. Teachers Sought More Information.

Teachers who observed student interns teach new strategies began initiating conversations about reading with other personnel knowledgeable about specific reading strategies. Many teachers wanted additional information. Some asked the student intern for more information or for the primary source of the strategy; others asked the university instructor in the graduate courses on reading; and still others asked the district staff development coordinator for information. The reading strategies that the interns were introducing became an initial point of shared conversation between the teachers and personnel delivering staff development.

3. Teachers Suggested Ways for the Student Interns to Use New Ideas.

Many teachers were interested in new strategies but found they needed to have the strategy adapted for their classroom. When the strategies were new for the teachers, they learned about the strategy from their student intern and worked with the student intern to adapt the strategy for their grade level and to fit the content of their teaching lessons.

For example, student interns in the reading methods class were introduced to the Predict-O-Gram (Blachowicz, 1986). The strategy was modeled for use with intermediate grade students. Student interns in primary grades asked their mentoring teachers for ways to adapt the Predict-O-Gram in their classroom. Teachers worked with student interns to modify the strategy for their particular grade level and often suggested texts for students to use with the strategies.

4. Teachers Began to Use New Ideas Themselves.

Teachers in the PDS program began to use many of the ideas that were presented by the student interns in their own classrooms. In the interviews, teachers discussed strategies that were new for them and ways they had used the strategies in their teaching. Teachers reported that they began using specific strategies like the Story Impression (McGinley & Denner, 1987) and that they began using questioning strategies like the DR-TA (Stauffer, 1969).

5. Teachers Initiated Conversations About Reading Instruction With Non-Mentoring Teachers.

The teachers who began to use new ideas discussed them with other teachers on their staff. Mentoring teachers reported that they had recommended ideas to other teachers that they had learned from the student interns. Since most schools had three or four interns teaching similar reading strategies, several mentoring teachers in each school observed these lessons. In informal conversations, some of these teachers began discussing what they had learned with other teachers. The shared focus of these conversations began discussions with mentoring and non-mentoring teachers about the teaching of reading.

Limitations

Although the belief that student interns supported by university faculty can make a difference in schools has been the primary reason the Wheeling administrators have enthusiastically welcomed a Professional Development School, no data have been available to substantiate that claim. Teaching behavior is complex, and identifying causes of influence can be elusive. This study did indicate that student interns, in some small way, are influencing the self-reported literacy behaviors of teachers.

One of the limitations of this study was that no attempt was made to observe the mentoring teachers to find out whether they were using the strategies. The study, therefore, indicates that teachers intended to use new ideas and even discussed ways they used new reading strategies in their classroom. However, there was no follow-up made on the teachers' discussions.

A second limitation to the study was that increasing the knowledge of reading strategies by mentoring teachers does not constitute real change in schools, and, consequently, improved classrooms in which student interns can observe and teach. While increased knowledge of the teaching of reading may be a stepping stone to real school improvement, change could also stop at this point. Therefore, a second limitation to this study is that the identification of small change may or may not lead to more substantial change.

A third limitation concerns identifying causes of change. Although we believe that the student interns were part of the reason why teachers reported that they intended to use and did use new reading strategies, teachers were simultaneously exposed to new ideas through other staff development projects, including the graduate courses offered by the university. As a result, this study cannot claim that student interns were the sole cause of increased knowledge of teachers.

Conclusions and Implications

A primary reason for the interest of the school district in forming a partnership with the university was to make changes in the school culture. Although deep changes have not yet occurred, the change process is beginning. Teachers are learning and discussing new ideas and are making the step toward adapting them for their classrooms. Our premise was that personnel from the university and the schools need to respect the knowledge each brings to the PDS and to learn from each other. Learning has not been a one-way street; we at the university have learned and changed in as many ways as have the teachers in the schools. We do believe, however, that the intentional "bumping together" of schools and universities can indeed change both institutions and that the change process has begun in schools in the ISU-Wheeling Professional Development School.

The assumption that 39 student interns spending a year in a school district under the direction of university faculty and school personnel can institute changes in schools is an important thought for professional development, and, in turn, for systematic change in the deeper structures of schooling. In-depth studies investigating school change in Professional Development School setting need to be conducted. Case studies of mentoring teachers who have had a student intern should also be conducted to learn whether the influence of new ideas brought by student interns is lasting. Finally, the amount of time the student intern spends in a mentoring teacher's class as it relates to teacher change needs to be explored to determine whether a specific amount of time is necessary to build trust for reciprocal learning. These and other studies recording school changes in PDS settings will add to the knowledge base about the effectiveness of Professional Development Schools.

References

Blachowicz, C. L. Z. (1986). Making connections: Alternative to the vocabulary notebook. *Journal of Reading, 29*(7), 643-649.

Cochran-Smith, M. (1991). Reinventing student teaching. *Journal of Teacher Education, 42*(2), March-April, 104-118.

Darling-Hammond, L. (1994). Developing professional development schools: Early lessons, challenge, and promise. In L. Darling-Hammond (Ed.), *Professional development schools: Schools for a devaluing profession* (pp. 1-27). New York: Teachers College Press.

Glaser, B. & Strauss, A. (1967). *The discovery of grounded theory.* Chicago, IL: Aldine Publishing.

Goodlad, J. I. (1993). School-University partnerships and partner schools. *Educational Policy, 7*(1), 24-29.

Hardy, J. T. (1993). The effects of a school-university collaborative change project on teacher behaviors: A case study. *Mid-Western Educational Researcher, 6*, 8-13.

Holmes Group. (1986). Tomorrow's teachers: A report of the Holmes Group. East Lansing, MI: Author.

Holmes Group. (1990). *Tomorrow's schools.* East Lansing, MI: Author.

Jones, M. G., & Vesilind, E. M. (1996). Putting practice into theory: Changes in the organization of preservice teachers' pedagogical knowledge. *American Educational Research Journal, 33*(1), 91-117.

McGinley, W. J., & Denner, P. R. (1987). Story impressions: A prereading/writing activity. *Journal of Reading, 31*(3), 248-253.

Miller, L., & Silvernail, D. L. (1994). Wells Junior High School: Evolution of a Professional Development School. In L. Darling-Hammond (Ed.), *Professional development schools: Schools for a devaluing profession* (pp. 28-49). New York: Teachers College Press.

Oldfather, P., Bonds, S., & Bray, T. (1994). Stalking the "fuzzy sunshine seeds": Constructivist processes for teaching about constructivism in teacher education. *Teacher Education Quarterly, 32*(3), 5-14.

Smith, S. D. (1992). Professional partnerships and educational change: Effective collaborations over time. *Journal of Teacher Education, 43*(4), 243-256.

Stauffer, R. G. (1969). *Directing reading maturity as a cognitive process.* New York: Harper and Row.

Wolcott, H. F. (1988). Ethnographic research in education. In R. M. Jaeger (Ed.), *Contemporary methods for research in education.* Washington, DC: American Educational Research Association.

Improving Elementary Teachers' Ability to Implement Reading Strategies in the Teaching of Science Content

William Dee Nichols

University of North Carolina at Charlotte

William H. Rupley
Sandra L. Mergen

Texas A&M University

Abstract

This study examined the extent to which primary grade teachers involved in a one hundred-hour staff development project reported familiarity, utility, perceived applicability and attitude towards the implementation of reading strategies in teaching science content. A total of 30 primary grade teachers representing 6 elementary schools in a Texas school district participated in a staff development program focusing on the integration of reading strategies in their teaching of science. Each participant responded to a pre- and post-survey and completed daily evaluations focused on determining the effectiveness of the professional development seminar. Analysis of variance and qualitative analysis of written evaluations revealed that teachers involved in the staff development experience made significant gains in their understanding and familiarity with several reading strategies and procedures. Furthermore, teachers reported that they would implement these strategies and techniques in their daily classroom instruction.

Over the past two decades, many investigations have examined the extent to which teachers in their content area teaching implement reading strategies. Much of this research has examined the strategies readers use in order to comprehend expository text (Jetton, Rupley, & Willson, 1995; Kletzein, 1991; Weaver & Kintsch, 1991). Reading is seen as a process in which the reader constructs meaning through the interaction of stored knowledge and the text information. Skilled readers construct mental representations of the text by using their existing knowledge along with their application of flexible strategies (Rupley & Willson, 1997). When their comprehension breaks down, good readers monitor and change strategies so that comprehension has a better chance of occurring. As readers reach a level of expertise they use rapid decoding, large vocabularies, phonemic awareness, knowledge about text features, and a variety of strategies to aid comprehension (Paris, Wasik, & Turner, 1991; Rupley & Willson, 1997).

Skilled readers use a variety of strategies before, during, and after reading to comprehend. While most content area reading strategies have traditionally been viewed as the domain of secondary education (Armbruster, Anderson, & Meyer, 1991; Gee, Olsen, & Forester, 1989; Moore, Readence, & Rickelman, 1983), many students acquire strategies between the ages of 7 and 13 (Paris, et. al. 1991; Rupley & Willson, 1996). While many of these strategies are taught explicitly, others are generated through practice with increasingly difficult text (Paris, et. al. 1991). Young children need guidance and assistance to use strategies, whereas children 10 years old and older become more spontaneous, selective, and self-controlled in their use of strategies (Jetton, Rupley, & Willson, 1995). Skilled readers are better equipped to look back in the text to monitor their comprehension, while less skilled readers often do not realize that their comprehension has failed. One problem that often occurs when trying to get students of all ages to use strategic monitoring is that even when students realize that the strategy helps them successfully complete the task, they still fail to utilize the strategy in similar reading situations (Alexander & Judy, 1988). Two reasons that this lack of strategy use may occur is that readers are either unaware of how to use the strategy or that they fail to see the importance of it (Paris, Lipson, & Wixson, 1994). In order for a strategy to be selected, it must be perceived as a valuable means toward accomplishing a task. Research conducted by Paris, Newman, and McVey (1982) indicated that children who were instructed in strategy use, told the importance of the strategy and how the utilization of this strategy helped them to remember information were more likely to use the strategy on subsequent assignments than students who just received strategy training. For reading instructional strategies to be used, the reader had to perceive benefit with it in relation to a valued reading purpose; therefore, if there is absence of strategic use, it is not always attributable to the knowledge of the strategy (Paris, et. al., 1994). Children need to be convinced that the reading strategies they are learning are useful, and they also need to learn the conditions under which strategies are applied and not applied (Paris, et. al., 1994; Paris, et. al., 1982). When instruction occurs that has these components, students will know when and why to use strategies and will more likely associate value with them (Paris, et. al., 1994).

A widely held belief of a cognitive view of reading recognizes that comprehension occurs when readers use a range of cues from the text, along with their existing knowledge and strategic monitoring. It is their knowledge of language that enables readers to process sentences and their meanings (Heilman, Blair, & Rupley, 1998), and it is their knowledge of the world that supplies them with the background for understanding both the implicit and explicit information in the text. Furthermore, it is their strategic knowledge that allows readers to monitor the quality of their comprehension and to verify that the information makes sense and that it meets their specific purpose (Ehri, 1992).

Even though comprehension requires prior and strategic knowledge, these forms of knowledge are difficult components for students to use (Willson & Rupley, 1997). It appears that beginning and less skilled readers have difficulty monitoring comprehension, which is partially due to their lack of awareness about the appropriate measures for evaluating their own comprehension. Beginning readers focus their attention on decoding and word meaning, and their strategies for monitoring comprehension usually revolve around these two areas rather than multiple monitoring strategies (Rupley, Willson & Nichols, in press). Another reason that beginning readers have difficulty monitoring comprehension is due to the fact that they often have a superficial understanding of the task of reading. For most readers in the elementary grades, reading remains a mysterious activity. Young and less capable readers, who often do not use good reading strategies, need to be provided with direct instruction and set purposes to guide their application of reading skills. Without monitoring, applying prior and strategic knowledge, and having meaningful reading purposes, beginning and poor readers will have a difficult time comprehending as they continue to encounter increasingly difficult content texts.

McKenna and Robinson (1990) assert that the most effective way to ensure the implementation of content literacy capabilities is to acquaint classroom teachers with a range of reading and writing strategies. By improving teachers' knowledge of reading and writing strategies, they can see their functions and uses while developing an understanding of the value of such strategies in order to foster content literacy in their classrooms. It is essential that teachers are able to communicate content strategies in order to better prepare their students in using successful strategies in their reading encounters.

The purpose of this study was to determine: (a) the extent to which content area reading strategies were being implemented by primary grade teachers in their instruction of reading and science, and (b) how professional development in the implementation of using reading strategies affected teachers' perceptions about the use of these strategies within their classrooms. Five research questions were addressed:

1. Are kindergarten through fourth grade teachers familiar with content area reading strategies?

2. How frequently do kindergarten through fourth grade teachers use content area reading strategies in their classrooms?

3. How did educating teachers in the implementation of integrating reading strategies into science content increase their familiarity with content area reading strategies?

4. How did educating teachers in the implementation of integrating reading strategies into science content increase teachers perceived use of content area reading strategies?

5. How did teachers involved in the professional development program view the overall effectiveness of such development?

Methodology

The sample consisted of 30 teachers from a school district in Texas who completed the pre- and post- questionnaire and participated in an "Integrating Reading Strategies with Science Content" staff development program. The primary teachers included in the sample represented kindergarten (n = 6), first grade (n =6), second grade (n =3), third grade (n =12), and fourth grade (n =3). Participants ranged from first year classroom teachers to teachers with 30 years of experience.

Instrumentation

The Reading Instructional Features Questionnaire (RIFQ) was developed by the researchers and the local school district in order to determine classroom teachers' existing knowledge of reading strategies and perceived time of use in reading instruction dedicated to strategy indoctrination. The first part of the instrument focused on demographic information related to number of years teaching experience, number of years in the school district, number of years teaching at present grade level, previous grade levels taught, and certifications/specialization or endorsements. The second part of the instrument consisted of a 69-item questionnaire that asked teachers to identify their familiarity with and uses of reading strategies and terminology. The questionnaire was divided into sections that examined the extent to which teachers reported their use of: (a) various types of reading methods in their instructional programs, (b) grouping practices, (c) reading and study strategies in their literacy programs, (d) reading and study strategies in their content area instructional programs, and (e) trade and resource books in the content areas. The pre- and post- surveys were administered in a group setting and took 30 minutes to complete. The items in the RIFQ were compiled after a review of the extant literature, which included a search of ERIC citations, textbooks, and examination of *The Literacy Dictionary: The Vocabulary of Reading and Writing* (Harris & Hodges, 1995). The reading strategies that were identified from this review were included as items in the questionnaire (see appendix A) with specific sources of information supporting inclusion of the items. The questionnaire was field-tested using a sample of 30 teachers who participated in an earlier staff development program. These participants responded to each item on the survey instrument and made suggestions for additions and revisions. Their suggestions were incorporated into a revised instrument.

Professional Development

The staff development sessions, which provided teacher education on ways to integrate reading strategies with science content, were six hours daily for two weeks and focused on the following goals:

1. To improve and enhance elementary teachers' knowledge of content and instructional strategies for reading, writing and science in grades K-4, and

2. To create model instructional units that integrated reading skills and teaching strategies in grade-appropriate science content.

Each session began with large group reflective discourse. During this reflective time, participants and facilitators analyzed the daily evaluations and discussed the integrative nature between the reading strategy implementation and the science content lessons. Participants then developed science content lessons that integrated reading strategies into the teaching of that content. Qualified teachers who participated in the staff development the previous year were lead educators during these sessions. These lead teachers developed units around an instructional science problem and, on a daily basis, developed hands-on-lessons that integrated reading strategies in order to solve the science question. These active classroom demonstrations of alternative instructional techniques allowed the participants to use and value learning strategies in science content.

An example of a typical integrated instructional science lesson can be viewed on day 4's integrated lesson. The kindergarten through second grade teachers were developing science units around the scientific problem of finding a solution for setting up a ten gallon aquarium that would be relatively self sustaining and would cost under $15.00. During the process of solving this scientific problem the teachers investigated the content of fish extensively. On day four, the lead teachers used the instructional strategy of jigsaw grouping to allow the participants to answer the following questions: What are the structures inside a fish?, What do fish use these structures for? What are the names of these structures? What is the special structure that allows fish to stay up and move throughout the water? The participants were then divided into expert groups and investigated the following fish structures: external anatomy, swim bladder, digestive system, respiratory system, and circulatory system. The participants then researched their topics using expository text and information found at various internet sites. The expert groups were then jigsawed into their original groups the next day so that they could identify the anatomy of the fish during the group dissection.

The third- and fourth-grade teachers also used the jigsawing technique during the morning session to help them solve the scientific problem of what type of energy would be the best solution if Texas could no longer use fossil fuels as a means of energy source? The participants were divided into expert groups and researched the following energy types: wind energy, water energy, solar energy, and nuclear energy. The expert groups were jigsawed the following day and deliberated on which method of energy would have the most positive results.

Participants then received instruction and practice focusing on reading strategies for both literature and the content area. Professional development sessions were led by reading experts who placed a strong emphasis on the integration between the morning and afternoon lessons. For example, if during the morning instructional period the lead teachers used semantic mapping and webbing during the creation of the science activity, then, in the afternoon session, participants would learn the theory behind using such strategies, how to use the strategies successfully, and how to create their own lessons using the various strategies. Using the jigsawing example described above, during the afternoon session, the reading expert described the theory behind cooperative grouping and the jigsaw technique and then selected a piece of literature and had the participants use the jigsaw technique to identify story schema in the selected literature. The participants were divided into the following expert groups in order to identify the following components of story schema: setting, characterization, conflict, rise in action, climax and resolution. The expert groups were then jigsawed so that in each literature circle an expert could lead the discussion over one of the story components. Practice and application were always provided using the strategies in both literature and content area reading material selected to go along with the science units, Fishy Business and Solar Solutions (See Appendix B for book list).

Daily evaluation/reflections regarding the content area reading strategy implementation training were developed in order to evaluate participants learning and perceptions of the training. Each day the participants responded to the following 5 statements:

1. The BEST THING about today was . . .
2. One thing I'll remember for a long time about TEACHING READING is . . .
3. One thing I'll remember for a long time about TEACHING SCIENCE is . . .
4. A SUGGESTION for tomorrow . . .
5. A CONCERN/COMMENT I have . . .

At the conclusion of the staff development workshop, the daily evaluations were analyzed inductively through multiple readings resulting in four coding categories. The four categories that emerged were:

1. Impressions of instruction and planning
2. Group participation
3. Reflections about reading
4. Reflections about science.

These four categories were then clustered based upon frequency of response and natural headings that emerged. After various sorts of participant responses the patterns were examined in regards to the five research questions.

Data Collection and Analysis

During the first and final meeting, each teacher completed the pre-test form of the RIFQ, and after the completion of the training program each teacher completed the post-test form of the RIFQ. Pre-test and post-test comparisons on the RIFQ were used to perform analysis of variance (ANOVA). The descriptive analysis and analysis of variance for the data are displayed in tables 1-5.

In order to examine the responses to the pre- and post-questionnaire the data were analyzed using descriptive statistics and a one-way analysis of variance (ANOVA). Descriptive statistics provided a mean score and a standard deviation for each of the 69 items. Analysis of the pre-test was intended to answer the following research questions:

1. Are teachers in grade levels kindergarten through fourth grade familiar with content area reading strategies?
2. How frequently do the teachers use content area reading strategies?

In order to answer the following research questions and examine the pre- and post-test forms, daily written evaluations, descriptive statistics, analysis of variance, and qualitative analyses were used.

1. Did educating teachers in the implementation of integrating reading strategies into science content increase their familiarity with content area reading strategies?
2. Did educating teachers in the implementation of integrating reading strategies into science content increase perceived use of content area reading strategies?
3. Did teachers involved in the professional development view the overall effectiveness of such training?

Tables one through five points out teachers' familiarity and perceived use of the reading strategies, as well as the effects of the staff development on their use of strategy implementation. In addition to performing statistical analyses on the pre- and post-test forms of the RIFQ questionnaire, the daily evaluations were inductively analyzed through multiple readings. In order to complete this process, the daily evaluations were transferred onto a word processor where the researchers could unitize and categorize the raw data (Glaser & Stauss, 1967; Holsti, 1969; Lincoln & Guba, 1985). After unitizing the data, individual sorts were performed based upon the commonality of the participants' responses. These provisional categories led to propositional statements that served as a basis for inclusion or exclusion (Lincoln & Guba, 1985). After negotiated discussions between the facilitators and the participants, a reached consensus was established and the categories that emerged were used to address the five research questions. The categories used to address the effectiveness of the training are found in Appendix C.

Results

The results in Table 1 reveal that teachers were at least familiar with and occasionally used worksheets, running records, computers, audio tapes, reading curriculum guides, pre-reading activities, reading conferences, personal journals, and portfolios. Results also indicated that continuing to educate teachers in content area reading strategies made a statistical difference in the familiarity and perceived use of the following: strategy checklists, reading surveys, self-evaluation forms, video tapes, personal journals, and literature response. The results also denote that, due to the professional development, teachers perceived that they would use fewer worksheets in their daily instruction.

The analysis of variance and descriptive statistics used to create Table 2 indicates that teachers were at least familiar with and occasionally used cooperative groups, literature circles, whole class instruction, skill groups, and ability groups. Results of the ANOVA indicated that the professional development made a statistical difference for the familiarity and perceived use of

Table 1. Types of Reading Methods

Items	Pre-Survey Means	Std. Dev.	Post-Survey Means	Std. Dev.
1. Worksheets etc.	3.34	.86	3.10	.55
2. Strategy Checklist	2.50 *	1.14	3.67 *	.88
3. Reading Surveys	2.13 *	.86	3.30 *	.70
4. Running Records	3.37	1.30	3.80	1.00
5. Self-evaluation forms	2.57 *	1.22	3.30*	.79
6. Computer	4.07	.83	4.17	.70
7. Audio tapes	3.55	.78	3.57	.68
8. Video tapes	2.50 *	.78	2.97 *	.61
9. Reading Curriculum guides	3.21	1.29	3.30	.88
10. Pre-reading activities	3.97	.85	4.33	.48
11. Reading conferences	3.40	1.07	3.87	.68
12. Personal Journal	3.43 *	1.07	4.27 *	.69
13. Literature Response	2.80 *	1.06	3.87 *	.78
14. Portfolios	3.10	.96	3.77	.68

*Note. The * indicates items that were found significant at the .001 level.*

Table 2. Grouping Practices

Items	Pre-Survey Means	Std. Dev.	Post-Survey Means	Std. Dev.
15. Cooperative Groups	3.77	.68	4.00	.45
16. Literature Circles	3.00	1.23	3.40	.62
17. Whole Class	3.70	.88	3.50	.68
18. Interest Groups	2.77 *	.94	3.47 *	.51
19. Skill Groups	3.03	.89	3.33	.55
20. Ability Groups	3.03	.81	3.07	.83
21. Research Groups	2.17 *	.79	3.33 *	.76
22. Author Studies	2.37 *	.89	3.27 *	.69
23. Genre Studies	2.37 *	.85	3.10 *	.66

*Note. The * indicates items that were found significant at the .001 level.*

the following grouping strategies: interest groups, research groups, author studies, and genre studies. Table 2 also indicates that teachers perceived, due to the professional development, a decrease in whole class instruction.

Table 3 illustrates that teachers were at least familiar with and occasionally used the following reading and study strategies in literature instruction prior to the professional developmant: DRA, DRTA, KWL, setting purpose, guided reading, fix-up-strategies, story maps, Venn diagrams, and webbing. At the conclusion of the professional development, the results indicated that

Table 3. Reading and Study Strategies in Literature

Items	Pre-Survey Means	Std. Dev.	Post-Survey Means	Std. Dev.
24. DRA	3.50	.86	3.60	.56
25. DRTA	3.23 *	.82	3.77 *	.43
26. KWL	3.30 *	.84	4.10 *	.48
27. LEA	2.90	1.06	3.53	.68
28. Setting Purpose	3.80	.89	4.27	.64
29. Guided Reading	3.53	.90	3.80	.71
30. Fix-up-strategies	3.43	1.07	3.97	.63
31. Story map	3.03	.68	3.60	.50
32. Venn diagram	3.07	.69	3.57	.50
33. Readers theater	1.97 *	.96	3.20 *	.66
34. Semantic maps	2.63 *	.85	3.28 *	.59
35. Skim-Scan	1.83 *	.95	2.90 *	.99
36. SQ3R	1.87 *	.90	3.17 *	.87
37. Anticipation Guide	2.00 *	1.05	3.77 *	.43
38. Reciprocal Teaching	2.13 *	.97	3.27 *	.58
39. Outlining	1.93	.87	2.60	.86
40. Note-taking	1.80	.85	2.30	.84
41. Learning logs	2.00 *	.98	3.23 *	.82
42. Webbing	3.00 *	.96	3.70 *	.53
43. Graphic organizers	2.93 *	1.11	3.83 *	.65
44. Test taking strategies	2.90	1.24	3.48	.99

*Note. The * indicates items that were found significant at the .001 level.*

a significant difference for the familiarity and value of the following strategies occurred: DRTA, KWL, reader's theater, semantic maps, skim-scan, SQ3R, anticipation guides, reciprocal teaching, learning logs, webbing, and graphic organizers.

Table 4, which presents the familiarity with and perceived use of reading and study strategies in the content area, indicated that teachers were at least familiar with and occasionally used the following reading and study strategies in their content instruction prior to the professional development:

Table 4. Reading and Study Strategies in Content Area

Items	Pre-Survey Means	Std. Dev.	Post-Survey Means	Std. Dev.
45. DRA	3.50	.73	3.80	.41
46. DRTA	3.40	.77	3.80	.41
47. KWL	3.47	.90	4.07	.45
48. LEA	2.73*	1.08	3.57*	.73
49. Setting Purpose	3.90	.84	4.13	.57
50. Guided Reading	3.57	.86	3.73	.74
51. Fix-up-strategies	3.23	1.28	3.79	.73
52. Story map	2.80*	.81	3.53*	.51
53. Venn diagram	3.30	.92	3.67	.55
54. Reader's theater	1.80 *	1.06	3.10 *	.71
55. Semantic maps	2.70	.95	3.30	.75
56. Skim-Scan	2.17	1.18	2.87	1.07
57. SQ3R	2.00 *	.95	3.23 *	.90
58. Anticipation Guide	2.10 *	1.06	3.77 *	.57
59. Reciprocal Teaching	2.23 *	.97	3.30*	.60
60. Outlining	2.03	1.16	2.67	.88
61. Note-taking	2.07	1.17	2.40	1.00
62. Learning logs	2.30*	1.02	3.13 *	.78
63. Webbing	2.93 *	.87	3.70 *	.60
64. Graphic organizers	2.83 *	.99	3.87 *	.73
65. Test taking strategies	2.77	1.22	3.37	.93

Note. The * indicates items that were found significant at the .001 level.

Table 5. Use of Trade Books in the Content Area

Items	Pre-Survey Means	Std. Dev.	Post-Survey Means	Std. Dev.
66. Science	4.10	.92	4.43	.50
67. Math	2.97 *	.81	3.80 *	.76
68. Social Studies	3.93	.83	4.37	.56
69. Technology	3.77	1.01	3.93	.83

*Note. The * indicates items that were found significant at the .001 level.*

DRA, DRTA, KWL, setting purpose, guided reading, fix-up-strategies, and Venn diagrams. After the professional development, there was a significant difference for the familiarity and perceived use of the following strategies: LEA, story maps, reader's theater, SQ3R, anticipation guides, reciprocal teaching, learning logs, webbing, and graphic organizers.

The final analysis (Table 5) examined teachers' familiarity with and perceived use of integrating trade books into their content area teaching. The analysis indicated that teachers were already familiar with using trade books in the areas of science, social studies and technology. Upon completion of the teacher development, teachers also indicated that they perceived that they would use trade books in math instruction also.

The evaluations that were analyzed inductively through multiple readings and various sorts were broken down into four categories. The four categories were:

1. Participants' impressions of instruction and planning. (I really appreciate the positive, enthusiastic attitude of the presenters. It influences everyone around.)

2. Participants' grouping practices. (The best thing about today was getting to work in my research group. I really enjoyed working with new friends and sharing their input. I also learned a lot about solar energy that I can pass on to my class.)

3. Reading reflections. (Using different strategies to teach is so important to help the child learn. These are all new terms to me, so I'm taking it all in and trying to understand how to teach these strategies.)

4. Science reflections. (Use graphic organizers for science projects to stress sequence of events and informative narratives.)

Further results of these clusters are located in Appendix C.

Discussion

The results of this study support the idea that teachers are using some reading strategies in their teaching of science content in the primary grades. What is most noteworthy is that teachers who received professional development focused specifically on the use of reading strategies in content area instruction predicted a higher classroom use and value for such strategies. The results of the RIFQ and the analysis of the teachers' daily evaluations with regard to familiarity, perceived applicability, and utility reflect the impact of such continuing education.

Upon examination of the pre-test form of the RIFQ, the teachers reported familiarity and utility of several strategies. These strategies included worksheets, running records, computers, audio tapes, reading curriculum guides, pre-reading activities, reading conferences, personal journals, portfolios, cooperative grouping, literature circles, whole class instruction, skill groups, ability groups, DRA, DRTA, KWL, setting purposes, guided reading, fix-up-strategies, story maps, Venn diagrams, and webbing. In response to research question 1 and 2 it appears that teachers in the primary grades are familiar with and use several content area reading strategies in their instruction.

When comparing the results of the pre-test and post-test forms of the RIFQ regarding the effectiveness of the professional development seminar, it is evident that such training does help teachers increase their perceived value and utilization of reading strategies, supporting the research of McKenna and Robinson (1990). The participants in this study indicated that the professional development made a significant difference in their familiarity and perceived utilization of the following instructional strategies: strategy checklists, reading surveys, self-evaluation forms, video tapes, personal journals, literature responses, interest groups, research groups, author studies, genre studies, DRTA, KWL, readers' theater, semantic maps, skim-scan, SQ3R, anticipation guides, reciprocal teaching, learning logs, webbing, graphic organizers, story maps, and LEA.

The descriptive statistics suggested that while the professional development did not make a significant difference in the familiarity and perceived utilization of every strategy, the training did increase the mean score associated with both the value and the knowledge, while decreasing the standard deviation of responses for all of the strategies.

Furthermore, the results of the multiple readings of the daily evaluations led us to conclude that teachers not only became familiar with and planned to utilize more strategic instruction in their classrooms, but they also valued the workshop as well as the strategies they would be teaching. This is a crucial element in strategy instruction because not only should teachers be able to communicate content area strategies, they must also assist their students in seeing the value of implementing such strategies in order to foster content literacy in their classrooms.

Although teachers at the onset of the educational program reported familiarity with and utilization of certain content area reading strategies in their classroom, many of the strategies that are recommended in the literature were unknown to them. As a result, teachers may not use certain strategies that have shown to be beneficial in content area reading for elementary grade students. These teachers report using general strategies, such as journal writing, pre-reading activities, and directed reading instruction with content area reading. However, strategies such as self-evaluation forms, semantic mapping, and graphic organizers, which have been successfully developed to help with content area reading were not known at the beginning of the staff development. Thus, professional development programs, such as that described in this study, would make a significant difference in the perceived type of instruction that teachers would use in order to incorporate learning and reading strategies into their daily content area instruction.

References

Alexander, P. A., & Judy, J. E. (1988). The interaction of domain-specific and strategic knowledge in academic performance. *Review of Educational Research, 58,* 375-404.

Armbruster, B. B., Anderson, T. H., & Meyer, J. L. (1991). Improving content-area using instructional graphics. *Reading Research Quarterly, 26* (4), 393-416.

Ehri, L.C. (1992). Reconceptualizing the development of sight word reading and its relationship to recoding. In P. Gough, L. Ehri, & R. Treiman (Eds.), *Reading Acquisition,* (pp. 35-48). Hillsdale, NJ: Lawrence Erlbaum Associates.

Gee, T. C., Olson, M., & Forester, N. (1989). A survey of content reading program development in U.S. schools. *Reading Research and Instruction, 28(3),* 30-44.

Glaser, B. G., & Strauss, A. L. (1967). *The Discovery of Grounded Theory.* Chicago, IL: Aldine.

Harris, T. L., & Hodges, R. E., (1995). *The Literacy Dictionary: The vocabulary of reading and writing.* Newark, DE: International Reading Association.

Heilman, A., Blair, T. R, & Rupley, W. H. (1998). *Principles and Practices of Teaching Reading (9th ed.).* Columbus, OH: Merrill.

Holsti, O. R. (1969). *Content Analysis for the Social Sciences and Humanities.* Reading, MA: Addison-Wesley.

Jetton, T., Rupley, W. H., & Willson, V. L. (1995). Comprehension of narrative and expository texts: The role of content, domain, discourse, and strategy knowledge. In K. Hinchman, D. J. Leu, & C. K. Kinzer (Eds.), *Perspectives on literacy research and practice 44th Yearbook of the National Reading Conference.* Chicago, IL: NRC, pp.197-204.

Kletzien, S. B. (1991). Strategy use by good and poor comprehenders reading expository text of differing levels. *Reading Research Quarterly, 26(1),* 67-86.

Lincoln, Y. S., & Guba, E. G. (1985). *Naturalistic Inquiry.* Newbury Park, CA: Sage.

McKenna, M. C., & Robinson, R. D. (1990). Content literacy: A definition and implications. *Journal of Reading, 34(3),* 184-186.

Moore, D. W., Readance, J. E., & Rickelman, R. J. (1983). An historical exploration of content reading instruction. *Reading Research Quarterly, 18(4),* 419-438.

Paris, S. G., Lipson, M. Y., & Wixon, K. K. (1994). Becoming a strategic reader. In R. Ruddell, M. Ruddell, & H. Singer, (Eds.), *Theoretical models and processes of reading IV,* (pp. 788-819). Newark, DE: International Reading Association.

Paris, S. G., Newman, R. S., & McVey, K. A. (1982). Learning the functional significance of mnemonic actions: a microgenetic study of strategy acquisition. *Journal of Experimental Child Psychology, 34,* 490-509.

Paris, S. G., Wasik, B. A., & Turner, J. C. (1991). The development of strategic readers. In R. Barr, M. Kamil, P. Mosenthal, & P. D. Pearson, (Eds), *Handbook of Reading Research* (Vol. 2, pp. 609-640). White Plains, NY: Longman.

Rupley, W. H, & Willson, V. L. (1997). The relationship of reading comprehension to components of word recognition: Support for developmental shifts. *Journal of Research and Development in Education, 30,* 255-260.

Rupley, W. H., Willson, V. L., & Nichols, W. D. (In Press). Exploration of the developmental components contributing to elementary children's reading comprehension. *The Journal for the Scientific Study of Reading.*

Weaver, C. A., III, & Kintsch, W. (1991). Expository text. In Barr, Kamil, Mosenthal, & Pearson (Eds.), *Handbook of Reading Research: Vol 7.* (pp. 230-245). New York: Longman.

Willson, V. L., & Rupley, W. H. (1997). A structural equation model for reading comprehension based on background, phonemic, and strategy knowledge. *Journal for the Scientific Study of Reading, 1,* 45-64.

Appendix A

Please complete the following items by marking your scantron. Any numbers left unmarked indicates "don't know".

To what extent do you use the following *types* of reading methods in your reading instructional program?

1. daily work in the classroom (written work, worksheets, reading book lists, etc.)
   a. never   b. seldom   c. occasionally   d. frequently   e. always
2. reading strategies checklist
   a. never   b. seldom   c. occasionally   d. frequently   e. always
3. reading surveys
   a. never   b. seldom   c. occasionally   d. frequently   e. always
4. running records
   a. never   b. seldom   c. occasionally   d. frequently   e. always
5. self-evaluation forms
   a. never   b. seldom   c. occasionally   d. frequently   e. always
6. computer
   a. never   b. seldom   c. occasionally   d. frequently   e. always
7. audiotapes
   a. never   b. seldom   c. occasionally   d. frequently   e. always
8. videotapes
   a. never   b. seldom   c. occasionally   d. frequently   e. always
9. reading curriculum guides
   a. never   b. seldom   c. occasionally   d. frequently   e. always
10. pre-reading activities
    a. never   b. seldom   c. occasionally   d. frequently   e. always
11. reading conferences
    a. never   b. seldom   c. occasionally   d. frequently   e. always
12. personal journal/notebook
    a. never   b. seldom   c. occasionally   d. frequently   e. always
13. literature response journal
    a. never   b. seldom   c. occasionally   d. frequently   e. always
14. portfolios
    a. never   b. seldom   c. occasionally   d. frequently   e. always

To what extent do you use the following grouping practices in your classroom reading instructional program?

15. cooperative groups
    a. never   b. seldom   c. occasionally   d. frequently   e. always

16. literature circles
    a. never   b. seldom   c. occasionally   d. frequently   e. always
17. whole class
    a. never   b. seldom   c. occasionally   d. frequently   e. always
18. interest groups
    a. never   b. seldom   c. occasionally   d. frequently   e. always
19. skill groups
    a. never   b. seldom   c. occasionally   d. frequently   e. always
20. ability groups
    a. never   b. seldom   c. occasionally   d. frequently   e. always
21. research groups
    a. never   b. seldom   c. occasionally   d. frequently   e. always
22. author studies
    a. never   b. seldom   c. occasionally   d. frequently   e. always
23. genre studies
    a. never   b. seldom   c. occasionally   d. frequently   e. always

To what extent do you use the following *reading and study strategies during literacy instruction?*

24. Directed-Reading-Activity (DRA)
    a. never   b. seldom   c. occasionally   d. frequently   e. always
25. Directed-Reading-Thinking-Activity
    a. never   b. seldom   c. occasionally   d. frequently   e. always
26. Know-Want to Learn-Learned (KWL)
    a. never   b. seldom   c. occasionally   d. frequently   e. always
27. Language Experience Approach (LEA)
    a. never   b. seldom   c. occasionally   d. frequently   e. always
28. Setting Purposes
    a. never   b. seldom   c. occasionally   d. frequently   e. always
29. Guided Reading
    a. never   b. seldom   c. occasionally   d. frequently   e. always
30. Fix-up Strategies
    a. never   b. seldom   c. occasionally   d. frequently   e. always
31. Story Map
    a. never   b. seldom   c. occasionally   d. frequently   e. always
32. Venn Diagram
    a. never   b. seldom   c. occasionally   d. frequently   e. always
33. Reader's Theater
    a. never   b. seldom   c. occasionally   d. frequently   e. always

34. Semantic Maps
    a. never   b. seldom   c. occasionally   d. frequently   e. always
35. Skim/scan
    a. never   b. seldom   c. occasionally   d. frequently   e. always
36. SQ3R
    a. never   b. seldom   c. occasionally   d. frequently   e. always
37. Anticipation Guide
    a. never   b. seldom   c. occasionally   d. frequently   e. always
38. Reciprocal Teaching
    a. never   b. seldom   c. occasionally   d. frequently   e. always
39. Outlining
    a. never   b. seldom   c. occasionally   d. frequently   e. always
40. Note-taking
    a. never   b. seldom   c. occasionally   d. frequently   e. always
41. Learning Logs
    a. never   b. seldom   c. occasionally   d. frequently   e. always
42. Webbing
    a. never   b. seldom   c. occasionally   d. frequently   e. always
43. Graphic Organizers
    a. never   b. seldom   c. occasionally   d. frequently   e. always
44. Test-taking Strategies
    a. never   b. seldom   c. occasionally   d. frequently   e. always

To what extent do you use the following *reading and study strategies in your content area* (social studies, science, math)?

45. Directed-Reading-Activity (DRA)
    a. never   b. seldom   c. occasionally   d. frequently   e. always
46. Directed-Reading-Thinking-Activity
    a. never   b. seldom   c. occasionally   d. frequently   e. always
47. Know-Want to Learn-Learned (KWL)
    a. never   b. seldom   c. occasionally   d. frequently   e. always
48. Language Experience Approach (LEA)
    a. never   b. seldom   c. occasionally   d. frequently   e. always
49. Setting Purposes
    a. never   b. seldom   c. occasionally   d. frequently   e. always
50. Guided Reading
    a. never   b. seldom   c. occasionally   d. frequently   e. always
51. Fix-up Strategies
    a. never   b. seldom   c. occasionally   d. frequently   e. always

52. Story Map
    a. never   b. seldom   c. occasionally   d. frequently   e. always
53. Venn Diagram
    a. never   b. seldom   c. occasionally   d. frequently   e. always
54. Reader's Theater
    a. never   b. seldom   c. occasionally   d. frequently   e. always
55. Semantic Maps
    a. never   b. seldom   c. occasionally   d. frequently   e. always
56. Skim/scan
    a. never   b. seldom   c. occasionally   d. frequently   e. always
57. SQ3R
    a. never   b. seldom   c. occasionally   d. frequently   e. always
58. Anticipation Guide
    a. never   b. seldom   c. occasionally   d. frequently   e. always
59. Reciprocal Teaching
    a. never   b. seldom   c. occasionally   d. frequently   e. always
60. Outlining
    a. never   b. seldom   c. occasionally   d. frequently   e. always
61. Note-taking
    a. never   b. seldom   c. occasionally   d. frequently   e. always
62. Learning Logs
    a. never   b. seldom   c. occasionally   d. frequently   e. always
63. Webbing
    a. never   b. seldom   c. occasionally   d. frequently   e. always
64. Graphic Organizers
    a. never   b. seldom   c. occasionally   d. frequently   e. always
65. Test-Taking Strategies
    a. never   b. seldom   c. occasionally   d. frequently   e. always

**Indicate your use of trade books/library books
in the following content areas:**

66. Science
    a. never   b. seldom   c. occasionally   d. frequently   e. always
67. Math
    a. never   b. seldom   c. occasionally   d. frequently   e. always
68. Social Studies
    a. never   b. seldom   c. occasionally   d. frequently   e. always
69. How often do you use technology in supporting your reading instruction?
    a. never   b. seldom   c. occasionally   d. frequently   e. always

Appendix B

Expository Text, Fish Unit

Andrews, C. (1995). *A Fishkeepers Guide to Fancy Goldfishes*. Blacksburg: Tetra Press.

Axelrod, H. R. (1993). *Your Tropical Fish*. New Jersey: T.F.H Publication.

Baensch, U. (994). *Digest for the Successful Aquarium*. Blacksburg: Tetra Press

Boyd, K. (1990). *The Complete Aquarium Problem Solver: A Total Trouble Shooting Guide for Freshwater Marine Aquariums*. Blacksburg: Tetra Press.

Cole, J. & Wexler, J. (1978). *A Fish Hatches*. New York: William Morrow and Co.

Harrison, C. (1995). *Keeping Tropical Fish*. Toronto: Copp Clark Pitman, Ltd.

Lodewijks, J. M. (1963). *Tropical Fish in the Aquarium*. New York: Blandford Press Ltd.

Overbeck, C. (1978). *The Fish Book: An Early Nature Picture Book*. New Canton: Lumar Publishing. Company.

Palmer, J. (1989). *Knowing Your Pet Aquarium Fish*. New York: The Bookwright Press.

Parker, S. (1990). *Fish*. New York: Alfred A Knopf Books.

Ricciuti, E. (1993). *Our Living World: Fish*. Utica: Blackbird Press. Inc.

Scheurmam, I. (1993). *Aquarium Plants Manual*. Hauppauge: Barron's Educational Series, Incorporated

Narrative Text, Fish Unit

Afanasyer, A. (1990). *The Fool and the Fish: A Tale from Russia*. New York: Dial Books for Young Readers.

Aliki. (1990). *My Visit to the Aquarium*. New York: HarperCollins Children Books.

Bush, J. (1990). *The Fish Who Could Wish*. Brooklyn: Kane/Miller Book Publishers.

Clements, A. (1991). *Big Al*. New York: Scholastic, Incorporated.

Edwards, R., & Wickstrom, S. (1989). *Five Silly Fishermen*. New York: Random House for Young Readers.

Ehlert, L. (1990). *Fish Eyes*. San Diego: Harcourt Brace & Company.

Fowler, A. (1991). *It Could Still Be a Fish*. Danbury: Children's Press.

Giff, P. (1983). *Fish Face*. New York: Dell Publishing Company.

Hall, K. (1985). *Fishy Riddles*. Pines Plains: Live Oak Media.

Lionni, L. (1970). *Fish is Fish*. New York: Pantheon Books.

Lionni, L. (1973). *Swimmy*. New York: Alfred A. Knopf Books for Young Readers.

Luenn, N. (1998). *Nessa's Fish*. Paramus: The Center for Applied Research n Education.

McKissack, C. (1992). *A Million Fish . . . More or Less*. New York: Alfred A. Knopf Books for Young Readers.

Pfister, M. (1997). *Rainbow Fish*. Carson: Books Nippan.

Pfister, M. (1997). *Rainbow Fish to the Rescue*. New York: North-South Books, Incorporated.

Expository Text Energy Unit

Bendick, J. (1979). Putting the sun to work. Champaign, IL: Garrard Publishing Co.

Berger, M. (1976). *Energy from the Sun. New York: Thomas Crowell Co.*

Branley, F. (1988). *The Sun: Our Nearest Star*. New York: HarperCollins Children's Books.

Branley, F. (1964). *The Sun: Star Number One* New York: HarperCollins Children's Books.

Grohskopf, B. (1977). *Children in the Wind*. New York: Simon & Schuster Trade.

Knight, D. (1976). *Harnessing the Sun: The Story of Solar Energy*. New York: The William Morrow & Company.

Narrative Text Energy Unit

Carle, E. (1992). *Draw Me A Star*. New York: The Putman Publishing Group.

Cleary, B. (1988). *Dear Mr. Henshaw*. New York: Bantam Doubleday Dell Books for Young Readers.

Gibbons, G. (1983). *Sun Up, Sun Down*. San Diego: Harcourt Brace & Company.

Krensky, S. (1992). *Children of the Earth and Sky: Five Stories about Native American Children*. New York: Scholastic, Incorporated.

Leedy, L. (1991). *The Great Trash Bash*. New York: Holiday House Incorporated.

Lionni, L. (1992). *A Busy Year*. New York: David McKay Company.

McDermount, G. (1997). *Flecha al Sol (Arrow to the Sun)*. Pine Plains: Live Oak Media.

Pfister, M. (1998). *Sun and Moon*. New York: North-South Books, Incorporated.

Appendix C. Participant Comments

Impressions of instruction and planning:

"I really appreciate the positive, energetic attitude of the presenters. It influences everyone around." (Day 1)

"I am thoroughly enjoying this workshop! Very refreshing!" (Day 2)

"Very organized. Presenters are knowledgeable and confident." (Day 2)

"Keep up the great work! We did a lot! My brain is tired!" (Day 2)

"This is a fun workshop!" (Day 1)

"Today was GREAT! I like all the INTERACTION!." (Day 1)

"Thank you for everything . . . The great ideas and the great materials!!" (Day 2)

"I think it is great that you included teachers as presenters because it really creates a great bridge between philosophy & real teaching—it's been great!" (Day 3)

"You are doing a nice job because you are listening to our ideas and comments and treating us like we are 'semi' experts. I like the way you are teaching the afternoon for all subject areas. The ideas you have, are made easily understandable with your examples for the different areas." (Day 4)

"I have enjoyed the expertise of the lectures. Not only do they know their material, but they have used it in various ways in their own classrooms and share that." (Day 4)

"I feel like the teachers have put so much effort into solar solutions—activities & field trips have been great!" (Day 5)

"You make the reflections so valuable because we see and experience your response. How often do we, as teachers, fail to follow through on what we assign." (Day 5)

"Thanks for the thoughtful consideration when choosing the books you ordered." (Day 6)

"I love all the reference books that tie reading and science together. Thanks for all your hard work!" (Day 6)

"Thanks for the reference books that comment literature to science topics! They look great!" (Day 6)

Group Participation:

"Working in groups and bonding is important for the students." (Day 1)

"Keep up the interaction!" (Day 1)

"I really like all of the cooperative group work." (Day 2)

"Loved the group work and sharing of ideas." (Day 3)

THE BEST THING about today was . . . ."Working in my research group. I really enjoyed working with new friends & sharing their input. I also learned a lot about solar energy that I can pass onto my class." (Day 4)

"All the group work is wonderful. We have created some good projects through brainstorming and sharing. Definitely a plus having this time allotted in daily schedules." (Day 7)

THE BEST THING about today was . . . "The interaction with peers and actual hands on activities." (Day 3)

"I like the group effort in working on the research project. We felt that our contribution was important. I will use this model with my students." (Day 4)

"Working in my research group. I really enjoyed working with new friends and sharing their input. I also learned a lot about solar energy that I can pass on to my class." (Day 4)

Reflections about reading:

"The purpose of reading is dependent upon the situation." (Day 1)

"Reading is a life skill that opens up a new world to a child . . ." (Day 1)

"Reading can open the world for a child, and it is my responsibility to make that world accessible." (Day 1)

"I need to make reading fun! I need to 'model' reading daily!" (Day 1)

"A variety of reading strategies must be applied to differentiate and meet individual needs." (Day 1)

"Reading must result in meaning." (Day 1)

"Learning styles determine which reading styles work best." (Day 1)

"What's reading for a 3 year old & what's reading for a 30 year old are different. Fit (reading instruction) to the learner not the teacher." (Day 1)

"There are a lot of strategies that I don't utilize." (Day 1)

"Reading must be meaningful and personalized to each individual." (Day 1)

'Reading integrates to all subjects." (Day 7)

"As a newer teacher in practice. I have not seen or practiced these reading strategies. I feel I am now ready to go in and mix things up a bit. Thank you." (Day 7)

"Never forget to make my lesson on the level of my students and to ensure that it incorporates some of their previous knowledge." (Day 1)

"Already believed this, just remembered. . . . You have to teach reading in a variety of ways to match a variety of needs and learning styles. Strategies need to be varied accordingly." (Day 1)

"Graphic organizers and sequencing are such great ways to repeat and review the reading activities. Great way to evaluate students' understanding also." (Day 2)

"There are many strategies and other ways to incorporate reading into everything." (Day 2)

"Reading is a very detailed process for children that requires many different skills that children may or may not have." (Day 2)

"Teaching reading continues through all areas (Language, Arts, Science, Math, Social Studies, Health)" (Day 3)

"Reading is incorporated in all subjects." (Day 3)

"I love using actual literature with everything!" (Day 3)

"It is always important to do pre, during, and post reading activities." (Day 3)

"Using different strategies to teach is so important to help the child learn. These are new terms to me so I'm really taking it all in and trying to understand how to teach these strategies." (Day 4)

"Researching in any context area incorporates the use of many reading skills." (Day 4)

"This is a good review of stuff I learned a while back. Or I forgot them. Or (heaven forbid) ha, ha, something new!" (Day 4)

"I definitely like and will use the learning log. This is a great way to build background knowledge and to transfer knowledge to other concepts and skills." (Day 5)

"Reading frees the mind from direct experiences." (Day 6)

"The Guided Reading Procedure (GRP) is a good way to introduce a difficult text. Allow your 'low level' readers to contribute early because they may have understood something and they need to contribute." (Day 7)

"Using anticipation guides even with kindergartners will be a great motivator and mind set before reading a story. Understanding and using a variety of questions and letting students know what kind of questions seems like another great way to keep kids interested and excited about reading and participation!" (Day 7)

"The anticipation guide is something I haven't been using, but am excited about using it in my classroom. I see how you can use it with all kinds of literature." (Day 7)

Reflections about Science:

"Science is understanding that living is observing. Observing is learning. Learning brings responsibility and responsibility brings action. Action is living." (Day 1)

"Science can be made fun and integrated with other subjects." (Day 1)

"To show students there is 'science' in everyday living. There are many things that use energy or other science with that you may not even notice if you aren't aware of all that science entails." (Day 1)

"Hands-on activities bring clear understanding and high interest." (Day 1)

"Hands-on experience approach gets you thinking and motivated." (Day 1)

"Get to know the subject well so that I can be a facilitator." (Day 1)

"You need to know what the students know and build upon their prior knowledge." (Day 1)

"Don't give students everything. Let them figure out some things out on their own or in a group." (Day 2)

"Make sure as a teacher that you show students how to find answers to questions." (Day 7)

"The GRP is another excellent reading practice to use to recall information and to organize it. It seems to be challenging because it challenges one's memory and ability to organize what they can remember." (Day 7)

"Take the questions we asked as teachers and have the students 'prove' their answers. This develops higher level thinking." (Day 8)

"I really enjoyed the reading strategies, especially the DRA and DRTA. I can think of students who would have benefited from this last year in my classroom." (Day 8)

"How it feels to try to make something work and not get it to work. It's frustrating, and I know the students got frustrated easily too." (Day 2)

"Science is not a passive subject. Science is always new and you must be active with it. " (Day 2)

"Science can be implemented throughout the day and not just as an isolated subject." (Day 2)

"Solar solution activities and the awesome discussions and realizations that came from being in a learning environment and watching someone else do the facilitating." (Day 2)

"Science cannot be separated from the other disciplines. It includes math, reading, etc." (Day 2)

"Reading is truly integrated into science in so many fun ways." (Day 2)

"Science is a hands-on subject. Learning needs to be a participation sport!" (Day 2)

"Use the graphic organizers for science projects to stress sequence of events and informative narrative." (Day 2)

"There are more literature books to deal with science than I thought. I learned that I love science and I'm redeveloping my love to teach it." (Day 3)

"Think through each activity to anticipate the problems and the solutions." (Day 3)

"Science can be so much fun; not the way I was taught science!" (Day 3)

"You can find some thing scientific in almost every science book. I feel much better about teaching science now!" (Day 3)

The BEST THING about today was . . . "The jigsaw grouping and participation in the dissection of the fish." (Day 4)

MULTIPLE VIEWS OF CASE TEACHING: TEACHER EDUCATORS REFLECT ON THEIR TEACHING PRACTICES

Victoria J. Risko

Peabody College of
Vanderbilt University

Kay Camperell

Utah State University

Lois Degler

Lesley College

Marilyn Eanet

Rhode Island College

Janet Richards

University of Southern Mississippi

Abstract

The authors describe their rationale for incorporating case methodology into their literacy methods courses. They identify specific design features of the cases they use. Reflecting on their teaching practices, they discuss methods they follow to invite teachers' inquiry and problem analysis. Additionally, they provide an analysis of potential benefits and challenges associated with case teaching.

During the last decade, the five of us have been keenly interested in examining our own teaching practices within our college courses. Influenced by theories about constructivist learning, critical pedagogy, and collaborative learning, each of us became interested in different forms of case methodology. We define *case methodology* (and *case methods*) as the teaching strategies we use when teaching with cases. We began using cases within our literacy methods classes to encourage our students' independent thinking and to enhance their ability to apply what they are learning to real world problems. Each of us looked for ways to help us demonstrate instructional strategies that we hoped our prospective teachers would adopt in their own classrooms—strategies that support inquiry-oriented and collaborative, learning communities.

More recently, we began to compare and contrast the cases we use and our teaching methods. These discussions have been useful for at least three reasons. First, our sharing has helped us articulate reasons for choosing particular types of cases and specific design characteristics associated with each type. Second, our discussions encouraged us to specify teaching methods we follow for developing cases within our classes. (These teaching methods are referred to as case methodology, case teaching, or case methods throughout this paper.) And third, they helped us identify particular benefits and challenges we have experienced. We believe that these three areas—case characteristics, methods for case teaching, and benefits and challenges—are underrepresented in the teacher education literature. We share what we have learned from our teaching and each other.

Reasoning in Support of Case Teaching

Enhancing teachers' professional knowledge and abilities to respond to complexities associated with classroom instruction are common goals for teacher development programs. Too often, though, our college methods courses, designed around lecture formats, are designed to "tell" future teachers and those who are already teaching what they need to know rather than facilitating their ability to construct their own understandings of instructional and learning issues. Goodlad (1990), Lee Shulman (1992), and others argue that teachers often have difficulty connecting information learned in teacher development programs to information needed for recognizing and responding to problems and unexpected events that occur in classrooms. One goal for reform efforts within teacher education programs is to engage teachers in problem-solving activities that invite critical thinking and flexible use of newly-acquired knowledge for achieving problem resolution.

Recently, some teacher educators have argued that the use of case methodology provides an approach for helping teachers make connections between theory and practice. Cases are developed to represent realities of classroom events and invite reflection (e.g., Kleinfeld, 1995; Merseth, 1991; Shulman, J., 1995; Silverman & Welty, 1996). Typically developed in narrative formats, the "stories" of actual happenings and teachers' problems are shared to help teachers explore their personal beliefs about teaching and learning (e.g., Connelly & Clandinin, 1990; Knowles & Holt-Reynolds, 1991; Noori, 1995). They are designed to encourage teachers to spontaneously refer to relevant information when it is needed for responding to instructional dilemmas. Case methodology, as described by Christensen (1991), Shulman, L. (1995), Merseth (1996) and others, is a process-oriented approach that enables teachers' problem formulation and problem solving. In this paper, we propose to address several issues and questions related to benefits and limitations of case-based teaching. First, there is the issue of case design. Multiple designs are possible; we describe the cases we use and methods we follow to develop their power in our classes. Next, we discuss benefits and challenges of case teaching. We conclude with a summary of issues we are exploring. In the following section, we describe our cases.

Cases are Different in Design, Yet Similar in Intent

Case methodology is discussed frequently within the teacher education literature. It is a popular topic at conferences focusing on professional development, and numerous books containing teaching cases have been written. Yet case designs adopted by researchers, theorists, and teacher educators vary greatly. Furthermore, descriptions of case methods often provide few details about specific teaching procedures and applications. In this section, we describe our methodology and characteristics of the four types of cases we use. Each is different in design. One set was written by experienced teachers for the education of prospective teachers; another set is written by the prospective teachers as they experience their own teaching dilemmas. A third is embedded in literary sources, mostly fictional stories of events experienced by teachers and students. The fourth was developed within multimedia formats to display actual classroom happenings within video presentations.

Stories Written by Others: The Study of Recurring Dilemmas

Kay typically uses three to five cases in her undergraduate content area reading course that are written by practicing teachers from graduate sections of the course. The graduate students are required to write a case about a critical incident that happened to them which is related to principles of content reading instruction. These cases reflect recurring dilemmas of secondary teaching, as described below. The cases, approximately three to five pages long, have a basic plot structure but are not necessarily highly elaborate or vivid stories. The specific dilemmas are not directly stated nor is a solution provided.

Each case is used to situate students' study of particular course concepts. For example, one case used most frequently is about a first-year history teacher, "Shauna", who is required to use an outdated, advanced placement history textbook with students who are average to poor readers. Shauna faces criticism from students, parents, and counselors when students have difficulties reading the text, and eventually stops giving any reading assignments. A second case, focusing on "Tim", is about a student teacher who is expected to teach a state-mandated marketing curriculum. Since there are no texts for them to read, Tim has to provide most of the curricular material within a lecture format. A third case describes happenings within an elective keyboarding class. In this class, "Gayle" focuses on teaching word processing skills (e.g., function keys, merging, formatting), but the state assessment test requires students to read an Employee Manual and independently follow instructions for creating various kinds of documents. Most students are unable to pass the state test because they don't know how to read the manual.

The "Shauna" case serves as a prereading activity at the beginning of each term. Students read the case outside of class and then read an assigned chapter to identify some immediate and long-range suggestions for resolving some of the problems Shauna faced. At the beginning of the next class session, students are asked to write what they see as major dilemmas of the case, followed by possible recommendations for resolving these dilemmas based on the assigned reading. Discussions about the case often take over an hour. Generally, students bring out issues about the difficulty of Shauna's text, her lack of support from parents and counselors as well as issues related to the politics involved in beginning teaching (e.g., Shauna was given old AP books to use so her department head could purchase new books). Following the discussion, students are asked to reflect on their original analysis of the case and to describe any new ideas gained from the discussion. A similar procedure is followed with the other cases. However, depending on the class, students may be involved in either whole-class or small group discussions. Generally, the first case is discussed in a whole-class format.

"Tim's" case provides a vehicle to explore differences between modern and postmodern curriculum issues. Furthermore, this case has been used to contextualize a NCREL webpage reading assignment (http://www.ncrel.org/tandl/change.htm) that emphasizes knowledge construction and student-centered learning. Students readily see that Tim is required to teach from a mandated, "modern" curricular perspective (e.g., direct instruction followed by memory tests), and gradually, issues related to student notetaking skills and alternatives to lecture are brought out in the discussions. In addition, dilemmas linked to student teaching arise as the class talks about the cooperating teacher's inability to help Tim because the curriculum was new to both of them. The teachers' frustration was compounded by the fact that potential funds for student editions of the material were tied to student performance on mastery tests. Emphasis on these issues seems to be particularly important given findings of other teacher educators who argue that sociopolitical constraints add to preservice teachers's reluctance to use content reading methods (Stewart & O'Brien, 1989). O'Brien, Stewart, and Moje (1995) suggest that it is important to address sociocultural influences that shape how preservice secondary teachers think about teaching and learning as well as the role content literacy plays in maintaining, and perhaps altering, traditional school practices.

Finally, the "Gayle" case provides a framework for discussions about teaching content but not the literacy/learning skills that are specific to a content area (McKenna & Robinson, 1993). Gayle taught her students word processing skills but failed to teach them how to read manuals that would help them learn how to process documents in unfamiliar formats.

As these cases and others are discussed, Kay's students learn to express their fears and concerns about their teaching expectations. As they discuss issues and resolve embedded dilemmas they learn that there are no methods which will work in every situation (Burbules, 1993) and that teaching requires that they learn problem-solving/decision-making skills (Lacey & Merseth, 1993).

Writing for Self: Learning from One's Own Problems

Janet's cases invite personal descriptions of teaching problems and reflection. Prospective teachers enrolled in her field-based literacy courses write their own cases to describe concerns and problems they are experiencing while teaching elementary students who are culturally and linguistically diverse. She initiates case writing early in the semester by discussing the purposes and benefits of writing one's own "teaching" cases. First, she models the process by identifying and reflecting on teaching problems she has experienced. Second, she shares several well constructed cases that were written by former preservice teachers, and she identifies particular attributes embedded in each narrative—attributes that constitute a good case. Then the following specific guidelines are shared.

> *Write in the first person.* Identify who you are, the context for the case, and the problem or series of related problems you are experiencing as a literacy teacher. If appropriate, supply some background information about your student(s) or the curriculum. Write as vivid an account as you can. Include authentic dialogue. Your cases will be more interesting to read if you exclude extraneous details and if you choose a topic about which you feel strongly and passionately. Write at least three double-spaced pages.

Janet then adds information to guide her students' thinking about case development. She wants them to understand that there are many definitions and beliefs about what contributes to a "good case" (Merseth, 1991, p. 7). While examining previously written cases, Janet illustrates that each of these is focused, engaging, and describes "a wide variety of situations, decisions, dilemmas, and difficulties that routinely confront teachers and teacher educators" (Sykes, 1992, p. ix). Janet asks her students to write in the first person to tell one main story, even though other problems can be "embedded" and developed (J. Shulman, 1992, p. 2), and to follow a narrative format in which they should "portray characters that seem real, contain dialogue and rich detail, present a problem or a series of related problems that unfold over time, and are contextualized in time and place" (L. Shulman, 1992, p. 21). Janet wants her students to differentiate "cases" from more simplistic teaching stories that are limited in depth and content. Class discussions and examinations of previously developed cases provide a way to help her students develop cases that exemplify "an instance of a larger class [or category] of knowledge [such as multicultural issues, social promotions, instructional problems, or relational conflicts among preservice teachers and their university supervisors,] and therefore merit more serious consideration than a simple anecdote or vignette" (L. Shulman, 1992, p. 17).

Janet and her colleagues find that the prospective teachers' cases provide rich sources of information concerning contextual conditions of the schools in which they work (Richards & Gipe, 1997). For example, recurring discipline problems in one of the practicum sites is often discussed in their cases. Other cases focus on situations in which the prospective teachers are developing literacy lessons for learners of English as Second Language, questions about group management during shared reading times, and dilemmas related to a teacher's inability to read her students' invented spelling.

Janet's own understandings of case methods have broadened considerably since she first added case writing to her courses. Because of the evolution of her own perspectives, she now urges her students to include relevant resources in their teaching narratives, such as outside readings and conversations with peers that may help them come to some conclusions about their teaching dilemmas. Additionally, she promotes case writing as a process. She schedules class time for her preservice teachers to engage in peer reviews, she provides feedback on several drafts, and students continue to edit their case until their final draft is polished.

Janet's prospective teachers share their case dilemmas in a whole class format. This provides opportunities for them to consider and reflect upon a myriad of authentic teaching concerns and feedback regarding possible solutions to their particular dilemmas.

The Importance of Story: Learning with Literature

Marilyn's written cases are narratives, mostly fictional, about teachers and students that she selects from various literature sources. The decision to use these materials with teacher education students was most recently inspired by Michael Cole's *The Call of Stories* (1989). The roots of using literature lie further back in Marilyn's own experiences as a novice teacher in the 1960's, and her eagerness to read stories about teachers and teaching, whether fiction or non-fiction, to gain insights and to feel less alone in her struggles. Similar to Isenberg (1944), Marilyn found material like Kohl's *36 Children*

(1967, 1988) and *Up the Down Staircase* (Kaufman, 1964) enlightening, challenging, inspiring, and even reassuring.

For several years, Marilyn has been collecting appropriate short stories to use as cases in her classes (Eanet, 1991). Three general criteria guide her selection of literature cases—a story needs to be well written, have literary merit, and contain teaching issues. It usually includes teacher-student interactions and/or classroom scenes. She finds that stories from the past, such as some of the short stories of Jesse Stuart, can be appropriate if they contain issues that are still relevant today. Blanchard and Casanova's *Modern Fiction about Schoolteaching: An Anthology* (1996) offers a good starting place for locating stories. Also useful are excerpts from longer fiction, such as *To Kill a Mockingbird* (Lee, 1960) and non-fiction such as *Lives on the Boundary* (Rose, 1989).

Case discussions centered on two or three selected stories have been a part of Marilyn's undergraduate reading classes for several years. A recent experience with a graduate course is currently influencing her thinking about how to expand her use of literature cases within her undergraduate course. This most recent revision involves organizing the class around a workshop format. Her graduate course, entitled "Learning from Teacher Stories: Using Classroom Narratives to Examine Issues of Teaching and Learning," is taught as a reading/writing workshop. Socratic Seminars (Ball & Brewer, 1996) and Literature Circles (Daniel, 1994), as described below, are the major instructional strategies developed within the workshop format.

Four elements guide Marilyn's workshop organization. First, most of the literature reading is done outside of class so that discussion and process writing activities can take place in class. Students share log entrees and drafts of papers. Peer editing helps them give each other feedback about their writings. Second, although some readings are required, students have choices, both individually and as members of small literature circles, in what they read and write about and in the selection of themes to explore. Third, classroom structure, routine, and expectations are designed to build a community of learners and to support active engagement in these literacy activities. Fourth, the instructor serves as a facilitator and resource person who provides mini-lessons first, to introduce the key strategies such as the Socratic Seminars and the Bolman and Deal frames (described below), and then later only as needed.

Readings consist of selections from the Blanchard and Casanova (1996) anthology, from the literature collection as described above, and from supplementary articles from the professional literature. The materials are previously analyzed by Marilyn according to themes. Marilyn requires that "Instruction" be one theme, and she gives students choices for other themes. "Family and School Relationships," "Classroom Management," and "Brain-Based Learning" are often selected.

Within the workshop format, two frameworks are provided to help students consider story content. The first is to use traditional case teaching questions (i.e., What are the issues?, What should the teacher do now?, In the long run?). The second framework comes from the work of Bolman and Deal (1994) who recommend using four frames for looking at issues related to teaching and schools. These are (a) the human resource frame (with focus on needs and motives, creating a trusting environment, and shared decision making); (b) the political frame (having to do with resources and power); (c) the structural frame (emphasizing productivity, authority, policy, rules); and (d) the symbolic frame (with focus on school as a way of life—informal, symbolic understanding like rituals, stories, and ceremonies). Discussions are enriched when students examine a story from these different viewpoints. For example, Marilyn often says the following, "We've been discussing what happened from a human resource viewpoint; I think there is also a political issue here . . ." to enable a discussion of different perspectives.

Discussion of cases follows several procedures. Adhering to a Socratic Seminar format (Ball & Brewer, 1996) within whole-class discussions, Marilyn introduces each literature selection with a variety of prereading strategies (e.g., prediction, anticipation guides). Then each class or "seminar" focuses on one or more of the literacy selections. Marilyn poses key questions, such as those suggested by Gentile (1993) (e.g, What are the facts?, What have we left out of our conversation?, and What could we write to express how we feel about this?) to facilitate discussions. Students' questions and ideas are encouraged, and Marilyn assumes the role of a facilitator as she asks students to elaborate on or clarify their understandings and interpretations. Following each seminar, students are asked to record their reactions and reflections within a reading log.

Additionally, Marilyn often follows Daniel's (1994) literature circle guidelines to enable small group discussions. She divides her students into literature circle groups based on their background (teaching) experiences and interests, and within each group, students are asked to make decisions about their readings. Each student assumes a role, as suggested by Daniel, of either the discussion leader, illustrator, vocabulary developer, literary luminary, travel tracer, or vocabulary enricher. Using Daniel's role sheets (that describe duties for each group member), students discuss the targeted literature selection. Roles are rotated across students for different literature selections. As students become more confident with their participation and more competent in their role-taking, they are developing firsthand knowledge about methods for implementing literature circles within their own future teaching.

Engaging in the study of these stories encourages taking multiple perspectives on teaching problems, supports the view of teaching as an (extremely) complex activity, and encourages an inquiring, reflective approach to practice. The sharing (that occurs in the discussions and other workshop activities) of information from professional readings and other courses, and from practical experiences serves to build a true sense of a professional community among the students. Further, these teachers are learning strategies they can use when developing their own student-centered literacy activities.

Multimedia: the Value of Video Stories

For several years, Lois and Vicki and their colleagues have been involved in a project directed toward the development of eight video cases, pressed on videodiscs and compact discs, and accessed by computer software (Risko & Kinzer, 1999). They use video cases because they allow students to observe classroom happenings as they are occurring and to interpret factors contributing to these events; there are no narrators who describe or explain what is occurring in the classroom situations. This use of multimedia to enhance students' analysis of authentic problems and generative learning is influenced by theories about anchored instruction. Anchored instruction is characterized by providing rich informational sources, presented in multimedia formats, to facilitate students' sustained exploration of embedded concepts and problems (Bransford, Vye, Kinzer, & Risko, 1990; CTGV, 1990).

Videodisc and CD-Rom technology is used because it has random-access capabilities. Different from videotape applications, scenes on videodiscs and compact discs can be accessed and revisited quickly and frequently. Therefore, the ability to examine the same content for different reasons is facilitated with these random-access capabilities.

The videos for these cases were recorded in actual classrooms and are accompanied by print materials that contain teachers' lesson plans and records of children's performance on assessment instruments and actual reading and writing activities (e.g, writing samples, journals, performance on text-based materials, and so on) collected over time. Each video case is one-hour in length and begins with a twelve-to-fifteen minute coherent story about the teacher and students situated within the classroom literacy instruction. These narratives are followed by additional video segments that can be accessed to learn more about classroom instruction and to observe interviews with principals, parents, teachers, children, and with educators and literacy researchers who provide brief, focused commentaries about each case. Each case represents a unit of instruction to illustrate how it develops over time and across multiple classroom formats (e.g., whole-class and small-group instruction, individual conferences, peer tutoring, and so on). Four cases present various approaches that support literacy development (e.g., literature-based curricula, language experience and process writing approaches) and four focus on literacy instruction for diverse learners within classrooms and pullout programs.

In addition to the study of these cases, their college students are required to read theoretical, research, and professional literature corresponding to the cases and topics of the course. Often, several choices of readings are available for student selection according to interests and target issues.

Usually only a subset of these cases (typically three) is used by Lois and Vicki, respectively, in an elementary developmental literacy course taught by Lois and in a remedial reading methods course taught by Vicki. Viewing and discussing these cases occur during almost every class session by the whole class. There are very few class sessions when the cases are not used and most content that is discussed in class is related directly to issues embedded within the cases. Students and the instructor frequently revisit the cases to analyze the content from different perspectives. For example, students in Lois' class may first watch the "Ms. Gift" case (situated within a fourth grade literature-based class) to analyze her questioning techniques as she engages her children in a discussion of a novel. They may return to the case to examine Ms. Gift's classroom organization techniques, and again to study the types of literature chosen for this particular unit.

In Vicki's class, students may initially watch Ms. Kingery's case to identify dilemmas two teachers face when they are required to team teach within an inclusion setting. They may then examine the diagnostic data collected on several children and review the video material to study how these children are participating in the literacy activities. Analyzing cases from different viewpoints is useful for building deep understandings of complex information and dilemmas embedded within each of the cases. And, as students cross-reference information across several cases, they begin to develop flexible understandings of procedural information. The process of comparing and contrasting how two teachers develop story comprehension, for example, helps these future teachers build conditional knowledge (Bransford, at. al., 1990)—the understanding that applications of newly-acquired information is dependent on many factors, including the conditions of the instructional setting, the beliefs of the teacher, and the learning characteristics of the children.

The video situations present a compelling reality to students as they explore many facets of problems. Students are engaged in thinking typical of a professional who sees situations in their complexity and then chooses from a variety of alternatives, the response judged most appropriate. The depth of student discussion and their lively participation contrasts strikingly with our pre-case teaching experience.

Different, Yet Similar

As can be readily noted, each of the cases described previously is different in form. Each design allows us to develop instructional situations that are compatible with our own teaching goals, beliefs, and needs. Yet our individual applications of case methodology have much in common. First, our respective use of cases provides a way for us to contextualize the content of our courses so that our students can build understandings of the relevance and importance of course content for classroom teaching. All of our cases, rich with embedded data, are open-ended and invite discussion, reflection, and further study of authentic problems. All invite students to generate characteristics of problems that teachers face and to synthesize multiple viewpoints to guide their problem solving and decision making. Furthermore, our use of cases helps us develop communities within our classes— communities that have rich exchanges of information and that support individual and collaborative growth.

Not a Panacea: Benefits and Challenges

From our earliest experiences, our students have been very enthusiastic about their involvement with teaching cases. All of our students have told us that the cases help them develop insights about teaching and learning that are difficult to generate from reading traditional textbooks alone. The stories of the case teachers invite much reflection. Our cases provide a powerful tool for developing ways to address problems and, as Marilyn suggests, the cases may well serve to make learning about teaching more memorable because of their authentic, affective, and aesthetic characteristics. And as Kay notes, our attempts to use cases have made us more reflective about our own teaching and have moved us to a more dialogical stance where we have learned how to listen and learn from our students.

Case teaching also has its challenges, many of which we continue to consider. One challenge relates to *discussion*. Each of us knows that involving students in discussions is absolutely important, but often difficult to accomplish. We want to engage students in conversations by (a) inviting them to pursue issues *they* identify as important, (b) facilitating spontaneous interaction among students but ensuring that the conversations revolve around a few cohesive issues, (c) encouraging student participation and reasoning through use of nonjudgemental language, and (d) moving the discussion from surface issues of a case to deeper analysis and evaluation. We have learned that developing such conversations demands careful planning on our part. We need to study each case carefully prior to a class even if we have used the case on numerous occasions. Classes differ, and we want to ensure that the alternative viewpoints raised in class are relevant to what has been previously discussed and to help the class revisit case content to learn in depth and understand additional, even contradictory information.

Each of us plans for our discussions. Kay, for example, uses note cards with questions that *open conversations* (e.g., Central Issues?, Important characters?, Ways the situation developed?, Different takes on the situation?), *facilitate analysis* (e.g., What do you suppose that . . . ?, Give me an example of . . . , What assumptions are you/the teacher making?), and *encourage evaluation* (e.g., . What suggestions would you give for improving the situation?, What makes you think that was a good/poor, adequate/inadequate decision?). Marilyn uses the Socratic methods and Daniel's literature circle for similar reasons. Janet supplies her prospective teachers with a list of specific questions to help structure their case discussions, such as "Can you distinguish between the symptom and problems in the case?", "From whose perspective is the case written?", and "What could this teacher have done differently?"

Lois and Vicki follow similar procedures with the video cases. Students initially watch the entire video case story and discuss it as fully and freely as possible, generating issues and problems they observe. Then they revisit the scenes. During the revisiting, Lois or Vicki may pose a broad question that corresponds to a teaching goal for that segment, such as "These are beginning readers. What is happening to help these beginners learn to read?" Or they may refer to one of the questions generated during an earlier viewing to guide reasons for revisiting a segment. A full discussion follows these revisits. Supplementary video segments and/or accompanying printed materials (e.g., records of children's daily performance) often support students' study of particular issues.

Another method involves keeping notes on chart paper or on the chalkboard to keep track of points and issues raised in order to facilitate returning to the multiple embedded themes. We have found that this procedure is important because students often rush to proposed solutions rather than taking time to thoughtfully analyze the people and dilemmas involved in a case. Allowing students to think through issues and to develop conclusions over time can be challenging for the instructor, as well.

A second challenge is *evaluation*. One suggestion comes from Marilyn. Students in her workshop course are evaluated on the basis of their participation and their informal and formal written work. To do this, she is experimenting with her own version of procedures recommended by Ball and Brewer (1996) for evaluating participation in the Socratic Seminar procedure. Her purposes are twofold—to improve her own observation and recording techniques and to demonstrate to the students a way to evaluate this type of activity in their own classrooms. Marilyn's criteria for evaluating include: 1— introduced a key issues; T—referred to text of story; E—referred to own experiences; TE—related text to own experiences; S—suggested solution; SS—suggested and supported solution; R—referred to research in support of suggestion. She then prepares a chart with student names and records responses during the seminars. To check accuracy and improve recording skills, Marilyn audio records the sessions. Kay uses similar criteria but finds that applying such criteria is easier within small group discussions than within whole class discussions.

Marilyn's major source of evaluation for grading purposes are two essays that students write. These 3-5 page essays are designed for students to synthesize their reactions to the readings, class discussion, and personal classroom experiences. The class and reading logs that are kept daily serve as "raw material" for this formal writing. These short essays serve to demonstrate students' reflection on the stories read and discussed, their consideration of the themes, and the connections they made between course material and their teaching practice.

Students are evaluated in the video case courses through papers they generate and exams they complete. Additionally, in the developmental course students might independently watch a new video case and respond to this in weekly journaling and on a take-home exam question. Students in the remedial class write a case report in which they describe their teaching situations and decisions they made while developing instruction in the practicum setting.

It was apparent early in the video case teaching that students weren't as clear at the end of the course on some terminology and specific information as in pre-case teaching semesters. Since the course is so discussion oriented, students find they have few "lecture" notes at the end of the semester. This can be unsettling to some of the students. The use of study guides to highlight important topics from class discussions and the text provides clarification and helps students to be more clear and feel secure about what they are expected to know. Subsequently, students do as well on course exams as they did previously.

Conclusions

In this paper, we discuss design characteristics and instructional strategies associated with our teaching with cases. The cases we use differ from traditional paper and pencil cases that provide both the stated problem and how the author resolved that problem. Our cases are open-ended and provide a context for the study of course content. As we discussed earlier, the content of our cases is presented in different forms (e.g., teacher-written, literature-based, multimedia). Yet each of our cases is embedded with concepts that relate to course readings and help future teachers analyze the complexity of information associated with teaching and learning. Rather than "telling" our students what they need to "know" and "do" as teachers, our students are invited to analyze cases that represent authentic classroom happenings and to pose issues and questions they want to pursue. Our use of cases involves modeling a more conversational style of teaching that encourages collaborative learning, development of shared knowledge among class members, and the building of community. Students experience for themselves the power of learning and the meaningfulness of their own contributions within an instructional setting that does not involve lectures or memory testing.

Teaching with cases has helped us reflect on our own instructional beliefs and become more precise in our understanding of issues we face as teacher educators. Our goal to balance literacy methods content with socially constructed knowledge is consistent with our beliefs about constructivist teaching. Situating course content within our cases enables us to invite students' generative learning, active participation in class discussions, and in-depth analysis and reflection of instructional problems.

And while we maintain our course goals and emphasis on developing our students' knowledge of course content, our ordering of course topics is arranged to correspond to case content. Topics associated with each case are examined within the analysis of that case and often revisited as we cross-reference concepts across cases. We have moved away from lecture-formats and course syllabi that prescribe precise and sequential development of course content. Our former methods of teaching followed a linear presentation of topics that often remained unconnected for our students. Too often these methods presented theory and research as information that is separate from information needed to resolve practice issues and/or students were required to formulate their own applications (e.g., theory to practice teaching). And while we know that cases, too, can follow similar prescriptive formats in which content sequences are predetermined and presented in a linear style, the methodologies we describe are implemented to illustrate a dynamic interrelatedness of theory and practice. Theory, research, and practice issues are examined simultaneously as students frame and analyze instructional dilemmas embedded within our cases.

We want our students to understand that teaching is problematic and requires decision-making. We want them to know that what they are learning in their readings and our class discussions is useful for helping them resolve dilemmas they will face. Applications of information require careful examination of situational conditions and factors. Different circumstances require different responses, and teachers need to approach dilemmas from a problem-solving perspective with the knowledge that several adjustments and resolutions may be required of them. We use cases to help our students understand a wide range of problems that may confront them as teachers and to help them apply concepts they've read about and observed in classrooms. Our students generate their own understandings of these problems and ways to draw on what they are learning to formulate resolutions.

We know that is important to be explicit about our goals for case teaching and explain why our methods may differ from others that our students may experience. We have learned that some of our students initially will be uncomfortable with instructional strategies associated with case teaching. Collaborative discussions replace lectures. Students are required to analyze and synthesize case information and to integrate course readings into their reflections. We find that anxieties associated with these changes can be ameliorated when we explain potential benefits of case teaching, focus discussions on applications of theory and research, and guide students' connections between text and case information. Discussions about what we are learning from these cases occur often during the semester, and we find that our students are quite positive about their involvement in case analysis.

In this paper, we describe our case designs and teaching methods. Across applications, we identify methods for creating shared, learning communities within our college classes—communities that value students' participation in their own learning and that demonstrate the importance of inquiry and use of information to solve problems.

References

Ball, W. H., & Brewer, P. (1996). Socratic seminars. In Canady, R. L., & M. Rettig, R. D., (Eds.). *Teaching in the block: Strategies for engaging active learning.* Princeton, NJ: Eye on Education.

Blanchard, J. S., & Casanova, U. (1996). *Modern fiction about schoolteaching: An anthology.* Boston: Allyn and Bacon.

Bolman, L. G., & Deal, T. E. (1994). *Becoming a teacher leader: From isolation to collaboration.* Thousand Oaks, CA: Corwin Press, Inc.

Bransford, J. D., Vye, N., Kinzer, C., & Risko, V. (1990). Teaching thinking and content knowledge: Toward an integrated approach. In B. G. Jones & L. Idol (Eds.), *Dimensions of thinking and cognitive instruction* (pp. 381-413). Hillsdale, NJ: Erlbaum.

Burbules, N. (1993). *Dialogue in teaching: Theory and practice.* New York: Teachers College Press.

Christensen, C. (1991). The discussion teacher in action: Questioning, listening, and response. In C. Christensen, D. Garvin, and A. Sweet (Eds.), *Education for judgment* (pp. 153-174). Boston: Harvard Business School.

Cognition and Technology Group at Vanderbilt (CTGV). (1990). Anchored instruction and its relationship to situated cognition. *Educational Researcher, 19,* 210.

Coles, R. (1989). *The call of stories: Teaching and the moral imagination.* Boston: Houghton Mifflin Co.

Connelly, F. M., & Clandinin, D. J. (1990). Stories of experience and narrative inquiry. *Educational Researcher, 19* (4), 2-14.

Daniel, H. (1994). *Literature circles: Voice and choice in the student-centered classroom.* York, MA: Steinhouse Publishers.

Eanet, M. G. (1991). Expanding literacy by the use of imaginative literature in the teacher-education classroom. In B. L. Hayes & K. Camperell (Eds.), *Literacy: Interna-*

tional, national, state, and local (pp. 57-66). Twelfth Yearbook of The American Reading Forum, Logan, UT: Utah State University.

Gall, J., & Gall, M. (1990). Outcomes of the discussion method. In W. Wilen (Ed.), *Teaching and learning through discussion* (pp. 25-44). Springfield, Il: Thomas.

Gee, T., & Forester, N. (1988). Moving reading instruction beyond the reading classroom. *Journal of Reading, 31,* 505-511.

Gentile, L. M., & McMillan, M. M. (1992). *Literacy for students at risk: Developing critical dialogues.* Paper presented at the annual meeting of the College Reading Association. St. Louis, Missouri.

Goodlad, J. I. (1990). Better teachers for our nation's schools. *Phi Delta Kappan, 72,* 184-194.

Goodrich, H. (1996/1997). Understanding rubrics. *Educational Leadership, 54,* 14-17.

Irvin, J., & Connors, N. (1989). Reading instruction in middle level schools: Results of a U.S. Survey. *Journal of Reading, 32,* 306-311.

Isenberg, J. (1994). Going by the book: The role of popular classroom chronicles in the professional development of teachers. Westport, CN: Bergin & Garvey.

Kaufman, B. (1964). *Up the down staircase.* New York: Prentice Hall.

Kleinfeld, J. (1995). Our hero comes of age: What students learn from case writing in student teaching. In J. A. Colbert, P. Desberg, & K. Trimble (Eds.), *The case of education* (pp. 79-97). Boston: Allyn & Bacon.

Knowles, J. G., & Holt-Reynolds, D. (1991). Shaping pedagogies through personal histories in preservice teacher education. *Teachers College Record, 93* (1), 87-113.

Kohl, H. (1967, 1988). *36 Children.* New York: Plume.

Lacey, C., & Merseth, K. (1993). Cases, hypermedia and computer networks: Three curricular innovations for teacher education. *Journal of Curriculum Studies, 25,* 543-551.

Lee, H. (1960). *To kill a mockingbird.* New York: Warner.

McKenna, M., & Robinson, R. (1993). *Teaching through text: A content literacy approach to content area reading* (2nd ed.). White Plains, NY: Longman.

McNabb, M. L. "Perspectives about Education." [http://www.ncrel.org/tandl/change.html].

Merseth, K. (1990). Case studies and teacher education. *Teacher Education Quarterly, 17,* 53-62.

Merseth, K. (1991). *The case for cases in teacher education.* Washington, D.C. American Association of Colleges of Teacher Education and American Association of Higher Education.

Noori, K. K. (1995). Understanding others through stories. *Childhood Education,* 134-136.

O'Brien, D., Stewart, R., & Moje, E. (1995). Why content literacy is difficult to infuse into the secondary school: Complexities of curriculum, pedagogy, and school culture. *Reading Research Quarterly, 30,* 442-463.

Richards, J. C., & Gipe, J. P. (1997). *Themes in preservice teachers' cases: Rich sources of information for literacy teacher educators.* Paper presented at the annual meeting of the National Reading Conference, Scottsdale, Arizona.

Risko, V. (1996) Creating a community of thinkers within a preservice literacy education methods course. In K. Camperell and B. Hayes (Eds.), *Literacy the information highway to success* (pp. 3-16). Sixteenth Annual Yearbook of the American Reading Forum. Logan, UT: Utah State University.

Risko, V., & Kinzer, C. (1999). *Multimedia cases for reading education*. Boston: McGraw-Hill.

Rose, M. (1989). *Lives on the boundary*. New York: Penguin Books.

Shulman, L. (1992). Toward a pedagogy of cases. *Case methods in teacher education* (pp. 1-30). NY: Teachers College Press.

Shulman, J. (1992). (Ed.). Case methods in teacher education. New York: Teachers College Press.

Silverman, R., Welty, W. , & Lyon, S. (1996). *Case studies for teacher problem solving* (2nd ed.). New York: McGraw Hill.

Spiro, R., Vispoel, W., Schmitz, J., Somarapungavan, A., & Boeger, A. (1987). Knowledge acquisition for application: Cognitive flexibility and transfer in complex content domains. In B. C. Britton & S. M. Glynn (Eds.), *Executive control processes in reading* (pp. 177-199). Hillsdale, NJ: Erlbaum.

Stewart, R., & O'Brien, D. (1989). Resistance to content area reading: A focus on preservice teachers. *Journal of Reading, 32*, 396-401.

Sykes, G. (1992). Foreword. In J. Shulman (Ed.). *Case methods in teacher education* (pp. vii-ix). New York: Teachers College Press.

When Teachers Change Alone: Case Studies of Literacy Teachers in a Non-Supportive School Environment

Patricia Bloem

Cleveland State University

Evangeline Newton

The University of Akron

A. Lee Williams

Slippery Rock University

Jacqueline Peck

Cleveland State University

Vicki Parsons Duling

George Mason University

Abstract

What happens when teachers change their pedagogical practices in environments that offer them little support? Using a qualitative case survey method, this article describes the change process of five classroom teachers (from grades 1, 3, 4, 6, and 8) and documents their search for validation of their instructional choices. Cross-case analysis suggests that teacher preparation classes could mitigate the isolation and better prepare teachers by attending to the fluid nature of knowledge and to thoughtful pedagogical change.

Calls for reform of education, and especially literacy education, are ubiquitous—they come from the government, from business, from religious groups, from the public and the media, and from educators themselves (Carnegie Task Force, 1989; Goodlad, 1984; Schafly, 1984; Timar & Kirp, 1989). Oftentimes these calls for reform are for entire schools to rethink practice. Educational change is a complex issue; the relationships among innovation, change and progress, of imposed versus self-initiated origins, and of the meaning of change for the participants who will be affected—the teachers, students, parents and administrators—is rarely straightforward. Yet administrators, staff developers, and teachers themselves are caught in the dynamics of these complex processes in any educational change initiative. The perception remains that change is elusive, and successful change is encountered in institutions only (Cuban, 1992). However, educational change is not only wide-scale institutional reform. It also describes the actions of teachers themselves to rethink, refine and change their individual classroom practices.

Models for stages that teachers experience as part of the adoption of educational changes show that change is a process. The Concerns-Based Adoption Model (Hall & Loucks, 1978, based on work in Hall, Wallace & Dossett, 1973) describes six stages in the innovation adoption process that individuals move through: awareness, informational, personal, management, consequence, collaboration, and refocusing. Routman (1991/94) described her own change process with five stages from "It's too hard; I can't do this," through following and then adapting expert advice, and finally to "I'll trust myself as observer-teacher-learner-evaluator." Adoption of innovation is affected by time and experience with the innovation as well as by support provided during the discomfort that people feel when moving from proficiency in the old method to initial inadequacy in the new (Fawcett, 1994; Joyce & Showers, 1980; Weaver, 1992). However, both time and support are often ingredients missing from teachers' repertoires for coping with change. Support appears to be a particularly critical issue, even for those whose change is self-directed. In a study of nine teachers who had elected to move from traditional to whole language instructional practices, Pace (1992) found that the teachers all experienced three identical roadblocks. Not surprisingly, the teachers struggled between old beliefs and new ideas. But reconciling this conceptual tension while "maintaining existing curriculum" and interacting with peers "who were not making changes" proved to be an enormous hurdle (p. 471). In fact, Pace (1992) concludes that the "tension between individual innovators and other teachers may be the most important factor to address in accomplishing classroom reform" (p. 471).

Additionally, individual changes affect the structure of the institution, which in turn influences the change of individuals. Because of this reciprocal relationship, even maverick teachers do not truly develop in isolation since social and bureaucratic structures influence what can and will be done (Cuban, 1992; Fullen, 1991; Sparks & Loucks-Horsley, 1990). Current beliefs about teaching and learning—both among individuals and in the socially held vision of the institution—also affect how change is perceived and tolerated (Fawcett, 1994; Sharer, 1992; Williams, 1996). Research documents the difficulty of change for teachers, especially for teachers who act to change their individual practice in a school that otherwise remains unchanged (Kraus, 1992; Levande, 1991).

The authors of this paper have had the fortune of closely observing teachers who have changed their pedagogy and have become out of step with the typical practice of their school buildings. The question we have asked about them and their situations is this: What happens when teachers change alone, without substantial support? Subsumed in that primary question are these elements: How does the solo aspect of their work affect them after a period of years? And finally, what is their impact on their school communities?

The research project followed the methodology of a qualitative case survey (Merriam, 1988), a form of cross-case analysis. The scope of a case survey is narrow and focuses on a single question. Researchers review data to look for evidence of that single phenomenon. Like all qualitative research, the case survey does not test a pre-arranged hypothesis. Thus, the researchers in this project first looked at data as it pertained to the question and then compared what was found individually, identifying commonalities across cases.

Four of the authors served as participant observers in the various classrooms over a period of at least several months and up to several years; all have maintained contact with the teachers through occasional classroom visits and observations, through joint conference or classroom presentations or other research projects. Subsequently the four authors interviewed the individual teachers about their change process and current teaching situation, with each researcher ascertaining that the individual teachers have maintained their changes. The fifth researcher writes about her own change process, reflecting on her own support network and practice and reanalyzing the elements of her pedagogy that put her at odds with the majority of her school colleagues. In each of the following case studies, each writer speaks in her own voice, and each credits the teacher in a way distinctive of her own study.

Sharon, a First-Grade Teacher

I first met Sharon in 1991 through a partnership project involving inquiry-oriented curriculum in a technology-rich environment, when she was teaching first grade in an urban school. Sharon's concern with the 20% of each class who were not readers by the end of each school year initiated her curricular changes. Her involvement in the partnership project legitimized them because it forced her to

> reexamine my entire philosophy of learning. . . . It forced me to become a learner and to experience things from the learner's perspective. And the one thing that it helped me to see was that as a learner, I also now have a responsibility to be a teacher. (Reflection, 9-29-94)

I asked Sharon if she was uncomfortable with the curricular changes she was making; she articulated the pain of change, but not without a healthy laugh. "Oh, yes, it was horrible! But I was already uncomfortable . . . when I saw what [the experts] were saying should be going on in the classroom, and I saw what I was actually doing. . . . It means I've got to change . . . and that can be expensive and risky and frightening" (Log 9-29-94).

Throughout Sharon's change process she has asked "Am I doing those children a service or disservice in having them so involved in curricular decisions, in being responsible for some of their own learning . . . ? (Reflection 11-2-94). She has frequently heard the pejorative comment, "Oh, your children couldn't have done that work . . . they aren't even gifted." Sharon's changes have increased her sense of responsibility for the teaching and learning of all children in her classroom. Her stance has created in her a sense of loneliness, a position that has been documented in other studies (Padak & Davidson, 1993).

> Many times I hear my peers saying, "What's wrong with these children?" There isn't anything wrong with the children . . . they haven't had enough time to catch on to it yet. . . . As an educator it is my job to figure out what I need to do to help the children acquire the skills and information that they need" (Reflection 9-6-94).

Despite being out of step with her colleagues and despite feeling lonely, Sharon recognizes how her changes have positively affected others in the school community. The Title I teacher asked to come into her classroom to better coordinate their teaching (Reflection 9-22-94). Also, a special education teacher, who had previously criticized Sharon's approach as being too stimulating, began to use more literature in her own classroom and had exciting revelations to share (Reflection 11-17-94). And this school year, Sharon has ventured into a new position in her building—that of curriculum resource teacher.

Gretchen, a Third-Grade Teacher:

Gretchen teaches third grade at an elementary school in a small Ohio town where the student body is diverse culturally, racially, and economically. While most of the teaching in her building is traditional, Gretchen describes herself as a "whole language" teacher. Her classroom is a literature- and print-rich environment in which children are offered many opportunities to grow through a variety of personal and interactive literacy activities.

I have known Gretchen for several years. She has been my son's third grade teacher, my partner in an action-research study, and my friend. Gretchen's ability to sustain antithetic practice comes largely from strong beliefs about learning based on her early life. Despite being the daughter of two educators, Gretchen struggled as a reader: "I was not able to track back smoothly and accurately to get to the line below." Her parents, however, "knew that I was bright in other ways" and "helped me learn by taping things for me so that I could hear them rather than read." Their response to her reading difficulty convinced her that "kids are different. You don't teach as if all of the children in the classroom are on the same page."

When Gretchen returned to teaching after several years as a full-time parent, she tried to follow the traditional practices of her district. She recalls it as "skill-and-drill" that was "killing" her readers. She began reading about whole language. While she found whole language practices consistent with her beliefs about learning, colleagues were unreceptive. In fact, they deliberately excluded her from "the planning, the programs, and the sharing of ideas" in ways that felt mean-spirited.

Feeling alone but with nothing left to lose from her peers, Gretchen decided to "get away from the basal for awhile" and teach a novel. When she returned to the basal, one child asked, "Why are we doing this?" As students clamored for more novels, Gretchen realized that whole language supported "the way I learned in my home . . . you reach the child where the child is, where that child's interests are, and then you go." The children's enthusiasm was relayed to administrators through positive parental feedback. Their enthusiasm gave Gretchen confidence and protected her from the criticism of colleagues. The next year Gretchen started her masters program because "I wanted to learn more."

Today, although in a different building, Gretchen is still a maverick in her instructional approach. While the teachers "ask me questions about what I do," Gretchen's ideas have had little impact on her colleagues' practice. But now Gretchen draws boundaries between her professional beliefs and her peer relationships and is able to state that her fellow teachers "are her best friends."

Robert, a Fourth-Grade Teacher:

Robert had taught for 17 years, ten in his current fourth-grade placement, when his rural Pennsylvania school adopted a literature-based reading series. His administration asked the teachers to use more holistic approaches in teaching reading and to encourage students to learn a process approach to writing. I interviewed and observed on a weekly basis during the first three years that Robert changed his teaching practices in response to the new reading mandate and occasionally during the following two years.

Robert began his new approach to teaching reading—using stories from the anthology, fewer skills worksheets, more actual reading, and a daily writing workshop—with both positive and negative anticipation. He had attended a workshop given by Carol Avery and was excited to implement new strategies. When he saw the children responding, he knew his efforts were worthwhile:

> I learned in the workshop that the most important thing you'll do in your reading and writing is to convey meaning. So when we read the story about the Royal Canadian Mounted Police and stumbled over some of the words, like the name of the town, we discovered it wasn't im-

portant. What mattered was that we knew it was the name of a town in Canada. How to pronounce it didn't matter (Interview, January 1993).

Two months later he wrote,

> They've [students] really gotten to appreciate stories, to predict outcomes, to think of how a story could end. If they were told before to sit and read, they wouldn't. But now I can give them a theme book on Monday and say, "Have this read by Friday" and know that they will read it (Interview, March 1993).

Robert had previously used worksheets and tests to evaluate students, and he was unsure of how to assess this new kind of reading. Then, too, he wondered how his students would fare on the standardized achievement tests that the district and parents took so seriously.

> As the year progresses, I am feeling more comfortable with evaluation. I understand my purpose for what I was doing and discussed with the kids what they should be trying to accomplish. I went back and compared what their scores were in the language areas to the norms for previous years. The scores showed the same type of progress (Interview 1994).

By the third year with the new reading program, Robert was growing comfortable with his teaching proficiency, but was becoming dissatisfied with the lack of change among colleagues. Students came to fourth grade with no more experience with reading literature and process writing than they had the first year. The district still had a curriculum document that stressed the teaching of isolated skills, and few other teachers were using the type of classroom organization Robert now felt was in the best interest of students. After five years of living with changes in reading instruction, Robert's practice has become fundamental to who he is as a teacher. However, his enthusiasm is dampened by the political realities of teaching.

> I feel so ambivalent about what I do know because the district takes the Iowa test scores and passes them around the schools, and everyone is looking at everyone else's scores. But standardized tests don't measure what is important. Can they tell if kids love reading? Can they tell if a kid will pick up a book in his spare time? Can they tell if we've created life-long readers? (Interview, November 1997).

Fran, a Sixth-Grade Teacher

Fran teaches 6th grade reading and math at the same urban, Catholic elementary school that she attended as a child, a school that has changed from an all-white, all-Catholic student body to a diverse community, both ethnically and religiously. Plotting Fran's change process from her first day on the job would be a bit like following a roller coaster that finally discovered the highway. She was originally eager to try the methods she'd studied in her masters—cooperative learning, thematic instruction, using a multitude of trade books—but quickly realized that they were not acceptable in her building. Thus she adapted to the status quo of her school's graded course of study, basals, and skill and drill. After a couple of rocky years, she began worrying and grieving about the aliteracy of her 6th graders, and as she abandoned the basals, we joined forces on a young adult literature/history project.

It was her third year of teaching, and Fran had become ready to try anything that would turn her students into eager readers and writers. So she implemented a thematic unit that allowed students plenty of choice of reading materials and of ways of responding to books, cross-disciplinary applications, and writing to parents as journal buddies; she found her students transformed into excited learners and their parents delighted with the change. Although she had new classroom management issues to deal with, she found even the poorest students beginning to read and write and participate.

But Fran, fretting over her students' abilities to do well in standardized and frequent testing, was constantly aware of the criticisms of her teaching, since her beliefs about learning and teaching were and are primarily at odds with the culture of her school. Other teachers rebuffed her cross-curricular efforts and seemed suspicious. Parents of students outside of her class began asking the principal why Fran's curricula did not match the others'. The principal had stated that Fran's unit "provides students with the kind of learning that goes beyond facts, beyond the proficiency tests, and is an experience which all kids really need." But over a few years and with administrative changes, that support seemed to be withdrawn. An edict was issued stating that all students within a grade must read the same books. The criticisms sapped Fran's confidence. After shifting to 7th grade, beleaguered with a group of exceptionally rowdy students, Fran considered quitting teaching.

Several events have helped Fran relax in her square peg role. For one, she was made aware of the solidarity she shares with her principal, who is also under fire for suspect educational philosophies. Second, in-service sessions led by a "very idealistic" outsider is helping her understand what changes will and will not be allowed in her building. Third, her former teaching partner requested that they share a grade again, and Fran realized that "although she didn't want to teach the way I do, it doesn't mean she didn't respect or support me. . . . Basically we aren't going to change each other, . . . but she wants me back." Fourth, she has found the confidence to speak for change in the staff room.

> When I'd been hearing one teacher go on and on about how to assess her students' reading, I just had to speak out. 'Ruth,' I said, 'I learn about

their reading in more ways than just the questions and answers of the tests, the stuff you'd do at the end of a basal. I can get a sense of how well they read just from a picture that they draw when they finish a book. Their journal entries are a great way for me to understand their comprehension.' Ruth was shocked. She said, 'I didn't know we could do that!'"

Because of her increased confidence, Fran is feeling the culture of the school change while she helps that change to happen.

Vicki, an Eighth-Grade Teacher

As a recent masters degree graduate and experienced teacher, I returned to the classroom after several years as a stay-at-home mom. Armed and excited about implementing my new ideas and changing pedagogy, I entered an eighth-grade social studies content area classroom in a suburban middle school in the northern Virginia area.

Many of these newer ideas and strategies were very different from the educational preparation of the early 1980s when I was a beginning teacher. Teaching was no longer a lecture-fact oriented environment, but rather one of facilitating group exploration, research, and discovery. I jumped right into the middle school environment and used innovative teaching techniques such as classroom read alouds, tying interesting and sometimes controversial literature studies with the civics curriculum, weekly literature circles, and consistent technology use. My students were encouraged to use multimedia software for projects, to do research on the Internet, and to e-mail me quarterly current event summaries.

It wasn't long before I gained a few followers and supporters while finding myself at odds with many of my colleagues. I was fortunate in befriending another eighth-grade teacher who had similar beliefs and ideals. We bonded, wrote, and won a substantial technology grant for the school. The collaboration and sharing sustained both of us in an unfamiliar and seemingly unfriendly adult environment. I was also physically isolated—teaching in a trailer in the back of the school and spending much of the day alone. Roadblocks appeared in the form of lack of computers in the classroom, supplies, and equipment, as well as uncooperative colleague comments including "You can't teach that novel!" or "That's not how we've always done it" or "Well, I'm not going to use that technology stuff." Yet throughout the year the students kept me going. Their enthusiasm and excitement for innovation and learning provided rewards along with the usual frustrations that occur in any teaching position.

Several aspects of teacher change became evident to me through self-reflection and introspection. Support and validation are crucial. I had the wise and constant guidance of my Ph.D. faculty advisor as well as my teaching friend in the building. The ability to discuss and bounce ideas off both a novice teacher and an experienced professor gave me the benefit of two very different points of view. Talks and discussions provided the fuel to keep the "fires" of change burning. Additionally, some experience in teaching, a solid, work ethic, confidence in the quality of one's teaching abilities, as well as having a personality that embraces risk are all elements that contribute to this teacher change.

I also learned that I needed collaboration and a friendly atmosphere to thrive and enjoy teaching. Even in this progressive northern Virginia school system, the administration is reluctant to embrace change or innovative ideas. Therefore I have left the middle school environment and returned to an elementary school faculty and environment that embodies many of the elements missing at the middle school. Interestingly, many elements of my changing pedagogy and teaching strategies are expanding and becoming more ingrained in my beliefs. So, too, is innovation. I am currently teaching in an unusual setting with multicultural, second language acquisition children in a multi-age group—another experience with innovation, controversy, and change.

Discussion

Even though each case study has distinctive elements, a pattern has emerged from the research. First, all of these teachers display an inquiry mindset. They were frustrated with the status quo, raised questions about other ways of teaching, and have explored, sometimes at personal cost, ways and methods to be more effective in their literacy teaching. These are not teachers who use the same set of lesson plans every year. Rather they have taken risks with their teaching, have observed student response, and have groped their way toward creating a teaching and learning situation that they feel will be of maximum benefit to their students. Their pedagogical changes have come about with deliberation, through trial and error, and through reflection and introspection.

Second, these teachers have all experienced either an epiphany or have had a catalyst spur them on to change. Robert's epiphany came about in a workshop that changed his way of thinking about the reading process. For Gretchen, the "aha" moment occurred when a student asked her why the class would have to return to basals after having read books. The partnership project between university and school was the catalyst for Sharon to reconsider her pedagogy. Both Fran and Vicki were influenced by masters degree programs, but it was Fran's worry about her students that propelled her into trying new methods.

For these five teachers, support and validation for the ways they conceive of teaching and learning are crucial to their well being as teachers. Yes, as innovators in their individual schools most of them have a fair amount of confidence or a willingness to take risks. But all of them need positive feedback from some quarter. For all of them the original validation for their change came from the children, and garnering support—or at least respect—from colleagues has been a major battle. Although Robert's administration gave the impetus for his change by sending him off to a workshop, his main line of support still comes only from the children, who validate for him his belief that he has found a powerful way to approach literacy. But he is frustrated that his colleagues still do not support him. Fran, too, has only felt steady support from her own students and their parents. But now that she is aware that certain colleagues respect her teaching beliefs, even if they do not share her attitudes, she may feel enough confidence to endure the mixed messages and lack of support from her administration. As long as their classroom pedagogy was not interfered with or the lack of support was not too blatant or destructive, all of these teachers have been able to survive in their solo roles. But it has not been easy, and for Vicki and Gretchen a job move has been necessary.

Implications

We need to learn a lot more about these mavericks if we are to be helpful to them. We can not make major assumptions from these data and from this study, but the compelling nature of these teachers' stories suggests fertile ground for research. It is a complex issue to study, partly because of the fluid nature of the change process, and partly because of the proactive ways individuals and institutions change each other. All five of these teachers are slowly causing the cultures of their school communities to change, but the cost on those individuals can be high. If teacher educators want to be a support to the mavericks, and certainly if we want to impact the kind of change that brings about wider-scale reform, we need more data and research. Perhaps this study could serve as a pilot for a more complete study that considers teacher change in a broader context.

As teacher educators we also need to think about various ways that we can help build the confidence levels of thoughtful, reflective teachers who feel as though they are isolated and unsupported. We need to be aware that those classroom teachers who seek us out perhaps after their graduate work is over, or who ask for validation through their conversations with us, may well be the ones playing a solo role in their buildings. Collaboration through university-school partnerships or mentoring must be built into staff development plans. Similarly, staff development must include participation of administrators and policy-makers so that they will be informed enough to trust and support teachers in their processes of change.

For preservice teachers, risk-taking in teacher preparation classes needs to be encouraged and supported to help novice teachers learn how to implement any professional changes with which they may be uncomfortable. In addition, since support of trusted colleagues was critical in each of these cases, preservice teachers can learn how to support each other by working collaboratively on university assignments or in the field.

Perhaps an even more important implication for teacher preparation may lie in the enormous gap between epistemology and praxis currently in our classrooms. Traditionally, teacher education programs have largely focused on instructional methods representing "best practice" according to current research. But the experiences of these teachers suggest that pedagogical knowledge evolves over time, influenced by a teacher's continuing reflection on his or her own contextualized classroom practice.

In the last several years, the notion of educator as "reflective practitioner" (Schon, 1987) has frequently appeared in scholarly journals. Similarly, the popularity of "constructivism" as a paradigm for teaching and learning suggests that understanding and "knowing" are individual constructions (Fosnot, 1996). Increasingly, preservice teachers are required to implement new methodologies in real classroom settings in order to understand the impact of context on instruction. Moreover, many courses now emphasize the value of teaching children metacognitive strategies that will enable them to reflect on their own learning processes. All of these trends support the need for teachers to recognize the organic and fluid nature of knowledge in education. Little research suggests that this epistemological insight is currently made explicit in university classrooms. We believe these case studies suggest that if it were, preservice teaching might come to view thoughtful change as an integral feature of their professional lives.

The authors give warm thanks to the four teachers who let us into their classrooms and their lives, and to Nancy Padak, whose encouragement to our own change processes and to our work feels boundless.

References

Carnegie Task Force. (1989). *Turning Points: Preparing American youth for the twenty-first century.* New York: Carnegie Corporation.

Cuban, L. (1992). Curriculum stability and change. In P. W. Jackson (Ed.), *Handbook of research on curriculum* (pp. 216-247). New York: Macmillan.

Fawcett, G. (1994). *A case study of eighth-grade students in transition between transmission and constructivist based language arts instruction.* Unpublished doctoral dissertation. Kent State University.

Fosnot, C. T. (1996). *Constructivism: Theory, perspectives, and practice.* New York: Teachers College Press.

Fullen, M. G. with Stiegelbauer, S. (1991). *The new meaning of educational change.* (2nd ed.). NewYork: Teachers College Press.

Goodlad, J. I. (1984). *A place called school.* New York: McGraw-Hill.

Hall, G. E. & Loucks, S. (1978). Teacher concerns as a basis for facilitating and personalizing staff development. *Teachers College Record, 80,* 36-54.

Hall, G.E., Wallace, R.C. & Dossett, W.A. (1973). *A developmental conceptualization of the adoption process within educational institutions.* Austin, TX: Research and Development Center for Teacher Education, University of Texas.

Joyce, B., & Showers, B. (1980). Improving inservice training: The message of research. *Educational Leadership, 37,* 379-385.

Kraus, C. (1992). Changes in primary teachers' instructional practices after year 1 of a collaborative whole language project. In N. Padak, T.Rasinski, & J. Logan, (Eds.), *Literacy research and practice: Foundations for the year 2000.* Fourteenth yearbook of the College Reading Association. Provo, UT: College Reading Association.

Levande, D. (1991). Transitions: Teachers moving into whole language. *Journal of Instructional Psychology, 18,* 266-269.

Merriam, S. B. (1988). *Case study research in education: A qualitative approach.* San Francisco, CA: Jossey-Bass.

Pace, G. (1992). Stories of teacher-initiated change from traditional to whole-language literacy instruction. *The Elementary School Journal, 92*(4), 461-476.

Padak, N.D., & Davidson, J.L.(1993, December). *Challenges in whole language teaching and learning: A view from teachers.* Paper presented at the meeting of the National Reading Conference, Charleston, SC.

Routman, R. (1991/1994). *Invitations: Changing as teachers and learners K-12.* Portsmouth, NH: Heinemann.

Schafly, P. (1984). *Child abuse in the classroom.* Westchester, IL: Crossway Books.

Scharer, P. L. (1992). Teachers in transition: An exploration of changes in teachers and classrooms during implementation of literature-based reading instruction. *Research in the Teaching of English, 26,*(4), 408-445.

Schon, D. A. (1987). *Educating the reflective practitioner.* San Francisco, CA: Jossey-Bass.

Sparks, D., & Loucks-Horsley, S. (1990). Models of staff development. In W.R. Houston (Ed.), *Handbook of research on teacher education.* (pp. 234-250). New York: Macmillan.

Timar, T. B., & Kirp, D. L. (1989). Educational reform in the 1980s: Lessons from the states. *Phi Delta Kappan, 70,* 504-511.

Weaver, C. (1992). A whole language belief system and its implications for teacher and institutional change. In C. Weaver & L. Henke (Eds.), *Supporting whole language: Stories of teacher and institutional change* (pp.3-26). Portsmouth, NH: Heinemann.

Williams, A.L. (1996). Living in the "real world" of instructional change in literacy: One fourth grade teacher and educational reform. In E. G. Sturtevant & W. Linek (Eds.), *Growing literacy.* Eighteenth yearbook of the College Reading Association (pp. 93-102). Commerce, TX: College Reading Association.

Portfolios, Learning Logs, and Eulogies: Using Expressive Writing in a Science Methods Class

Debby Deal

George Mason University

Abstract

Teachers' beliefs about teaching and learning science influence how and what they teach. Negative beliefs often result in limited time being devoted to science and the application of traditional transmission models of instruction. This paper discusses the symbiotic relationship which exists between literacy and science skills, and it illustrates how expressive writing can be used in a pre-service science methods course to influence positive teacher beliefs. The author identifies and supports three additional purposes for writing in a content methods course: to develop conceptual understanding, to provide diagnostic information, and to encourage creative curriculum integration.

Middle education students at my university are certified to teach all subjects in grades 4-8. Consequently, any of the students who pass through my science methods class could be teaching science as part of an elementary curriculum or science as a single subject in middle school. Over the years, I have found that many have negative feelings toward science and/or a limited science background. Often, they also have beliefs about science teaching that reflect their experiences as students in lecture-based science courses. Research has found that beliefs about science teaching and learning may strongly influence not only how and what new teachers teach (Anderson, 1992; Hashweh, 1996; Pajares, 1992; Enochs, Scharmann, & Riggs, 1995) but how much time they will spend teaching activity-based science (Enochs, Scharmann, & Riggs, 1995).

In addition, teacher's beliefs are often resistant to change (Anderson, 1992; Johnson & Hoffman, 1994; Kagan, 1992; Hashweh, 1996; Pajares, 1992;

Richardson, 1996). In the *Handbook of Research on Science Teaching and Learning* (1994), Anderson writes, "Change does not occur by simply altering such variables as how teachers feel and act. Rather these desired changes require teachers to learn, rethink, and adopt different knowledge, thought, and practices related to teaching" (p. 28). Richardson (1996) identifies three sources that contribute to the beliefs of pre-service teachers: personal experience, experience with schooling and instruction, and experience with formal knowledge which includes pedagogical knowledge. Although she suggests that formal knowledge has the least effect on belief formation and modification, she does acknowledge that "the influence is not negligible" (p.106). Consequently, developing a positive educational belief structure is a major focus of my science methods course.

For the purposes of this paper, I shall use Pajare's (1992) definition of beliefs: "Teachers' attitudes about education—about schooling, teaching, learning, and students—have generally been referred to as teacher beliefs" (p. 316). Pajares goes on to point out the distinction between teachers' educational beliefs and a more expansive general belief system. In this paper, I shall address teachers' educational beliefs. Kagan (1992) offers a similar definition of beliefs, stating, "Teacher belief is a particularly provocative form of personal knowledge that is generally defined as pre- or inservice teachers' implicit assumptions about students, learning, classrooms, and the subject matter to be taught" (p. 66).

Over the last four years I have implemented a variety of literacy-based practices, including expressive writing, to encourage preservice teachers to revisit and rethink their beliefs about teaching and learning science. About three years ago, I began collecting student artifacts. Since then, I have observed that, in addition to the original reason for the writing, each writing task serves at least one of several broad purposes: encouraging positive attitudes toward science, developing an understanding of science concepts, providing embedded diagnostic information, and creating "natural" opportunities for curriculum integration.

The research literature recognizes and encourages the connection between the teaching of science and literacy skills. The *National Science Education Standards* (1996) consider oral and written discourse to be an important stage of inquiry "that focuses the attention of students on how they know what they know and how their knowledge connects to larger ideas, other domains, and the world beyond the classroom" (p. 36). Casteel and Isom (1994) describe learning in science and literacy to be reciprocal processes and suggest, "the literacy processes are the means by which science content is learned because content information is rooted in written and oral language" (p. 540). In this paper, I will focus on how I have students use writing for each of these four purposes, and I will provide examples of student work.

Promoting Positive Attitudes

Depending on the purpose for writing, my students use a variety of formats, including learning logs, freewrites, poems, letters, and reading responses. One purpose, writing to develop a positive perspective of science, requires students to become aware of their current attitudes and to identify connections between their beliefs and their experiences (Kagan, 1992; Richardson, 1996). The first learning log prompt, "Reflect on yourself as a learner in science, and discuss your attitudes toward teaching science," addresses this need. Quite often, students discover a significant relationship between their experiences as a learner and their attitudes as a preservice teacher. For example, Mary wrote:

> I had all A's and B's in school so I must have done well in science—but I certainly did not find it interesting. I think it is because I was taught in the old traditional style of teaching—memorizing textbooks and not much hands-on.

Another student, Lydia, clearly connected an early memory to her own attitudes toward teaching science.

> She [my sixth grade teacher] said, "I don't like science because it's too much of a hassle, so we won't be doing it this year." I was very disappointed and felt like it wasn't fair. Now, remembering that, as a teacher, I know that I must try to expose all of my students to all aspects of education and learning without my personal bias.

Although each student has a different story to tell, what is obvious to me as I read the entries and obvious to the class during discussion, is that teachers' attitudes and how they present science significantly influences their students' attitudes toward science. Memorable teachers are sometimes those who inspire, but just as often, they are those who leave negative imprints. Particular hands-on activities are often remembered in detail, while only the existence of a textbook, used in a passive manner, is mentioned.

At the end of the semester, I ask students to once again write about their attitudes toward teaching science. By then, my students have discovered that writing in science can be a creative as well as a cognitive process. Not all choose to respond in a narrative format; some, like Kristen, prefer poetry.

> *Before*
> My boredom was grey like a rain soaked
> afternoon, and also like a dreary classroom.
> It reminded me of the science professor's
> voice droning on and on. It made me feel
> like yawning.

Now
My curiosity is bright yellow like the light
generated from the simple circuit, and also
like the dazzle of our science inventions.
It reminds me of exploring the owl pellet.
It makes me feel like "digging" in.

Weekly learning log responses are not graded; thus students can explore their thoughts and understanding of hands-on investigations in a non-threatening manner (Audet, Hickman, & Dobrynina, 1996; Dorroh, 1993). A dialogue in which students engage in sense-making and reflection emerges. I respond to their entries with comments, often in the form of questions. For example, I might ask a student, "How do you know?" or "What will you do next?" Sometimes I encourage students to probe further or to rethink their ideas, but I do not use the learning log for didactic teaching.

Reflecting on Teaching and Learning

At the end of the semester students compile a Science Learning Portfolio which provides a summative opportunity for students to reflect on their own growth as science learners and teachers, both cognitively and affectively. Portfolios provide another opportunity for instructor and student to observe changing attitudes (Oropallo & Gomez, 1996). Approximately two weeks before the end of the semester, students receive a list of inclusions (see Appendix A). The list requires students to think about what they have learned and about their attitude toward science. It is designed to allow choice within broad categories, such as "work that demonstrates your ability to collect, record, and interpret data" and an "example that demonstrates your growth over the semester." Students attach a 3 x 5 card to each selection explaining why they chose to include it as part of their portfolio. For her "growth" item, Anna described how her beliefs as a teacher and as a learner evolved during the semester:

> To show how I have grown over the semester I have included a learning log and an acrostic poem that I created. The learning log is about a strategy that I used during my independent teaching and [describes] how well the unit was going at the time. Through this learning log you can see how my confidence level about teaching science has increased from the first learning log and how my attitudes toward science were changing. This is when I actually began to like science. The students and I were learning to like science together. The poem that I have created starts out showing the feelings that I brought to the class with me and about how I felt about the class and teaching science. As you read further you will see how I began to settle in and actually ended

up enjoying teaching science. I still have a long ways to go with my lessons, however, I have grown to like teaching science and look forward to doing it again.

Lisa felt that she had grown most as a science learner, and she described her feelings in a letter. In part she wrote, "You have opened the door to my curiosity with regards to science. I find myself in situations all the time where I want to know how and why things work; it had been decades since I felt that way about anything pertaining to science."

Unlike Lisa, Rachel entered the class with an undergraduate degree in science, a positive attitude, and a traditional perspective on teaching. She discussed her changing beliefs about teaching, in her philosophy statement.

My view of teaching has changed in one significant way over the last year. I no longer believe that the primary job of the teacher is to provide information. I now believe that if the teacher creates an environment conducive to learning, the students will take an active role in their own learning . . .

She proceeded to describe five major components she considered essential: (a) making information accessible, (b) creating a safe, structured environment, (c) modeling enthusiasm, (d) having high expectations, and (e) teaching how to learn. Each of these examples, found in student portfolios, supports the use of reflective writing as a means to facilitate positive attitudes by pre-service teachers.

Learning Science Concepts Through Writing

Expressive writing allows students to explore ideas and to think on paper. Holliday, Yore, and Alvermann (1994) state, "Writing should glue thinking to paper, provide a public record of thinking, promote critical thinking, allow the transformation of vague ideas to clear conceptions, and stimulate the construction of understandings" (p. 885). In my science methods class, it provides a permanent record that students and teachers can revisit as students grapple with conceptual understanding, another purpose for content area writing. Because conceptual change requires a great deal of time (Driver & Bell, 1986; Watson & Konicek, 1990), the writing creates a concrete reference point from which change can be observed and documented. As students investigate, write, draw, discuss, listen, and read they have repeated opportunities to expand their understanding of science concepts.

Used in this manner, science and writing are connected in an authentic context, similar to how scientists study the natural world. Observations and data collection are part of each class investigation. Students are encouraged to ask and record questions that result from inquiry. As closure, they use

their data to summarize, analyze, draw conclusions, or suggest further inquiry. For example, as part of an energy-transfer investigation with owl pel-
lets, Maria wrote a eulogy for Vincent Vole that described the food chain she
had learned about. ". . . One of the oldest voles in our community surviving
many owl attacks, Vincent was known for his shrewdness. He always knew
where to find the insects for dinner . . ."

Following a multi-week investigation in which teams of students designed
air-powered vehicles, students were asked to write what they would do differently next time and what they would keep the same. Peggy's response
indicates reflective thinking and suggests that as a result of experience and
group interaction, she is developing an understanding of friction and energy
transfer. In part she wrote:

> I would use wheels that produced less friction as they rolled along the
> floor.
> I would try to experiment with different wheel designs.
> I would try to break the design down into parts: what would make the
> best wheel, the best body, the best energy "transferer" (straw,
> barrel?)
> I would do research on how to build a similar vehicle
> I would try to be more involved. I really didn't know what to do or
> suggest so I just observed most of the time.

Problem-Solving Through Writing

As students write about their ideas and strive to make sense of data,
their writing serves yet another purpose—to provide a continuous source of
embedded diagnostic information. Before introducing a new science concept, I often use writing to activate prior knowledge. I might ask students to
"tell everything you know about rocks and minerals" or to "use words and
pictures to explain a simple circuit." In order to use writing to collect an
accurate picture of what student's know, class experiences must support beliefs
about science learning and teaching which are compatible with risk-taking.

After hands-on experiences with batteries and bulbs, recording data,
and class discussions, Hank documented his problem-solving approach which
relied on prior knowledge, experimentation, and group interaction (see Figure 1). His description provided me with rich data for assessing his understanding and planning further exploration.

Opportunities for Creative Integration

Unfortunately, science is often not recognized or taught as the creative
process it is (Gallagher, 1991). Classroom environments in which literacy skills
are integrated with science and in which students are comfortable taking

Figure 1. Hank's Learning Log Entry Documented His Thinking Process with Bulbs and Batteries.

The only preknowledge I brought to this activity was how to put batteries in a flashlight. Using that knowledge, I immediately put the two batteries together like this:

Then, I ignored the wires to see what would happen if I just placed the bulb on top of the battery, because that is how a flashlight seems to work. It didn't work.

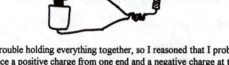

One person in my group said, "Remember, it's a circuit." So I held the wires to either end of both batteries and twisted them together and touched the bottom of the bulb. That did not work either, so I untwisted the wire ends and touched the bottom of the bulb with them separate from each other, but simultaneously. However, the bulb would not light.

I had a lot of trouble holding everything together, so I reasoned that I probably only had to use one battery since a positive charge from one end and a negative charge at the other end was all that two (or more) batteries really amounted to. I thought that maybe the problem was that the circuit was broken because of all my fumbling around. I retried touching the ends of the wires to the bulb, but it still would not light.

Then I remembered when I installed a new phone last year, I had to wrap the end of a wire around something that looked like a screw. So I tried wrapping the wire ends around the bulb. The bulb still would not light.

Figure 1 (continued). Hank's Learning Log Entry Documented His Thinking Process with Bulbs and Batteries.

I unwrapped one of the wires from around the bulb, intending to try twisting it again with the end of the other wire and then wrapping that whole thing around the neck of the bulb. However, before I did that, I accidentally touched the end of that wire on the bottom of the bulb and I saw a very quick flicker. For a moment, I wasn't sure what I had done to make it work. Then I deliberately touched the bottom of the bulb again and got the bulb to light.

Next, I wondered if I could reverse the wrapping wire and the bottom-touching wire to make the bulb light up. The bulb lit up this way as well.

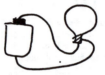

Next. I realized that my original "flashlight model" would work if I added a wire to complete the circuit, when working with my partner.

risks do promote creativity. Thus, a final purpose for writing in my science methods class is to model "natural" opportunities for curriculum integration and creativity. Tasks often support this purpose in addition to encouraging positive attitudes, building content knowledge, or providing assessment information. The three examples I will use in this section all involved curriculum integration and at least one other purpose.

In general, when new students first enter my class and discuss their experiences with writing in science, they mention traditional research papers and lab reports. One assignment is designed to expose students to multiple options for creative reporting as well as to address the National Science Education Standards (1996) on the history and nature of science. Students choose one of two tasks: (a) interview a scientist or an engineer or (b) research a female or minority scientist. If they opt to do the research project, they must present their information in a non-traditional format that includes both oral and visual components. Evidence of extensive research is found in the final products which have included: interviews (both live and taped), videotapes, eulogies, poems, news reports, letters, game shows, "scientist in a bag/box," first person monologues, HyperStudio presentations, and scrapbooks. In reflecting on this assignment, students frequently tell me that due to the open-ended nature of the task which is unlike report writing, they were highly motivated and collected much more data than needed. During the diverse oral presentations, I have observed that the audience maintains its interest.

I have also observed that students often learn content knowledge more readily when they can translate it into their choice of written or oral form. For example, after our hands on investigation of bulbs and batteries, students brainstormed vocabulary that they associated with electricity. We discussed the terms in relation to our hands-on experiences, and then students were asked to define the words and to use them in a creative way that would convey their meaning and aid learning. Carl chose to write these electrical limericks:

There once was this thing called a volt
Which could really provide quite a jolt
When turned way up high
It could light up the sky
Or cause so much noise that you'd bolt.

Another project, field trip guides, blend the disciplines of science, computer technology, writing, and art. This is a favorite assignment which contributes to positive attitudes and allows me to assess how well my students understand questioning strategies and diverse learning styles. The guides, intended to help students in grades 4-8 become actively involved during field trips, require my students to familiarize themselves with the site, understand the science principles involved, and generate productive questions that promote multiple levels of thinking. In Dana's field trip guide to NASA, she asked open-ended questions, promoted visual thinking, and connected the field trip to classroom studies (see Figure 2).

Many museums and parks have websites that offer teachers pre-visit or on-site activity suggestions. My students have found these to be a useful starting place. They then adapt the information to meet their objectives, encourage active learning, and format it to be "student-friendly." In addition to the expected field trip sites, students have created excellent guides to less likely places, such as a virtual field-trip guide to the San Francisco Exploratorium web-site, a guide to a local nursery, and a generic guide appropriate for any park.

Figure 2. Dana's Field Trip Guide Used Divergent Questions, Promoted Visual Thinking, and Connected to Classroom Studies.

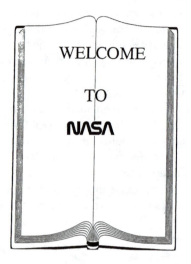

WELCOME

TO

NASA

1

Name five pieces of lab equipment you recognized in the lab. Draw a picture of any lab equipment you did not recognize and describe how the scientist used this equipment

2

SAFETY SYMBOLS

How many safety symbols did you recognize? Explain why the safety symbols were used in the lab today. Where would you find these symbols outside of a science lab?

3

What did you think of the lab? Compare and contrast the procedures, rules, and equipment in the NASA's lab to the procedure, rules and - equipment in the school's lab.

4

Conclusions

The use of writing in my science methods class seems to affect how my preservice students think about teaching and learning science. The artifacts generated suggest that for many students their beliefs about science education have been challenged, and they are beginning to reflect a positive attitude and an eagerness to learn. In their final learning log entry, students discuss how they feel about teaching science now. Although science is still not the first teaching choice of many students, most indicate that they would now feel comfortable teaching science. The reflective writing they do during my class seems to help students become aware of their own growth and beliefs regarding science. This is illustrated by Claire's acrostic poem which documents how her feelings about teaching and learning science changed from fear to growing confidence during the semester (see Figure 3).

In addition to expressing a more positive attitude toward science, stu-

Figure 3. Claire's Poem Showed How Her Feeling About Teaching Science Evolved.

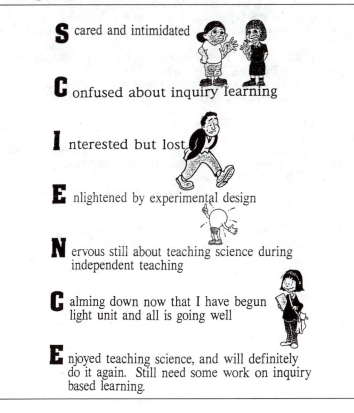

S cared and intimidated

C onfused about inquiry learning

I nterested but lost

E nlightened by experimental design

N ervous still about teaching science during independent teaching

C alming down now that I have begun light unit and all is going well

E njoyed teaching science, and will definitely do it again. Still need some work on inquiry based learning.

dents often use their writing to address their desire to further expand their science content knowledge. Thinking of themselves as life-long learners, many indicate that they feel confident in their ability to continue their own learning as practicing teachers. Sasha communicated this belief in her philosophy statement:

> I believe that teaching science
> must be a discovery learning
> experience for children. In fact,
> if it is done right, the teacher
> will probably learn something
> as well.

References

Anderson, R. D. & Michener, C. P. (1994). Research on Science Teacher Education. In D. L. Gabel (Ed.). (1996). *Handbook of Research on Science Teaching and Learning*. New York: Simon and Schuster Macmillan.

Audet, R., Hickman, P. & Dobrynina, G. Learning logs: A classroom practice for enhancing scientific sense making. *Journal of Research in Science Teaching, 33*, 205-222.

Casteel, P. C. & Isom, B. A. (1994). Reciprocal processes in science and literacy learning. *The Reading Teacher, 47*(7), 538-545.

Dorroh, J. (1993, summer). Reflections on expressive writing in the science class. *The Quarterly of the National Writing Project and the Center for the Study of Writing and Literacy, 15*, 28-30.

Driver, R., & Bell, B. (1986, March). Students' thinking and the learning of science: A constructivist view. *School Science Review*, 443-455

Enochs, L. G., Scharmann, L. C., & Riggs, I. (1995). The relationship of pupil control to preservice elementary science teacher self-efficacy and outcome expectancy. *Science Education, 79*(1), 63-75.

Gallagher, J. J. (1991). Prospective and practicing secondary school science teachers' knowledge and beliefs about the philosophy of science. *Science Education, 75*(1), 121-133.

Hashweh, M. Z. (1996). Effects of science teachers' epistemological beliefs in teaching. *Journal of Research in Science Teaching, 33*(1), 47-63.

Holliday, W., Yore, L., & Alvermann, D. (1994). The reading-science learning-writing connection: Breakthroughs, barriers, and promises. *Journal of Research in Science Education, 31*, 877-893.

Johnson, R. & Hoffman, N. (1994). Preservice teachers' efficacy beliefs, literacy definitions, and conceptions of literacy development. In E. G. Sturtevant. & W. M. Linek (Eds.). *Pathways for Learning: Learner Teach and Teachers Learn.*, 73-84. East Texas State University: College Reading Association.

Kagan, D. (1992). Implications of research on teacher belief. *Educational Psychologist, 27*(1), 65-89.

National Science Education Standards. (1996). Washington DC: National Research Council.

Oropallo, K. & Gomez, S. (1996). Using reflective portfolios in preservice teacher education programs. In E. G. Sturtevant and W. M. Linek (Eds.) *Growing Literacy*, 121-132. Texas A&M University-Commerce: College Reading Association.

Pajares, M. F. (1992). Teachers' beliefs and educational research: Cleaning up a messy construct. *Review of Educational Research, 62*(3), 307-332.

Richardson, V. (1996). The role of attitudes and beliefs in learning to teach. In T. Sikula, T. Buttery & E. Guyton (Eds.). *Handbook of Research on Teacher Education* (2nd ed., pp. 102-119). New York: Simon and Schuster Macmillan.

Watson, B. & Konicek, R. (1990, May). Teaching for conceptual change: Confronting children's experience. *Phi Delta Kappan,* 680-685.

Appendix A. Science Portfolio

Benefits of Portfolios
For teachers and parents, a student portfolio
- highlights individual growth over time; concepts, skills, and attitudes
- demonstrates evidence of self-directed learning
- provides examples of problem-solving and creative thinking
- identifies areas of interest
- clarifies student's perception of work completed

For the student, a portfolio
- establishes a vehicle to communicate how the student feels about science
- encourages active involvement in the learning process
- provides an opportunity to recognize personal growth
- provides an opportunity to contribute to the assessment process

Please include the following in your portfolio:
- table of contents
- statement or artwork that represents your philosophy of teaching science
- journal entry
- description of a successful hands-on activity
- work that demonstrates your ability to collect, record, and interpret data
- example of a performance assessment
- example that demonstrates your growth over the semester
- an item of your choice

*** Attach a 3 x 5 card to each piece which explains why you chose to include it in your portfolio.

THE MULTICULTURAL FAIR:
A CELEBRATION OF DIVERSITY
AN INNOVATIVE APPROACH TO
TEACHER EDUCATION

Denise H. Stuart
Monica Gordon Pershey
Linda D. Hayes
Cleveland State University

Abstract

Students in a teacher education program developed and participated in The Multicultural Fair, an innovative approach to instruction. Students selected topics in diversity awareness, collaborated with peers, and created resource handouts and constructed interactive displays. This paper describes the need for alternative approaches to teacher education and the evolution of a project that culminated in celebration of diversity and children's literature. Students' written vignettes revealed perceived outcomes of their experiences with this alternative approach. These include growing awareness of issues of diversity, gaining knowledge of teaching resources, working in a community of learners, and anticipating classroom applications of teaching ideas.

"I was surprised to discover how a fairy tale could reveal so much about cultures . . . when we actually found and read the same basic story from a variety of cultures . . . it was proof of the similarities that all cultures share . . . the differences . . . provided the means of appreciating the various cultures."

"Discover" was a key word as students engaged in self selected inquiry into topics of diversity while preparing to present activities and children's literature at The Multicultural Fair. The process of developing a fair may be one innovative approach to teaching that effectively prepares students and teachers for the diverse "villages" of the twenty-first century. Many issues emerged through reflective writing as students in two teacher education courses produced vignettes describing personally significant moments they had experienced while preparing for and participating in The Multicultural Fair. This paper will discuss the need for alternative approaches in teacher education, the evolution of the project that culminated in an event of celebration, and themes that emerged from students' vignettes which recount their perceived outcomes of this innovative, alternative teaching approach.

The theme "It Takes a Village to Raise a Reader" is a particularly powerful concept as our villages, our schools and our communities are becoming increasingly diverse. Children of color in our schools are anticipated to increase from 25% in 1980 to 42% by the year 2000 (CMPEAL, 1988) and comprise 49% by 2020 (Cushner, McClelland, & Safford, 1992). Research suggests that incorporation of students' language and culture into the school program is a significant factor in student academic success (Cummins, 1986; Diamond & Moore, 1995). Students' application of their life experiences and cultural backgrounds influences comprehension and reading development (Mason & Au, 1990). To facilitate learning and heighten student engagement, curricular materials and methods should reflect the diversity of students' cultures. Higher levels of reading and writing performance are attained and self-esteem in learners is improved as students encounter characters, settings and themes in multicultural literature that connect with their prior experiences (Bishop, 1987; Diamond & Moore, 1995).

Yet many of our preservice and inservice teachers have had limited exposure, either through literature or personal experience, to cultures outside of their own (Haberman, 1990). These are the teachers who will be in classrooms daily with a diversity of "villagers" into the next millennium. How can we develop meaningful experiences in our teacher education programs that encourage teachers to explore their own heritages and broaden and deepen their exposure, appreciation and understanding of diverse experiences and cultures? How can we better prepare teachers to meet the needs of the diverse students and readers who will be in their classrooms?

Teacher Education

Diversity and multicultural education, with ideological foundations in principles of pluralism, democracy, equity, civil rights, social justice, and global interdependence, have been subject to discussion about how to be actualized. Teaching and learning that challenge bias, intolerance, and social domination have been established as core precepts and ultimate intents (Barry & Lechner, 1992; Hildago, Chavez-Chavez, & Ramage, 1996; Lynch, 1989; Sleeter, 1993). However, preservice teachers may have had very little previous exposure to these notions of critical pedagogy and may need to spend time developing familiarity with these concepts and determining an individual sense and degree of personal commitment to these principles.

Lynch (1989) typifies multicultural education as a process of increasing sophistication. It begins by adding content about diverse cultures to a standard curriculum and broadens to include folkloric education where customs, foods, music, dress, and holidays are explored. Then multicultural education moves to a permeative phase where culturally diverse content, materials, and teaching approaches are infused across a learner-centered curriculum that promotes social cohesion and educational reform.

Preparing preservice teachers involves multiple processes that facilitate the phases of discovery proposed by Lynch (1989). This may include:

1. Preservice teachers begin to participate in scholarly discourse that enhances their knowledge of why and how information about diversity is included in school curricula. Introducing preservice teachers to large numbers of quality children's novels, picture books, and informational books can help them understand the concepts, issues, themes and problems inherent in affirming diversity in educational settings. Published guidelines for selection of quality materials (Dudley-Marling, 1997; Norton, 1990; Tomlinson & Lynch-Brown, 1996) can assist preservice teachers in finding resources that promote cultural awareness, with the implication that curricular diversity is a means to enrich learning experiences.

2. In a constructivist learning paradigm, learners are encouraged to work together to develop a sense of community and joint purpose and are invited to learn about themselves while learning about a subject area. The teacher guarantees intellectual freedom and has unlimited expectations for learners' potential. Hildago, Chavez-Chavez, and Ramage (1996) have elaborated on the model of constructivist inquiry posited by Lincoln and Guba (1985) and suggest that preservice teachers may participate in learning activities that provide a means for "gaining realistic perspectives on cultural groups and their social contexts . . . respecting the histories, perceptions, and practices of these groups . . . valuing multiple sources and interpretations of knowledge . . . [and] understanding other cultures as complex [and] dynamic" (Hildago, Chavez-Chavez, & Ramage, 1996, pp. 770-771). Preservice teachers are guided to reflect on their own backgrounds, beliefs, and repertoires of learning and teaching behaviors and assess how this uniqueness contributes to their own perspectives on diversity education.

3. Preservice teachers' active learning experiences may allow them to transcend views of multicultural education as a part of diversity education that merely carries on, as Lynch (1989) noted, additive ethnic studies and/or celebratory, "safe", "oversimplified", and "quaint" views of cul-

ture as ethnic manifestations (Hildago, Chavez-Chavez, & Ramage, 1996, p. 764). To attempt to orient preservice teachers to the position that educators need to permeate all aspects of school life with a sense of cultural responsiveness, preservice teachers need to have lived-through experiences that will promote, as Zimpher and Ashburn (1992) recommend, (a) an appreciation of diversity, (b) a belief in the value of cooperation, and (c) a belief in the importance of a caring community (Hildago, Chavez-Chavez, & Ramage, 1996). Although these qualities are difficult to promote, Zimpher and Ashburn (1992), Garcia (1996), and Hoffman (1996) suggest that a personal investment in multicultural and diversity education, modelled by university faculty and lived-through by teacher educators and preservice teachers in the context of the teacher preparation program, may motivate the genuine integration of teaching with respect for diversity when these preservice teachers assume teaching positions.

The Multicultural Fair

Two professors seeking to make assignments personally relevant to students and to build an awareness and appreciation of diversity, particularly multiculturalism, informally chatted only to discover that they had developed similar projects and goals. They concluded that students from the two classes should share their products. Students in the College of Education courses *Survey of Children's Literature* and *Teaching the Culturally Different Child* self-selected topics for diversity studies that then broadened to include ethnicity, language, class, gender, religion and exceptionality. They gathered resources and teaching ideas to use in the classroom. Their challenge was to create an interactive display that engaged an audience to consider issues of diversity as well as how these are portrayed in children's literature. Additionally, preservice teachers would make it possible for other teachers to implement the ideas in the classroom by developing a written handout that included background information on the topic, a description of the display, and activities and materials needed to recreate the display. The handout would also include a list of resources, print and nonprint, such as related children's literature, teachers' books and articles, Internet sites, community agencies, and contacts. Hence, a celebration and sharing of coursework at the end of the quarter became The Multicultural Fair.

This fair, open to the public, university students, and faculty, was held in a central location at the University. Native American dancers performed and talked about their culture as part of the culminating event. Over time a third professor joined the project, and internal funding was obtained to support the project from process to product. Assistance was made available to help students locate resources on the Internet. Students took field trips to the public library and visited the children's literature and foreign language departments, and an assistant was hired to create a resource manual, which was a compilation of all of the handouts developed by students. From this emerged a web page (http://prometheus.ed.csuohio.edu/mcf/mcweb2.html) which makes the ideas more broadly available. Students had an audience for the work they were doing. And as the fair grew year by year additional performers joined in the celebration. An African-American storyteller shared the oral history of her family's migration from south to north, a Latino percussionist shared the sounds and history of a variety of instruments, and an Irish dancer stepped the rhythms of her culture.

After self-selection of topics, students collaborated in small groups, meeting in and out of class to do research and to organize findings to prepare a handout and an interactive display. They read children's literature, searched the Internet, collected artifacts, interviewed people, and developed activities and lesson plans to support study and understanding of their aspect of diversity, including, in some displays, multiculturalism.

From this work a variety of interactive displays were created for the fair. Selected examples include the following.

1. Participants were exposed to the Cinderella story motif that can be found in traditional literature across cultures, and they were invited to read the literature to match and create cultural artifacts.

2. Participants created their own Kente cloths as they read *The Black Snowman* (Mendez, 1989), and they studied the symbolism of colors in the cloth.

3. A study of Korean culture was presented by interacting with a CD ROM on LC display using a lap-top computer.

4. Participants were exposed to African-American artists, musicians and authors as they listened to music, viewed art work and browsed related children's literature. They were challenged to check their knowledge through a matching game and were encouraged to refer to the materials presented.

5. An activity for building background knowledge of World War II was developed on Hypercard to extend the reading of Lois Lowry's (1989) *Number the Stars.*

6. Participants were invited to compare two versions of a popular story, Hill's (1987) *Where's Spot?* written in English and Arabic, as they took a "Journey Through the Middle East;" to read Heide's (1990) *The Day of Ahmad's Secret* to compare marketplaces; and to sample humus as they read about a family picnic in Heide's (1992) *Sami and The Times of The Troubles.*

7. Participants at a display about *Nightjohn* (Paulsen, 1993) engaged in simple but powerful response to the question, "If you could write only one word, what would that word be?" "Freedom," "love," "God," "Jesus," and other similar sentiments were their thoughtful responses.

8. Participants at a display on homelessness based upon *Monkey Island* (Fox, 1991) entered a refrigerator box with some newspapers and old blankets inside. Its "door" was closed. Sitting in this dim space, they completed a short questionnaire on their knowledge of and attitudes toward homelessness.

9. At "Breaking the Chain of Domestic Violence" participants were given strips of paper and asked to confidentially write down a situation of domestic violence that they knew. The strips were added as links in a paper chain strung across the front of the display. Near the conclusion of the Fair, the group held a "break the chain" ceremony, cutting the paper chain down in front of a group of cheering visitors.

Method
A Look at Students' Perceived Outcomes

To gather anecdotal information on how participation in The Multicultural Fair contributed to students' awareness of diversity issues, the vignette method of program evaluation was used (Jochums and Pershey, 1993). In the vignette method, a participant in a professional development program writes about a specific event or episode during the program that has contributed to his or her growth. The participant is asked to describe the episode and explain why it was important. The vignette method reflects a constructivist approach to learning, as the participant is invited to share how he or she acquired his or her own understanding of the area that has been studied (Lincoln & Guba, 1985). This method is useful in identifying experiences that contribute to professional growth and allows the evaluator to gain an informed understanding of the workings of a professional development program.

Data for two consecutive summer programs have been combined. Of the sixty-three participants most were preservice teachers, however a few were certified teachers enrolled in summer coursework. Most students were females; less than one-fifth were males. Most participants were white, although African-American students comprised about one-fourth of the students. A few Asian-American students were also in these classes. No student participated more than one summer.

Participants in The Multicultural Fair were asked to respond anonymously to this prompt:

A vignette is a short piece of writing that chronicles or describes an event or occurrence that someone has personally experienced. It can be likened to an anecdote or a brief story of what has occurred. Vignettes are told to reveal how an event, incident, circumstance, or occurrence was a meaningful or important personal experience.

Please take a few minutes to write a vignette about the most meaningful, educational, or thought-provoking event or occurrence that you have experienced in this class. Please focus your comments on something important that you experienced related to The Multicultural Fair, either before, during, or after the event.

Results

The process of inductive analysis (Patton, 1990) was used to glean categories and themes from these student-generated vignettes. The following themes and selected comments emerged from analysis of the vignettes.

Emerging Themes
Issues of Diversity.

"When Allison presented her grandmother's African dress to me, I felt honored. Even though I'm not African when I put on that dress I felt important and proud. This piece of African culture brought me closer to this whole project and purpose."

This statement captures the essence of many students' experiences at the fair expressing increased awareness of diversity, and in this case, multiculturalism. It is no surprise that two-thirds of the vignettes particularly described (a) cross-cultural experiences, (b) experiences where a student felt that his or own culture was affirmed, and (c) development of a broadened definition of diversity that moved beyond issues of culture and ethnicity.

"[The fair] . . . made me understand my Korean neighbors. especially adolescents who don't speak their parents' language—who I often criticized. I didn't try to understand their problems in two cultures before, but now I am willing to change my attitude toward them."

Several students described becoming more sensitive to different viewpoints, as in the above example. This was also evident in the description of a conversation that took place at the fair. A student wrote that he "actually got a chance to sensibly talk to someone who had a little bias in their heart" as he had the opportunity to explain to the visitor why it is important to have cultural sensitivity when teaching Puerto Rican children in public schools. Additionally, students became aware of close relations between African-Americans and Italian-Americans in turn of the century New Orleans due to common family values and musical interests, despite Jim Crow laws. One student "was surprised (at) how many different countries ate rice pudding."

Several wrote about expanded experiences such as sampling new foods. Many wanted to continue learning more and were surprised and appreciative of the diversity of peers in their own university classes.

> "Hearing the stories made me want to sit down with my aunt (who is somewhat the family historian) and hear stories about *my* family."

Students described increased interest in their own experiences and culture. One student shared her mother's experiences as an immigrant learning English as a second language, another "rekindled my love for African-American history," while another reflected on "how important my religion is to me as a culture." Students were reminded of previous opportunities: one reconsidered the possibility of teaching in Africa while another, on seeing a photo of a cafe in a remote part of Italy, realized he had been there and ". . . that we live in such a small world."

> "Prior to the fair I found myself categorizing all Native Americans into one culture. How wrong I was. . . . Each tribe has its own unique characteristics."

Students wrote about their own limited awareness, about broadening their definition and clarifying their understanding of diversity as including multiculturalism and as being more than "different ethnic and cultural groups, but of different lifestyles and experiences." Several came to view having "a different sexual preference as a different culture" while others addressed the "culture" of adopted children and of families without fathers in the home.

Resources: Print and Nonprint. "I really did not realize how many multicultural books are on the shelves of every library . . ." was a statement typical of one third of the students who addressed increased awareness of resources available and an emerging critical view of these resources. They became familiar with specific guides such as MacDonalds's (1982) *The Storyteller's Sourcebook: A Subject, Title, and Motif Index to Folklore Collections for Children*. They discovered children's literature written in other languages and read folk tales, traditional literature, and popular stories that can be found in many languages. They became committed to providing diverse literature in their classrooms. As one student articulated "everyone needs to feel validated and sometimes it comes through literature. It helps to see yourself in a book."

> "When I visited libraries to find books about Korea, [they] were published over 10 years ago. I came to realize why people have misunderstandings about Korea."

Students began to think critically about the resources related to their topics. "I have learned not to take all multicultural materials at face value." Another student expressed mixed feelings, wondering "how much positive material could [be] found to present about such a war torn area" as the Middle East. As she further explored her resources she "found a recurrent activity that surprised" her, that visiting family and friends was described as a favorite recreational activity in the literature. She concluded, "That would explain how the children survive. They have a strong support system."

> "I feel the most meaningful personal experience was when I went into the home of the family of another culture and 'connected'. I had the opportunity to visit several times. . . . After I returned the materials the family allowed me to borrow her son was there to interpret and he told me that his mom was so proud of me for learning about their culture. She said most people don't care about them. . . . She gave me a big hug with tears in her eyes."

Students discovered human resources for broadening their own perspectives, as in the example above. Another student who interviewed a Nigerian man learned that this culture wore masks because it was taboo to see a king's face. Many exchanges took place in preparation for the fair and at the fair as one student commented, ". . . .I had an opportunity to share an enlightening conversation with one of the Native American dancers."

Community of Learners.
> "One of the most meaningful events was when my group got together and brainstormed the questions for our display . . . the whole group had to cooperate and work together."

Nearly a third of the vignettes addressed issues of collaboration. Some experienced shared labor positively, saying "if we could share ideas successfully our project was successful." Several commented on the enjoyment of working together and the process of negotiating varying ideas to achieve consensus, being "impressed by everyone's creativity and surprised by my own." Others viewed it as "a personal lesson in working with others. Always trying to see the positive of a given situation can be challenging . . ." Several students commented on the need to remember that not all students like to work collaboratively and they must consider this in classroom planning.

> "I saw there were quite a few people that were truly interested in the subject we presented. It was heartening to see this. I was proud to be a part of this experience."

Many students described this sense of community at the fair event. "I felt a warmth at the fair of people sharing their culture and ideals with others." They were "engrossed with everyone's projects," had "underestimated the interest that would be generated," were delighted at the subsequent conversations their projects evoked, and generally felt "it was wonderful to interact with the other displays."

Classroom Applications.

"After seeing the Multicultural Fair come together, I began to think about what a great idea this would be to implement in my own classroom or even school-wide."

One-fourth of the students commented specifically about applying their experiences to teaching. They could now conduct useful literature searches, they could use specific activities and resources, and they themselves might even teach in other settings or countries. They expressed being "anxious to use [a display idea] with my students" and wanting to "become more expressive in my own oral reading" as a result of hearing the professional storyteller. They related the importance of addressing diversity in their own classrooms and across cultures and grade levels, acknowledged the importance of diversity awareness in building self-esteem in learners, and repeatedly expressed the need to understand the cultural ways of their own students.

"It struck me that multiculturalism is so easily intertwined with almost any topic. From the environment to fairy tales to food, educators have the opportunity to provide their students with meaningful multicultural experiences."

Discussion

The vignettes reveal that students have variously realized the three phases of multicultural awareness described by Lynch (1989). Students have begun to participate in scholarly discourse, have learned about themselves while they learned about multicultural education, have worked together in groups, have constructed their own research questions, and have met the high expectations set by their instructors, their groups, and themselves. Students also reported new understandings of the histories of cultural groups and gained awareness of differing perspectives. They have also come to see cultures as complex and dynamic.

Many of the vignettes reveal that these preservice teachers have reached the third stage described by Lynch (1989), which is to believe that educators need to permeate all aspects of school life with a sense of cultural responsiveness. Their personal investment in The Multicultural Fair has helped them discover the value of integrating multicultural teaching and teaching for diversity awareness.

Delpit (1995) suggests that university courses in teacher preparation be reorganized to allow for students' own thoughts to be explored, to enable the voices of diverse cultures to be heard, to teach preservice teachers to be aware of the practices of students' home cultures, and to inspire preservice teachers to work towards a school culture that honors diversity in all aspects of school life. These vignettes reveal that the students who participated in this innovative approach, The Multicultural Fair, had a thought-provoking experience that may influence their perspectives and behaviors when they assume teaching positions. In the students' words,

> "In our democratic society we are made to believe that we teach all people and include all people—we haven't gotten there yet."

> "I have always felt that experiencing another culture makes us more 'worldly' and more understanding of our foreign neighbors. This Fair is a great way for students to gain a sense of this responsibility."

References

Barry, N. H. & Lechner, J. V. (1995). Preservice teachers' attitudes about and awareness of multicultural teaching and learning. *Teaching and Teacher Education, 11*(2), 149-161.

Bishop, R. S. (1987). Extending multicultural understanding through children's books. In B. Cullinan (Ed.), *Children's literature in the reading program.* (pp. 60-71). Newark, DE: International Reading Association.

Commission of Minority Participation in Education and American Life (CMPEAL). (1988) One third of a nation. Washington: CMPEAL. In Gonzalez, R. D. (1990). When minority becomes majority: The changing face of English classrooms. *English Journal, 79,* 16-23.

Cummins, J. (1986). Empowering minority students: A framework for intervention. *Harvard Educational Review, 56,* 18-36.

Cushner, K., McClelland, A., Safford, P. (1992). *Human diversity in education: An integrative approach.* New York: McGraw-Hill.

Delpit, L. (1995). *Other people's children: Cultural conflict in the classroom.* New York: New Press.

Diamond, B. & Moore, M. (1995). *Multicultural literacy: Mirroring the reality of the classroom.* New York: Longman.

Dooley, N. A. (1991) *Everybody Cooks Rice.* Minneapolis: Carolrhodda Books.

Dudley-Marling,C. (1997). "I'm not from Pakistan": Multicultural literature and the problem of representation. *The New Advocate, 10*(2), 123-134.

Fox, P. (1991). *Monkey Island.* New York: Dell.

Garcia, E. E. (1996). Preparing instructional professionals for linguistically and culturally diverse students. In J. Sikula, T.J . Buttery, & E. Guyton (Eds.), *Handbook of Research on Teacher Education* (2nd ed.) (pp. 802-813). New York: Simon & Schuster Macmillan.

Haberman, M. (1990). The rationale for training adults as teachers. In C. E. Sleeter (Ed.), *Empowerment Through Multicultural Education* (pp. 275-286). Albany: State University of New York Press.

Heide, F. (1990). *The Day of Ahmad's Secret.* New York: Lothrop, Lee and Shepard Books.

Heide, F. (1992). *Sami and the Times of The Troubles.* New York: Clarion Books.

Hidalgo, F. Chavez-Chavez, R. & Ramage, J. C. (1996). Multicultural education: Landscape for reform in the twenty-first century. In J. Sikula, T.J. Buttery, & E. Guyton (Eds.), *Handbook of Research on Teacher Education* (2nd ed.) (pages 761-778). New York; Simon & Schuster Macmillan.

Hill, Eric (1987). *Where's Spot?* New York: Crocodile Books.

Hoffman, D. M. (1996). Culture and self in multicultural education: Reflections on discourse, text, and practice. *American Educational Research Journal, 33*(3), 545-569.

Jochums, B. L. & Pershey, E. J. (1993). Using the vignette method in formative evaluation. *Evaluation Practice, 14*(2), 155-161.

Lincoln Y. S. & Guba, E. G. (1985). *Naturalistic inquiry.* Newbury Park, CA: Sage.

Lowry, L. (1989). *Number the Stars.* New York: Dell.

Lynch, J. (1989). *Multicultural education in a global society.* New York: Falmer Press.

MacDonald, M. R. (1982). *The storyteller's sourcebook: A subject, title, and motif index.* Detroit: Heal-Schuman.

Mason, J. & Au, K. (1990). *Reading Instruction for Today.* Glenview, IL: Little, Brown Higher Education.

Mendez, P. (1989). *The Black Snowman.* New York: Scholastic.

Norton, D. E. (1995). *Through the eyes of a child: An introduction to children's literature* (4th ed.). New York: Merrill.

Patton, M.(1990). *Qualitative evaluation and research methods.* Newbury Park, CA: Sage Publications.

Paulsen, G. (1993). *Nightjohn.* New York: Bantam.

Sleeter, C. E. (1993). Multicultural education: Five views. *Education Digest, 58*(7), 53-57

Tomlinson, C. M. & Lynch-Brown. (1996). *Essentials of Children's literature.* Boston: Allyn and Bacon.

Zimpher, N. L. & Ashburn, E. A. (1992). Countering parochialism in teacher candidates. In M. E. Dilworth (Ed.), *Diversity in Teacher Education.* San Francisco: Jossey-Bass.

EMERGING
ISSUES

Insights in Implementing Family Literacy Programs

Jim Anderson

University of British Columbia

William T. Fagan

Memorial University
of Newfoundland

Mary Cronin

University of Regina

Abstract

The purpose of this chapter is to describe several key insights gained from the implementation of PRINTS (Parents' Roles INteracting with Teachers Support), a culturally responsive family literacy program with working class parents. The parents viewed the program quite positively, and overall, they and their children benefited from it. The ways in which the program supported parents in transferring the knowledge gained through their participation in the program into the contexts of their children's home literacy experiences are described. As well, the difficulties parents reported integrating certain strategies into their daily routines are explored, as is the parents', preoccupation with more traditional aspects of literacy learning such as letter and word recognition. Questions are also raised about some of the traditional ways of assessing the effectiveness of family literacy programs.

In implementing a family literacy program, what the initiators learn from the experience is as important as how the program affects the participants. Neuman and Gallagher (1994) have pointed out that research and theory in early literacy have not brought us to a point where we can identify causal chains. Factors or issues, while appearing simplistic, are often quite complex. In this chapter, the authors reflect on a number of insights attained during the implementation of a family literacy program, PRINTS (Parents' Roles INteracting with Teacher Support) in two low income communities.

The overall goals of the program were to empower parents through developing an awareness of literacy activities currently engaged in, and through becoming familiar with a range of other literacy activities and to foster literacy development for their preschool children. We also recognized the need to document the implementation of a family program in low SES communities. To do this we: had research assistants keep field notes of each session, kept our own field notes, kept journals in which we regularly reflected on our experiences, and held debriefing sessions which we audiotaped and transcribed at the midpoint and at the culmination of the program. It is from these sources that we drew the insights which we share here.

In this paper, we first share the intended outcomes of the PRINTS program and give a brief overview of the PRINTS model. We then describe the communities or contexts in which we implemented the program and briefly introduce the participants in the program. We then share the insights which we gained as we implemented the program. We conclude by suggesting that, based on our experiences and on issues being raised in the literature, there is a need to proceed cautiously in developing and implementing family literacy programs and a need for continued research in this area.

The PRINTS program

Intended Outcomes

Within the PRINTS program, intended learning include: (a) awareness by parents of current literacy support activities in their homes; (b) development of a positive self-concept and increased self-esteem; (c) knowledge of 34 literacy support activities across five contexts: talk, play, books and book sharing, scribbling/drawing/writing, and environmental print; (d) familiarity with certain technical literacy terms, like scaffolding, invented spelling, writing drafts; (e) greater confidence and less alienation in relation to schools and teachers; (f) greater commitment to involving themselves with their children in literacy support activities; (g) awareness or knowledge of literacy concepts for the children; (h) more participation by the children in literacy related activities; (i) more varied participation in literacy related activities by the children; and (j) development of a positive self-concept of the children as emergent readers and writers.

The outcomes of each of these intended learnings are delineated and described more fully elsewhere (Fagan, Anderson, & Cronin, 1997). In this paper we focus on what we believe to be key insights we gained as we implemented the PRINTS program and which we believe are important issues which other researchers and educators working in family literacy might consider.

The PRINTS Model

The PRINTS Program is based on a modified form of a model of early literacy development that originated in Britain (Hannon, 1995). The model consists of five strands or contexts in which early literacy develops (talk, play, environmental print, reading materials, drawing/writing materials), each of which encompasses five roles of parents or teachers (providing opportunity, recognizing, interacting, modeling, and setting guidelines). Sessions for each strand involve providing an overview of the strand, providing time for parents and teachers to share what that strand means to them and how they operationalize it, providing lots of positive reinforcement, discussing implications of certain home-based activities for school learning, and sharing a range of activities in each of the five strands for literacy development. Children's "small books" and educational toys are distributed periodically. The teachers and parents initially meet separately, but the facilitator is able to share information from one group to the other.

There are 13 two-hour sessions for the parents: an introductory session, 2 sessions for each of the five strands (10), and two wrap-up sessions involving parents and teachers. For the teachers, there is one session per strand plus the introductory and wrap-up sessions.

The program is suitable for parents of children ages 2-6 and for preschool teachers and teachers of kindergarten and grade 1.

Communities and Participants

This program was implemented in two community centres: Murphy Crescent and Beaverton in a small urban area of Canada. These are public-housing areas for low-income families, and in each community, a building has been designated by the Public Housing Authority as a centre in which various educational and community-based activities take place.

Eight parents and one grandparent, four in one centre and five in the other, participated in the program. The preschool teacher in Beaverton participated, as did two kindergarten teachers and a kindergarten helper in a school which most of the children from Murphy Crescent attended. There were nine target children who ranged in age from two to five years.

The program commenced in November, 1996 and concluded in March, 1997.

Implementing the Program: What We Learned
Differing Values

As we worked with the parents in this project, it became apparent that certain values they held which clearly lay outside the domain of literacy had a significant impact on their children's literacy learning. That is, while they clearly valued literacy and wanted their children to be successful at, and to enjoy reading and writing, certain values parents held appeared to constrain the activities in which they engaged their children.

For example, one gets the impression from the literature describing "family

literacy" in mainstream families (e.g. Morrow, 1995; Taylor, 1983) that children are constantly surrounded by literacy events, that they have ready access to the tools of literacy such as paper, pencils, markers, crayons, chalk-
boards, and so forth and that they integrate literacy into their play. In fact,
we suspect that when most of us think of a "literacy rich environment," we
conjure images of a household where literacy artifacts and materials abound,
where the home is littered with literacy.

However, this clearly was not the case for the parents in this program,
and in fact, they often lamented how some of the activities we discussed
(and often modeled) caused their homes to be untidy. For example, during
the sessions on play, we brought in playdough and talked about how children could use playdough to make objects as they played, how they could
make characters from storybooks, and how they could make letters and
numbers and construct words such as their own names out of this medium.
The parents were quite enthused about the activities, and one of them, D
remarked how "I would have never thought about doing this but I can see
how M (her son) would really learn from this." However, as the program
progressed, there was universal concern about how "dirty" playdough was,
how "untidy" the living room became as children left books and paper and
pencils lying around, and "what a mess" chalk made when children write on
a chalkboard. The following journal entries capture these sentiments cogently.

Journal, December 12, 1996

The brainstorming around play was interesting in that D and G talked
about how the untidiness that comes with play really bothers them. D
told of how one of her friends had once remarked to her, "D how do
you manage to keep the house so tidy? The house looks not lived in."
And D reported this without pride. She also commented later, in reference to how a chalkboard is valuable for young children, that G (D's
sister) had "put L's blackboard away" because it was messy.

Journal, January 30, 1997

I picked up on G's comment when we mentioned Junior Boggle [a
word game which we had provided each of the parents to use with
their children]. She mentioned she would have to "get that down again"
(from the attic) as her daughter L "really enjoys it."

Several points warrant mention here. First, on an intellectual level, these
parents appeared to understand how children's literacy could be enhanced
by these materials and activities, and in fact, D was very apologetic about
how she was unable to get past her preoccupation with tidiness. Secondly,
even when literacy materials are provided to the homes and when parents
understand and support their use, children still might have very limited, or
no, access to them.

On occasion, the parents expressed concern about the appropriateness, in terms of gender, of the activities which we discussed. For example, in one session we provided the parents with a booklet of nursery rhymes and a booklet of children's songs, and we talked about how children not only enjoy rhyme and music but also how they learn about language and literacy through them. B commented on how she "loved to sing to B (her child)" but that she had given up singing to him because her friends and relatives had chided her about how this was a "sissy" activity. On another occasion, we discussed how we could help children learn about print by having them participate in grocery shopping.

Journal, January 30, 1997

D remarked that although she takes M shopping, it would never occur to her to point out the product labels and the other print as she goes about picking up groceries. She mentioned that M really likes to play with a small grocery cart that he has and at that point, I told them about how we used to take Terri's [the daughter of one of the authors] small grocery cart along with us and actually let her collect some of the unbreakable and not too heavy items in her cart. D felt that was a good idea but G felt it would be "girlish" for M to take along his cart.

On occasion, some of the parents indicated difficulty finding time to engage their children in literacy activities. G, for example, often complained that there were still too many nights when she did not find time to read to L [her daughter] at bedtime. When we talked about the possibilities for literacy learning afforded by everyday events such as grocery shopping, M suggested that "it would take all day to pick up the groceries if I did that and I just don't have the time." On another occasion when we were discussing how to modify activities and games to meet the needs of the children, D who tended to be very open, commented on the issue of time:

Journal, December 12, 1996

"You know one of the problems with us is we don't take the time to spend with our kids." We talked about quality time and the like but I'm pretty convinced that D is aware of the importance of interacting with children and possibly feels that in the hustle and bustle of her life, she doesn't spend enough time talking with her kids.

Focus on Print

As was indicated earlier, a premise of this program was that literacy learning occurs in various contexts. For example, informed by research which suggests the foundational role of oral language development in children's literacy learning (Snow, 1991), we placed considerable emphasis on oral language and demonstrated and discussed with the parents ways in which they could facilitate their children's language development in enjoyable and engaging ways (e.g. games). Likewise, this program was informed by the extensive literature on the role of play in children's literacy development (Pellegrini, 1993; Stone, 1996). And for example, in one session, we had the parents make puppets to take home to their children. Of course, we also discussed ways in which parents could encourage children to use the puppets (e.g. to dramatize a character, to retell a story, to read a story).

Parents appeared to enjoy the activities such as those just mentioned while we were engaged in them during the sessions, but they appeared not to use them to any significant extent with their children at home. However, when we worked on activities or games which focused on print, they were much more enthused and in the subsequent session(s), would enthusiastically report how they and their children had used the activity or the materials or games. The journal entry for Thursday, January 16, 1997 reflects this dilemma:

> I talked to B [the other facilitator] after the session and I was telling him that I'm concerned that I'm not sure whether parents are understanding the significance of the strategies and activities that focus on creativity, role playing, language development and so forth. For example, G commented very positively about L's development since she has been attending the play group at the center: "She's now colouring inside the lines" That is, they really seem interested in activities that focus on print, words and reading in general but my sense is that they are much less interested in things having to do with more general development. B suggests that this is the message that the popular press (and indeed educators) send out and therefore it is natural that this rather narrow perception of literacy is the one that parents have.

This focus on print and the apparent lack of knowledge or awareness of the other factors in children's literacy development were brought home on several occasions. For example, during one of the sessions in which we discussed how children's oral language development and literacy development are intertwined, several of the parents talked derisively about how talkative their children were. It was also apparent that they were having difficulty understanding the different functions of language.

Journal, November 14, 1996

> I sense that parents . . . don't realize that the kind of talk and thinking engaged in at school is fundamentally different from daily chit-chat about the weather or what one is doing tonight. What is so difficult is that mainstream parents appear to engage their children in decontextualized language (and thinking) almost naturally or intuitively but as Heath's work so cogently shows, this kind of talk is not prevalent in the homes of many parents such as those with whom we are working.

In the sessions devoted to play, we provided parents with a number of games they could use with their children. Included was a home made alphabet game in which children were to match the letters of the alphabet printed on small apples made of construction paper with the letters of the alphabet printed on a tree. In addition, we provided each parent with Junior Boggle, a game in which children can spell words using letters printed on one inch cubes and supported by a series of cards containing words (e.g. car) with an accompanying picture. During the subsequent session, the parents raved about how "wonderful" these games were. And during a debriefing session held at the midpoint of the program and during a session held to review the program at the end, nearly all of the parents indicated that they saw these two particular games as the highlight of the program. Although we had presented a number of other games to the parents (e.g. games involving categorizing objects), little mention was made of them. When probed, parents indicated that they saw these other games as being "okay," but it was obvious that they ascribed far less value to them than they did to those which focused on print.

Program Support for Transfer

One of the factors supporting transfer of learning is program support. The PRINTS program supported transfer of learning in a number of ways. At the start of each session, parents were asked to talk about what was happening in the lives of their children and if they had an opportunity to use any of the literacy activities. Any literacy support tasks which they shared were highly praised by the facilitators. This sharing also provided an opportunity to introduce various literacy-related concepts. One such example is figurative language.

Journal, November 21, 1996

We were discussing how parent and child talk can draw the child's attention to sights and sounds.

M: "Yes, when Jennifer hears the kettle boiling, she says, 'The kettle is crying, Mom.'"

Parents were not told or trained how to engage their children in literacy activities; they became part of the knowing. For example, if an activity dealt with reading a story with children, the parents then read stories to the other parents to become familiar with the techniques. If the activity dealt with grouping or categorizing pictures from flyers, the parents cut out pictures and grouped them. The need for parents to be involved as much as possible during the learning became more obvious as the program progressed. In fact, involvement in an activity determined how long a particular session ran.

Since the ages of the preschool children ranged from 2 to 5, the parents were asked how they would modify an activity for their children. The significance of doing this is underscored by Rogoff (1990), who promotes the issue of intersubjectivity or mutual understanding of those involved in the learning, and who can better understand children than their parents? Two examples from the program support this mutual understanding. One activity, mentioned previously, was based on using an alphabet tree to build more familiarity with the upper and lower case forms of the alphabet. On a drawing of a tree on construction paper were printed the letters in upper case. On cut-out apples the letters were printed in lower case. The child's task was to put the apple on the tree so that the lower and upper case matched. One parent, knowing that her child did not know the upper and lower case forms, printed the upper case form on the reverse side of the apple. The child then engaged in a straight matching task, which she was able to do, and then turned the apple over and discovered the lower case form. On another occasion, after the parents were asked how they might change an activity to meet their children's level of maturity, one parent of a three year old said, "She'll grow into it." When asked what she meant, she explained that her little girl could not meaningfully participate in the activity then, but when she had reached that level of maturity, the parent would be familiar with the activity and could then involve her. According to Wood, Wood, and Middleton (1978), parents who are sensitive to the needs and abilities of their children and who structure activities accordingly are more likely to foster increased cognitive competence that are parents who do not show such sensitivity.

As indicated earlier, there were 13 sessions for PRINTS. The optimal length of an early literacy intervention program for parents is unknown. Would the same degree of transfer have taken place with 8 sessions or 18 sessions? Vygotsky's concept of zone of proximal development may help us understand the impact of session length on parents' learning and subsequent transfer. The facilitator is a key factor in supporting parents' learning, a point noted by Grimes and Davies (1997) in their study. The question is how long constitutes optimal time for withdrawal of support? As long as there is explanation, involvement, support, and positive feedback by facilitators, parents may learn and promote transfer. But if this is withdrawn too soon, parents may not have reached the level of confidence and independence necessary to become effective facilitators with their children.

The 13 sessions of PRINTS were spaced so that after two consecutive sessions addressing a context (for example, play), there was then a break of a week to give parents an opportunity to implement what had been learned. This goal was made explicit to the parents. Certainly, time is of the essence in promoting transfer.

Participants and Transfer

A second factor affecting the transfer of learning are the participants themselves. While the nine caregivers in the PRINTS study may be considered homogeneous in terms of socioeconomic status, education level, opportunity, and so forth, this was far from the truth. The parents from the two communities were very different on several dimensions. But even within each Centre, there were unique differences among parents. Roskos' (1997) ecocultural theory alerts us to the many micro-differences within apparent similarities. On a micro level, a Journal entry of December 12, 1997 provides an example.

> J: "D (her husband) can never get enough reading. He reads the books so quickly and then he is gone back to the library for more. All his family are bookworms. Before I got married when I would go to his house, they were all reading, his mother, and brother and sisters."
>
> C: "You wouldn't get J (her husband) to read if you paid him."
>
> K: "W (her partner) wouldn't be caught dead with a book."

The parents (all mothers/grandmothers) were also very busy. Because they were unemployed did not mean they were not involved. Many of them were involved in volunteer activities in the centre and in the community. In one centre, all of the parents from the PRINTS program had enrolled in a GED program. They also had their housework and cooking. And as one parent reported, in order to pay her power bill, she had to take three buses which was almost a full day affair. It could also be that there was not a tradition for making time for literacy related activities with young children to the same extent as occurs in middle and upper class homes. At one point, the facilitators discussed whether a discussion on time management would be appropriate so that parents could find more time to engage in these activities with their children.

Expectations set up in children are also crucial. Because of the enthusiasm for PRINTS on the part of some parents, the children were expected to look forward to the materials and activities which the parents brought home.

> Journal, February 13, 1997
>
> (J had missed the previous session.)
>
> J: " I was really upset that I had to miss the last session. But tonight A (J's daughter) said, 'Mom you're not going to miss PRINTS tonight. I want to see what you get.'"

The attitude or bias of the facilitator is also crucial in affecting transfer. Have facilitators already acquired a bias towards lower socioeconomic parents based on the prominence of this factor in the literature? Does the labeling of these parents produce a Pygmalion effect in working with them? From the accepted descriptors, the parents who participated in the PRINTS project could be labeled lower socioeconomic. But the parents did not perceive themselves as operating within this label. They did not feel that different from many others who were not so labelled and considered that under their circumstances, they were doing very well. They had not accepted that their expectations for themselves or their children were closed, and they were eager to seize any opportunity to provide a better future for both. Unless the expectations for them by the facilitator matched their own expectations, transfer may not be effectively promoted.

Congruency of Environmental Conditions

The degree of transfer depends to some extent on the distance from habitual to established behaviour. Intervention, by its very nature, is meant to interrupt habitual behaviour. Hannon (1993) points out that if the task does not come "naturally" to the parents, and the parents view it as an interruption in their lives, it may not lead to the intended outcome. An often repeated reason by the parents for why an activity had not been engaged in with the children was that there was not enough time; they just couldn't get around to it; it was not part of their normal routine. For example, the goal of unpacking groceries was to get them on the shelves and not to engage the children in sorting and categorizing.

Hannon (1995) discusses how context congruency and intended outcomes interact. He points out that the setting in which the program for parents is held may be a key factor. Whether parents are coached in their homes, as in the Neuman and Gallagher (1994) study, in a community centre setting, as in the case of PRINTS, or in a school setting, will make a difference as to what kind of learning is valued for transfer.

Transfer is also dependent on the meaningfulness of the activities in which the children are expected to engage. Post office play, for example, may not be meaningful to a large segment of the population who have never seen a post office nor a mail carrier, but who go a metal box near the corner store to get their mail. If they wish to purchase stamps, they can do so at discount rates at the drug store.

When books, games, supplies, etc., are no longer made available, how does the nature of the interaction between children and parents change? Do the parents regress to a former habitual state? In the case of PRINTS, a playtime group, through federal funding operated at the centres. At one of the centres, the parents who were involved in PRINTS were also involved in the playtime program. Many of the ideas introduced in PRINTS were incorporated in this program, especially the purchase of children's books and the involvement of the children with these.

The maintenance or sustainability of the program was frequently mentioned by one of the PRINTS advisory committee members. Perhaps university academics are the most inappropriate people to initiate and facilitate early literacy programs. Their goal is usually to "try out" something. When the "try out" time is passed, the facilitators and the project are gone. There is no ownership of the program on the part of the parents and the community, regardless of the degree to which the parents were involved. The parents know this, and it no doubt affects the transfer of learning. In the case of PRINTS, one group of parents lobbied for its continuance, promoted the program among other parents, and provided a list of parents who would participate. In order to maintain contact with the initial group, one session was planned in which these came together to talk about what was continuing to happen in the literacy lives of their children.

Providing other educational access for the parents encourages the sustainability of learning. By providing opportunity for the parents to improve their own educational standards, they are more likely to value education for themselves and for their children. In the case of one centre, a GED program was offered through the centre and all parents enrolled, each being very supportive of the others. However, a drawback with adult education programs is the model of learning to which parents are exposed. If the program relies on memorization of material to pass exams, which was the case with the program in which the parents in this project were involved, then this type of interaction may easily be incorporated into the parents' schemas for school learning and which they may habitually impose on their children.

Measures

What should be measured, when and how? This is no easy matter. University personnel tend to devise neat, cut-and-dried assessment measures, especially for children's learning. These often defy the concept of environmental context congruency. Perhaps it is not so much the actual concept learned or strategy implemented by parents or children, but the shift in schema, the change in values, the openness to new ideas, and the willingness to take chances, that may be important. Because parents do not immediately engage their children in a particular activity does not mean that they do not value it or that it does not eventually become a part of their repertoire of literacy activities. Towards the end of PRINTS program, parents were presented with a list of the 34 activities that had been explored and shared with them. They were asked for their help in implementing PRINTS again by choosing those activities which should be continued and those which should be deleted. All parents of both centres maintained that all the activities were important and should be kept.

Journal, February 27, 1997

K: "Oh, keep them all. They're all important. It's just that we did not get around to doing them all yet. But I can see how they are all valuable."

Journals by the facilitator (and/or by the parents) tend to provide a more holistic understanding of the nature of transfer. Observation is also important in this regard. Observation by one of the facilitators with the playtime group indicated a number of materials and strategies that were identical to those introduced during the PRINTS program. Talk and sharing by the parents also provide many insights.

Journal, February 6, 1997

After Environmental Print had been introduced.

K: (who had a four-month-old baby and a three-year old). "I was getting D's food ready when I noticed GERBER on the jar and I said to G, 'Look, G, it begins the same as your name; it's a G.'"

The unfortunate part of measures of learning is that the results of the measure may be interpreted without considering the total experience from which they arose. A cause-effect relationship may be inferred when it does not exist, or the results may focus educators on factors that, in actual fact, are no more important than others. Measuring transfer of learning in an early literacy program is walking a fine line between the evaluator's biases and the reality of the situation.

Summary and Conclusion

The need for family literacy programs to reflect a social-contextual orientation was an overarching principle of PRINTS, a principle supported by Auerbach (1989). That is, we attempted to make PRINTS meaningful and purposeful and functional in the lives of the families with whom we worked. And while the authors who facilitated the program came from working class backgrounds that in many ways approximated those of the families in the PRINTS program, it appeared that some of the strategies, materials and activities which we introduced were incongruent with the values held by the participants.

Furthermore, while transfer of learning is a significant issue in the implementation of early literacy programs, it is far from being a simple issue. How the program is implemented has implications for how transfer is measured, and how transfer is measured has many implications for describing the success or failure of the program.

Our experiences in implementing this program are consistent with research (e.g. Auerbach, 1995) which suggests that family literacy is a very complex area which needs careful scrutiny, thought, and analyses. This is especially so in light of the proliferation of family literacy programs despite a rather limited research base and the development of programs with little consideration for the socio-cultural context in which they are to be implemented (Auerbach, 1989). Furthermore, suggestions are emanating from some quarters that family literacy programs are "the solution" to "the literacy crisis" and a means of insuring the economic competitiveness of countries such as the United States and Canada (Auerbach, 1997). Indeed, until the complexity and the potentiality of family literacy programs are further understood, it seems prudent for those involved in such programs to have reasonable expectations as to what they can achieve.

References

Auerbach, E. (1997, May). *The rhetoric of family literacy: Reading between the lines*. Paper presented at the annual conference of the International Reading Association, Atlanta, GA.

Auerbach, E, (1995). Deconstructing the discourse of strengths in family literacy. *Journal of Literacy Behaviour, 27,* 643-666.

Auerbach, E. (1989). Toward a social-contextual approach to family literacy. *Harvard Educational Review, 59,* 165-181.

Fagan, W. T., Anderson, J., & Cronin, M. (1997, March). *Parents as copartners, learners, and helpers in early literacy development in two low income community centers*. Paper presented at the American Educational Research Association Annual Meeting, Chicago, IL.

Grimes, J., & Davies, C. (1997, March). *Understanding partnership with parents: Does the ORIM framework help?* Paper presented at the American Education Research Association Annual Meeting, Chicago, IL

Hannon, P. (1995). *Literacy, home and school: Research and practice in teaching literacy with parents*. London: The Falmer Press.

Hannon, P. (1993). Intergenerational literacy intervention: Possibilities and problems. *Viewpoints,#15, Family Literacy* (pp. 6-9). London: ALBSU.

Morrow, L. M. (1993). *Literacy development in the early years: Helping children read and write*. Boston: Allyn and Bacon.

Neuman, S. B., & Gallagher, P. (1994). Joining together in literacy learning: Teenage mothers and children. *Reading Research Quarterly, 29,* 382-401.

Pellegrini, A. (1993). Ten years after: A reexamination of symbolic play and literacy research. *Reading Research Quarterly, 28,* 162-175.

Rogoff, B. (1990). *Apprenticeship in thinking: Cognitive development in social context*. New York: Oxford University Press.

Roskos, K. (1997, March). *An ecocultural view of early literacy learning*. Paper presented at the American Education Research Association Annual Meeting, Chicago.

Snow, C. E. (1991). The theoretical basis for relationship between language and literacy development. *Journal of Research in Childhood Education, 6,* 5-10.

Stone, S. J. (1993). Collaborative literacy learning during sociodramatic play in a multiage (K-2) primary classroom. *Journal of Research in Childhood Education, 10,* 123-133.

Taylor, D. (1983). F*amily literacy: Young children learning to read and write*. Exeter, NH: Heinemann.

Wood, D., Wood, H. A., & Middleton, D. J. (1978). An experimental evaluation of four face-to-face teaching strategies. *International Journal of Behavioral Development, 1,* 131-147.

COLLEGIALITY IN HIGHER EDUCATION: TAKING THE RISK AND MAKING IT WORK

Scott Popplewell
Linda Martin
Sherry Kragler
Valerie Hall
Ball State University

Abstract

Collegiality has been a topic of discussion in education for decades. However, collegial issues in higher education have largely been ignored. Therefore, the purpose of this research was to fully describe collegial relationships in higher education. Qualitative data (journal entries, surveys, interviews) were collected. From this data, two main themes emerged: the characteristics of collegial relationships (compatibility, commitment, and communication), and the benefits of collegiality (quality, productivity, and personal growth) in higher education.

Collegiality, a professional relationship built on sharing, is not a new concept. According to Finkelstein (1981), collegiality is a complex phenomenon involving numerous types of interaction; collaboration is one example. For some time, researchers have known that working in collaboration creates rich learning experiences for all members of a team (Dewey, 1933; Vygotsky, 1978). Within the educational setting alone, different groups of individuals collaborate for various reasons. Students learn to work in teams to complete a task (Atwell, 1987; Routman, 1991; Slavin, 1983). Teachers collaborate to plan and to implement instruction (Little, 1984; Poole, 1995) and to form professional discussion groups in which to learn and to share new information in education (Jaeger, 1996). Teachers and administrators work collaboratively to make curricular and instructional decisions (Little, 1984; Poole, 1995). In addition, education specialists, such as school psychologists and reading specialists, work with teachers to make critical decisions about children (Villaume, Worden, Williams, Hopkins, & Rosenblatt, 1994).

With all the emphasis on collaboration, it is surprising that few have considered the value of collegiality in higher education facilities. In fact, when comparing the collegial interaction of faculty members in two colleges and a Ph.D.-granting university, Finkelstein (1981) found collegial relationships to be fewer in the Ph.D.-granting university that required research and publications. Intellectual isolation appears to be the pattern. Since little is known about how collegiality works in higher education, it is imperative to examine the dynamics of this phenomenon.

Purpose

The purpose of this research project was to fully describe collegial relationships in higher education. The guiding research questions were threefold: a) What is the process in working in collegial relationships? b) How do these relationships function? c) What are the benefits of working with colleagues?

Methodology
Theoretical Perspective

The theoretical perspective for this study is social interactionism. "Social interactionists understand social reality as a complex network of interacting persons, who symbolically interpret their acting in the social world" (Van Manen, 1990, p. 186). As professors work together, they share differing opinions and adjust their thinking based on new interpretations gathered from their social interactions. Their understandings are expanded and refined through group interchanges.

To build collegial relationships, teams develop various ways of working together. Therefore, the first guiding question is designed to determine the process of how each team member contributes during the social interaction to accomplish the goals set by a team. Understanding the way colleagues interact is important for assisting others in building collegial relationships. Thus, the second question is intended to gather information useful to other potential teams. Many benefits may result from these team efforts which motivate researchers to continue to work together. From the third question, numerous benefits of working with colleagues were generated. Together, responses to these questions provided a general picture of collegiality.

Participants

In the conception of this study, two literacy professors, working together for the first time at a midwestern university, kept journals to describe the collaborative process as they generated ideas for their classroom instruction.

The journal entries supplied rich details that stimulated additional thoughts and discussion. With time, the information found in the journals stimulated the beginning of this research project.

The professors' research training was very different. One conducted research predominantly through a quantitative approach while the other professor was trained to use a qualitative approach. Despite their divergent paradigm backgrounds, the professors were amazed at the positive effects of their working efforts. The strength of their collaboration was the common desire to improve their instruction.

Over time, two more literacy professors from the same university were brought into the project. They shared the workload by assisting with the data collection and analysis, which increased productivity. Because these professors were not involved in the study previously, their input added depth to the analysis of the data.

As the four colleagues worked together, it was determined that it would be valuable to confer with literacy professors who were known to work with others to publish and present their research. Surveys were sent to 50 literacy professors who were purposively selected. Pseudonyms were used to refer to the respondents in the presentation of the data.

Researcher Role

The researchers were participant observers in this study as they examined collegiality through various data sources. Patton (1990) describes the participant observer as the "researcher [who] makes firsthand observations of activities and interactions, sometimes, engaging personally in those activities" (p. 10). The two professors who began the study working together on a different project found that collegiality was an untapped resource. "People can move from one society or social setting to another where people are using different symbols. Without realizing it they become participant observers and interviewers; before much time passes, they have acquired the meanings of the new cultural scene" (Spradley, 1979, pp. 155-156). As Spradley asserted, without realizing it, these researchers had become participant observers. The four literacy professors had worked together on several projects and decided to compare their own experiences with those of other researchers.

Data Collection

Various data sources provided triangulation to support the results of the research. Initially, two college professors working together for the first time kept reflective journals over a six-month period to record processes and reactions to their collaborative efforts while planning an extensive research project.

Following the initial data collection of the two professors developing this study about collegiality, additional information was gathered from a survey that had been field tested and refined. The original survey of three questions was sent to three professors. The questions were:

1. What processes are involved in collaboration?
2. What factors support collaboration?
3. What are benefits of collaboration?

From the long, detailed responses generated, it was determined that the questions needed to be more specific to narrow the discussion. The revised survey was sent to purposively selected university literacy professors.

The participants were encouraged to describe different aspects of successful collegial relationships. The questions from the survey are listed below:

1. List factors that have made your collaborative relationships successful.
2. List steps that you follow in working with your partner (s).
3. List the benefits of your collaborative work as compared to your individual projects.
4. Why do you collaborate?
5. Briefly state how you determine who is first author of each article.

Follow-up surveys were sent to those who had not responded to the original survey. Of the 50 surveys, 23 were completed.

Finally, over the course of a year, unstructured interviews were conducted with a minimum of 20 literacy professors. "Ethnographers often gather most of their data through participant observation and many casual, friendly conversations. They may interview people without their awareness, merely carrying on a friendly conversation while introducing a few ethnographic questions" (Spradley, 1979, p. 58). Through professional conversations about collegiality, substantiating data were gathered.

Data Analysis

Using the constant comparative method of analysis (Glaser & Strauss, 1967), the reflective journals were examined for patterns in the recorded responses. Interrater reliability was obtained by two readers of the journals. From this initial examination of the journal entries, themes emerged that described how these colleagues successfully collaborated over the course of months as a research plan unfolded. Themes from the analysis of the journal entries included the importance of: shared beliefs, trust, similar work habits, shared work load, and similar interests.

Following analysis of the journal entries, four colleagues at a midwestern university analyzed the responses to the surveys and the interviews. Open coding was conducted to reveal all possible themes in the data. These themes included: caring, respect, expectations, balanced effort, trust, common goals and interests, dependability, flexibility, compatibility, better quality, community, productivity, energy, fun, satisfaction, division of labor, community, working on parts you like, compensate for weaknesses, and feedback. Next, selective coding resulted in the collapsing of categories into general themes that emerged from the data (Strauss, 1987). The many themes could be organized into two broad categories: characteristics and benefits. The themes that were similar were merged to create sub-categories.

Results

Analysis of the surveys revealed two general themes in the data the respondents considered important for successful collegial relationships in higher education: a) the characteristics that describe collegial relationships and b) the benefits of university professors working with colleagues. Within these two general themes, topics were collapsed into categories relating to collegial issues in higher education. Since the themes identified previously from the journal entries were similar to those identified in the surveys, they were collapsed within the data. Results of these analyses are seen in the Figure 1. Each of the general themes with the categories is described separately.

Characteristics of Collegial Relationships

Themes the respondents considered important characteristics of collegial relationships were collapsed into three sub-categories: compatibility, commitment, and communication. These are described with relating issues. The issues are italicized to show how they relate to the sub-category.

Compatibility Respondents described compatibility as the importance of team members having similar *philosophies*, *interests*, and *goals*. Of these, similar philosophies was considered by respondents to be the most important quality in forming collegial relationships. However, it was also recognized that, while there may be similar thinking about topics, not everyone has to agree about all issues related to the topic. As Sharon noted, "While having similar approaches to topics, it is not always necessary to have full agreement on all issues related to the topic, nor is it necessary to have similar work styles." Some disagreement improves the quality of the work, but a similar basic philosophy is essential.

Commitment. In addition to compatibility, respondents noted throughout the data the importance of team members having a mutual commitment to completing a project successfully. Hence, members of a team must be willing to follow through with their individual assigned tasks to a project. Mutual *trust* in a colleague's commitment is critical. *Balancing the workload* so that all team members feel that they are equally contributing to a project will effect individuals' commitment to its completion. *Dependability* is con-

Figure 1. The Characteristics and Benefits of Collegial Relationships in Higher Education

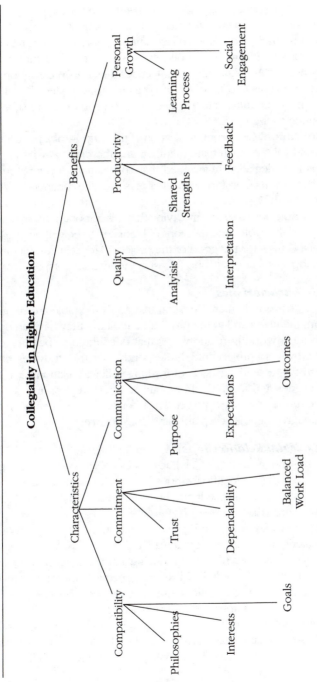

sidered an important characteristic. Dorothy stated, "One of the most important factors in successful collaboration is to be able to trust collaborators to follow through on their end of the collaboration." Therefore, commitment, not only to a project, but to one's colleagues is essential in completing a project. Kelly noted, "Accountability to my colleagues puts pressure on me to accomplish the goals and tasks." Consequently, for a collegial relationship to function successfully, each member must be committed to substantially contributing to the work.

Communication. Clear communication of the *purpose* of a project, the *expectations* and roles of each team member, and the *outcomes* are important first steps in collegiality. Julie noted that collegiality "develops out of long term discussions/relationships with other persons." She continued, "When team members mesh, it seems natural to do work together, and collaboration occurs." Bonnie added to this by saying that it is important for individuals to "understand their roles and divisions of labor and to be willing to adapt individual perspectives for the good of the project." Hence, team members need to share opinions honestly and to respect individual perspectives.

Summary of Characteristics

In essence, teams in higher education that are compatible are committed to the team members and to the project. In addition, they have an open dialogue and form working relationships that encourage respect for one another; trust grows as a project unfolds. Respondents in this study described respect and trust as essential aspects of forming collegial relationships. Respect for colleagues and for their efforts builds a positive working climate and keeps the momentum of a project. Trust between team members also assures that disagreement is acceptable and constructive.

Benefits of Collegial Relationships

Beyond the understanding of characteristics of a successful collegial relationship, respondents identified various benefits for continuing team efforts. These factors were collapsed into three categories: quality, productivity, and personal growth.

Quality. Collegiality was seen by respondents in this study to produce work with greater quality than work that was completed in isolation. Consistently, these efforts were described as producing a much richer *analysis* and *interpretation* of data. Jerry noted, "Ideas are generated and energy levels seem to be higher than working alone. Multiple perspectives create richer data." Daniel added, "I am able to develop ideas that I, alone, could never develop." Sarah contributed, "I collaborate because of the synergy that develops, which is energizing and which more often leads to a product that's bigger than the sum of its parts." Therefore, these respondents believe that higher quality work is produced by team efforts rather than work that is completed individually.

Productivity. Complex research topics are more likely to be success-fully completed because of the *shared strengths* offered by collaborators and the divided work load. As Jennifer stated, "You get the two-heads-are-better-than-one thing, many times over. Good critics give you invaluable *feedback*." Patricia stated, "We can tackle larger projects." Productivity is especially im-portant because of the pressure on university faculty to publish and to present research at conferences. Bergen and Connelly (1988) report a project at the Pittsburg State University in Kansas that promoted collegiality. Faculty mem-bers in this institution aided and supported their new colleagues' research efforts by acting as mentors to guide their professional development and growth.

Personal Growth. Respondents in this study described collegial efforts as a personal learning process; that is, as a means to continue to learn from one another. Stacey stated, "Collaboration allows groups of people to stimu-late each others' thinking and practice, and in so doing, this benefits more individuals outside the collaborative group." Rachel responded, "I learn new ways of knowing." Personal satisfaction and social engagement adds to the professional experience. Georgia stated, "Collaboration is usually more en-joyable. It strengthens and builds relationships. Working alone can be isolat-ing." Pollicino's (1996) findings support these data. Pollicino (1996) investi-gated different factors that effect university faculty satisfaction, and found collegiality was the strongest.

Summary of Benefits

Colleagues who worked together stressed several benefits. They felt they were sharing their strengths to create a quality product. Because of multiple perspectives, the final product displayed the strengths of all contributors. Also, through social engagement, respondents felt they were experiencing per-sonal growth. Thus, collegial relationships are mutually beneficial.

Limitations

Although the results of the study clearly indicate the value of collegiality in higher education, some limitations do exist. The small number who re-sponded to the survey (23 literacy professors) may not be representative of professors who work in collegial relationships. A greater number of partici-pants may have yielded more information about how collegial relationships are formed and how they work successfully. In addition, surveying literacy professors who choose to work alone may add insights into why collegial relationships do not always work. Finally, structured, focused interviews may have added depth to the interpretation of the data.

Conclusion

In this study, important topics and issues that affect successful collegial working relationships among literacy professors are described. The literacy professors discussed characteristics of collegiality and the many benefits from working with others on projects. Learning about the characteristics and benefits that make collaborations function well can assist all professors as they plan and implement research together. Collegial relationships are worth pursuing at all levels of education.

References

Atwell, N. (1987). *In the middle*. Portsmouth, NH: Heinemann.

Bergen, D., & Connelly, J. (1988). The collegial research mentor project: A model for faculty research and scholarship development. *Career Planning and Adult Development Journal, 4* (2), 3-8.

Dewey, J. (1933). *How we think*. Boston: D. D. Heath.

Finkelstein, M. (April, 1981). *The dimensions of colleagueship among college and university faculty*. Paper presented at the annual meeting of the American Educational Research Association, Los Angeles, CA.

Glaser, B., & Strauss, A. (1967). *The discovery of grounded theory: Strategies for qualitative research*. Chicago: Aldine Publishers.

Jaeger, E. L. (1996). The reading specialist as collaborative consultant, *The Reading Teacher, 49*(8), 622-629.

Little, J. W. (1982). Norms of collegiality and experimentation: Workplace conditions of school success. *American Educational Research Journal, 19*(3), 325-340.

Patton, M. Q. (1990). *Qualitative evaluation and research methods* (2nd ed.). Newbury Park, CA: Sage Publishing.

Pollicino, E. (1996). *Faculty satisfaction with institutional support as a complex concept: Collegiality, workload, autonomy.* (ERIC Document Reproduction Service No. 394 428)

Poole, W. (April, 1995). *Reconstructing the teacher-administrator relationship to achieve systemic change*. Paper presented at the annual meeting of the American Educational Research Association, San Francisco, CA.

Routman, R. (1991). *Invitations*. Portsmouth, NH: Heinemann.

Slavin, R. (1983). *Cooperative learning*. New York: Longman.

Spradley, J. P. (1979). *The ethnographic interview*. Fort Worth: TX: Holt, Rinehart and Winston, Inc.

Strauss, A. L. (1987). *Qualitative analysis for social scientists*. Cambridge, England: Cambridge University Press.

Villaume, S. K., Worden, T., Williams, S., Hopkins, L, & Rosenblatt, C. (1994). Five teachers in search of a discussion, *The Reading Teacher, 47*(6), 480-487.

Vygotsky, L. (1978). *The mind in society: The development of higher psychological processes*. Cambridge, MA: Harvard University Press.

THE INFLUENCE OF PORTFOLIO SELECTION ON REFLECTIVE THINKING

Diane M. Truscott

Buffalo State College (SUNY)

Barbara J. Walker

Oklahoma State University

Abstract

Portfolios can offer an opportunity for critical reflection. This study looked at the kind of artifacts student teachers selected for their cumulative portfolio, which artifacts they viewed a most important in describing them as a teacher, and which types of reflective thinking the artifacts represented. Participants were 63 undergraduate student teachers from various disciplines (elementary, secondary, and special education). Results indicated that the majority of students (95%) included artifacts that involved technical reflection. Experiential-based items like implemented lesson plans were included by the vast majority of students (88%) as well. Additionally, many student teachers (44%) stated that the Philosophy Toward Teaching Essay, which involved conceptual and critical reflection, was the most important item in describing them as a teacher. Thus, despite the opportunity for critical reflection, student teachers appear to focus on technical skills.

Theoretical Perspective

As teachers, reflective thinking is the cornerstone of our continuing development. A reflective teacher "inquires into his or her thinking and practice with an eye toward making improvements" (Bullough & Gitlin, 1994, p. 24). It is through reflectivity that we continue to expand our own knowledge of teaching and learning. Reflection occurs when we examine and think about our teaching by asking critical questions and analyzing our theory and practice. Reflectivity involves " . . . developing both . . . *orientations* (toward open-mindedness, responsibility, and whole-heartedness) and *skills* (of keen observation and reasoned analysis)" (Zeichner & Liston, 1987, p. 24). Thus, we think not only about the actual event of teaching, but also we crosscheck our practice with our theories. As we analyze our self-observations, we realize that our practice comes from a complex network of knowledge and beliefs and that this network undergerds our instructional decision-making. As teacher educators, we need to provide opportunities for reflectivity throughout the teacher education program.

Promoting Reflectivity in Teacher Education

Research in promoting reflective thinking in teacher education programs suggests that reflectivity is more evident when structured, supported opportunities are provided. Guillaume & Rudney (1993) report that student teachers often reflect upon and question their thoughts and practices when given specific activities which guide the reflective process. In this study, they used dialogue journals to provide this guidance. Walker and Ramesth (1993) asked preservice teachers to write reflective statements after they taught. They found that the preservice teachers could, in fact, connect statements revealing the dynamic relationships among instructional variables when asked to reflect about their instruction. Risko (1995) has suggested using highly participatory techniques such as observation, discussion and reflection of videotaped classroom instruction to encourage preservice teacher development. Others have recommended providing opportunities to teach and reflect in small discussion groups (Florio-Ruane & Lensmire, 1990) as an effective way to develop teachers' knowledge and reflection about teaching. Pultorak (1993) also found that structured procedures incorporated during student teaching produced reflective thinking across many levels of sophistication. Korthagen (1992) describes results of redesigning student teaching seminars in order to stimulate teachers to reflect on their practice and to promote cognitive change. Specific techniques were used during seminars to help preservice teachers begin to see the relationship between theoretical perspectives, beliefs, educational goals and means to achieve those goals. This study reported growth in student reflectivity.

As pre-service teachers move through a teacher education program, Black and Ammon (1992) suggest that they progress through stages of development that increasingly involve reflective thinking. From their studies, it is evident that as preservice teachers are developing pedagogical content knowledge, they are also developing their own thinking by reflecting on both theory and practice. Teacher education programs that encourage reflective teaching prepare students to view knowledge and situations as problematic rather than certain, and they emphasize reflecting on theories and practice rather than achieving competence in technical skills.

Using Portfolios in Teacher Education

Teacher educators have begun examining the use of portfolios as a means of encouraging reflective thinking that moves beyond the view of teaching as achieving competence in technical skills. Portfolios document and provide a means of evaluating learning using multiple contexts (education courses, field experiences, student teaching, . . .) in a systematic fashion (Tierney, Carter, & Desai, 1991). They are a collection of work through which preservice students can reflect on, take ownership of and evaluate their own progress as they develop professional competence. In doing so, preservice teachers begin to integrate ideas from multiple theoretical perspectives into a personal philosophy of teaching. Portfolios, then, can lead to "a more integrated stance in which preservice students are comfortable creating their own knowledge" (Christensen & Walker, 1992, p. 63) and can provide ". . . a connection to the contexts and personal histories of real teaching and make it possible to document the unfolding of both teaching and learning over time" (Wolf, 1991, p. 129). By attaching a reflective statement describing what the artifact shows about their development, preservice teachers rethink their understanding of teaching. Thus, the selected artifacts show how the preservice teachers view their own learning. In doing so, the focus of the portfolio is on the students' reflection rather than on competence in a technical skill.

By deciding what to include in their portfolio, preservice teachers analyze and reflect on the artifacts they have created, evaluating each piece as to its contribution to their development as a teacher. Oropallo and Gomez (1996) found that as preservice teachers constructed their portfolio, reflection was critical. To encourage the reflective process, it was important that the preservice teachers made the decisions regarding the contents of their portfolio. Thus, creating a portfolio representative of the entire teacher education program may lead to a reflective stance that ties together both educational theories and practice into a coherent whole. As preservice teachers select the artifacts and reflect on themselves as teachers, their conceptualization of teaching may be enhanced. In fact, the types of portfolio artifacts could represent opportunities for reflective thinking. Thus, this study was designed to examine the types of portfolio artifacts included in a teacher education portfolio as representative opportunities for reflective thinking. Specifically, we posed three questions:

1. What kind of artifacts would student teachers select for their cumulative portfolio?

2. Which artifacts would the student teachers view most important in describing them as a teacher?

3. What types of reflective thinking would these artifacts represent?

Method

Participants were 63 undergraduate education majors from various disciplines (elementary, secondary, and special education) enrolled in student teaching and a monthly seminar. As part of the seminar, students compiled a teaching portfolio. Various approaches to assembling a portfolio were presented. The Director of Student Teaching emphasized a presentation portfolio, while other invited guests presented concepts related to a cumulative portfolio of work across time. All teacher educators emphasized being reflective and selective. One instructor shared reflective statements from her personal portfolio; another emphasized reflecting on teaching standards and putting items that responded to these standards. Responses to questions from student teachers always reiterated being reflective and selective about their portfolio artifacts. These discussions were held in the large group rather than small groups, and student teachers were not required to bring an artifact to class and practice reflecting on it. Although artifacts were to have a reflection statement, some students did not include these on all artifacts.

At the end of the seminar, students presented their portfolio to their classmates, principals from surrounding schools, and education professors. At the end of the class, which was their last hour of their college education, the students completed the questionnaire which included categories of possible artifacts they might have included in their portfolio. The questionnaire is found as Appendix A. Of the 63 participants, only 43 answered the last three questions which required them to think again about their artifact selection. Since this was the last activity of their college education, 20 students just didn't answer the questions that asked them to reflect on what was the most important item in the portfolio as well as why it was important. The 43 that did respond became the pool of responses analyzed. Frequency counts and corresponding percentages were calculated across categories and within each category.

The type of portfolio artifact included, or excluded, was analyzed for the level of reflectivity that it could promote. Van Manen's (1977) three levels of reflectivity referenced frequently in literature dealing with levels of reflectivity (Core & Zeichner, 1991; Pultorak, 1993) provided the framework to ground this analysis. The first level is *technical* rationality where the focus is on the efficient and effective application of educational knowledge for the purposes of attaining ends; an emphasis is placed on technique and doing it right. This level of reflection is not concerned with the ends but rather proficiency in the means. Examples of portfolio artifacts that focus on the technical are letters of reference, a resume, lesson plans, and teaching units. The second level, *conceptual* reflectivity, addresses assumptions and predispositions involved in the actions student teachers take to achieve the desired outcomes, thus understanding theory relative to practice. Portfolio artifacts that may support this level of reflection include teaching narratives, position papers, lesson reflections that integrate one's personal philosophy on teaching, classroom observations, etc.. The third level is *critical* reflection. Here, the teaching process itself (ends and means) and the classroom, school, and societal contexts are considered. In this type of reflection the "teachers look critically at the ethical basis for what happens in the classroom" (Leland, Harste, & Youssef, 1997, p. 387). Some examples of artifacts that lend themselves to this type of reflective thinking include analysis of observations across classrooms, interviews, child study projects, and excerpts from dialogue journals.

Results

To answer question 1, we computed the percentage of students who included artifacts in each category (See Figure 1). The large majority of students (95%) included *personal data* in their portfolio such as letters of reference and resumes. *Experiential-based* items, lesson plans and classroom observations, were included by the vast majority of students (88%) as well. *Curriculum-based* projects (72%), including thematic and integrated units, and *writing assignments* from various courses (60%) were selected for inclusion in the portfolio by a large proportion of students. Other items selected were *out-of profession items* (53%) such as songs, awards; *class handouts*

Figure 1. Percentage of Student Selections by Category of Portfolio Artifacts

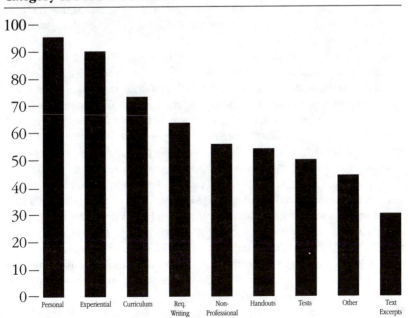

(51%); *formal course assessments* (44%); and *excerpts from textbooks* (28%). Only three portfolio items were "highly recommended" for inclusion by the professor for the seminar: a resume, letters of reference, and a Philosophy Toward Teaching paper. No item was required, but it appears the student teachers perceived the "highly recommended" items as required. All portfolio items were self-selected by the student teachers.

We further analyzed the specificity of the artifacts reported under each category. Frequencies or the percentage of artifacts were calculated using the total number of artifacts reported for that category. Lesson plans were the most frequently included experiential-based item (56%). Thematic units (63%) and content units (34%) were the main type of item selected as a curriculum-based project. Formal assessments that were included were essay (38%) or objective (33%) examinations from previous courses. An academic paper describing the student's philosophy toward teaching served as the main illustration of the assigned writing category (48%). Most of the samples in the personal data were references (27%), resumes (27%), and evaluations (27%) from student teaching supervisors. Awards (48%) represented the majority of items in the out of profession category and the miscellaneous category reported the use of personal photographs (55%).

To answer question 2, we analyzed the responses to the question, "Which item is most important in describing you as a teacher?" Table 2 lists in rank order the items selected by student teachers. Little variability was observed in this response. The majority of student teachers (44%) stated that the Philosophy Toward Teaching statement was the most important item, with lesson plans ranking second (14%).

To answer question 3, we used Van Manen's (1977) three levels of reflection to examine the types of opportunities student teachers had to reflect on based on the items they selected to include in their portfolio. Table 3 lists each category that was part of the end of the course questionnaire by rank order. It specifies under each category the most frequently included artifacts within that category. Artifacts were then independently analyzed by the two researchers to determine which level of reflectivity it fostered. Inter-rater agreement was 100% for 5 out of 8 categories. Consensus was reached on the three remaining categories (curriculum-based units, formal assessment, and excerpts from texts) resulting in qualifiers added to the coding scheme. For example, one rater considered curriculum-based units *technical* in nature, while the second rater viewed them as *conceptual*. Agreement was reached that while instructional units typically concentrate on demonstration of lesson design, if the unit included an illustration that the unit was based on theoretical principles and developmentally appropriate practices, it also represents conceptual understandings. Similarly, qualifiers were placed for the formal assessment and text excerpt categories. This requires an analysis

Table 1. Examples of Categories and Frequency of Portofio Artifacts

Experiential-Based	
Lesson Plans	56%
Teacher-Made Tests	13
Classroom Observations	11
Student Projects	8
Classroom Materials	7
Pictures	3
Curriculum-Based	
Thematic Units	63%
Units	34
Adapted Instruction	3
Formal Assessment	
Essay Exam	38%
Objective Exam	33
Short Answer Exam	14
Worksheet	5
Portfolio	5
Case Study	5
Assigned Writing	
Philosophy of Teaching	48%
Academic Paper	25
Professional Writing	10
Position Paper	8
Projec	6
Abstract	4
Personal Data	
Resume	27%
References	27
Supervisor Evaluations	22
Transcripts	9
NTE Scores	7
Cover Letter	4
Biographical Info.	3
Out of Profession	
Awards	48%
Certificates	20
Letters/Cards	10
Volunteer Work	8
Hobbies	5
Extra Curricular	5
Work Evaluations	3
Poems	3
Other	
Personal Pictures	55%
Memories	10
Community Involvement	10
Campus Leadership	5
Journal	5
Notes from Students	5
Senior Recital	5
Technology	5

Table 2. Frequency of Portfolio Artifacts Reported as Most Important in Describing the Student as a Teacher.

Philosophy of Teaching	44%
Lesson Plans	14
Personal Data	7
Both Lessons Plans & Personal Data	5
Pictures of Classroom Teaching	5
Teacher Evaluation	5
Philosophy of Classroom Management	5
Student Work Samples	5
Course Essays	5
Awards	5
All Items	2

Table 3. Levels of Reflectivity of Artifact Categories in Rank Order

Most Frequently Reported Categories and Specific Artifacts	Levels of Reflectivity		
	Technical	Conceptual	Critical
Personal Data			
Letters of Reference	✔*		
Resumé	✔*		
Supervisor Evaluation	✔*		
Experiential-Based			
Lesson Plans	✔*	✔*	✔*
Curriculum-Based Units	✔	✔	
Assigned Writing			
Philosophy of Teaching		✔*	✔*
Out of Profession Awards	✔*		
Classroom Handouts		✔*	✔*
Formal Assessments			
Essays	✔	✔*	
Objective Tests	✔*	✔	
Excerpts from Texts		✔*	✔

*Note. Items with 100% interrater agreement.

of the artifact itself (the kind of essay question asked, or the actual excerpt included) in order to classify it as technical, conceptual or critical.

The most frequently reported artifacts appear to focus on the technical aspects of teaching as opposed to conceptual or critical understandings. Personal data, the number one category, represents solely technical artifacts. Lesson plans (ranked second) are technical but also could support reflectivity at the conceptual level if the written reflections connect student actions with theoretical underpinnings. Also, lesson plans could foster critical reflectivity if students think about the contextual factors influencing the lesson. The plan alone does little to support reflectivity beyond a technical level. Curriculum-units (ranked third) illustrate technical proficiency and could support conceptual reflections if theory is clearly represented in the unit development. The Philosophy of Teaching paper is the one artifact that most of the students (60%) included that fosters reflectivity at the conceptual and critical levels.

Discussion

Considering the results of the portfolio questionnaire, a couple of observations can be made which lead to further questions rather than answers. First, most students included at least two of the highly recommended items in the portfolio. These included letters of reference and resume. This could be because the student teachers perceived these items as required rather than "highly recommended." Likewise, many of the students were seeking employment, and the inclusion of letters of reference and a resume would seem appropriate if you were seeking a position. It would be interesting to poll principals to see if they, too, believe that letters of reference and a resume are necessary components of a portfolio used in a job interview. Nevertheless, these items deal specifically with technical reflectivity. The students focused on how this information showed they "did it right." These products did not illustrate how they learned or their understanding of teaching.

The Philosophy of Teaching essay is even more intriguing. The student teachers were assigned to write a philosophy statement in a freshman education class and, again, as an entrance requirement to teacher education. These artifacts were not included in the portfolio, but rather a new philosophy was written. Unfortunately, we did not encourage student teachers to revisit and include previous philosophy statements they had written. The philosophy of teaching paper promotes the greatest opportunity for critical reflection and a way to demonstrate growth since student teachers had three similar artifacts across the teacher education program. Even though this was rated as the most important item for "describing themselves as a teacher," only 48% of the students included it in the portfolio. This was a missed opportunity for critical reflection by over half of the student teachers.

Experiential-based items that consisted mainly of lesson plans implemented during student teaching or practicum experiences ranked as the second most included category in the portfolio. However, only 14% of the students stated that implemented lesson plans were one of the most important items describing them as a teacher. Several reasons may exist for this. First, many of the plans were changed as they were implemented because the children in the classroom needed adaptations, a sign of responsive teaching. However, from the student teachers' points of view, this may have indicated that they "did not do it right" and, therefore, the plans were not indicative of their true abilities as a teacher. Second, it could be that theory rather than actual practice is more valued by student teachers. This would seem appropriate since they have been involved in the academic aspect of education rather than the world of practice. Third, the students' course of study may have influenced their perception of the "value of practice." Many content area teachers do, in fact, place little emphasis on student teaching and educational practice, in general.

Although curriculum-based projects were included in 72% of the student portfolios, no student mentioned it as an important item in describing himself as a teacher. Again, several explanations could account for this. The students might view curriculum planning as a necessary, but not important part, of teaching. Likewise, they may not value this planning after they have been teaching in the classroom. The actual practice might be more important than a well-thought out curriculum plan. However, several students did mention that they actually taught plans that were developed during campus course work. Perhaps this indicates the students growing understanding of the reciprocity between planning, implementing, and modifying instruction.

Finally, despite the emphasis on multiple sources or contexts in portfolio development, students are still focusing on concrete products such as lesson plans. Very few students included other revealing items such as photos (7%), projects (12%), or classroom materials developed (9%). The out-of-profession category illustrates students' use of multiple ways of demonstrating knowledge. However, in this category almost half of the items found related back to proficiency and at a technical level: awards.

Implications for Portfolio Design and Structured Guidance

"Reflection involves more than getting beginning teachers to think hard about what they are doing" (Bullough & Gitlin, 1994, p. 78). It involve helping students think carefully about the pedagogical means used to attain educational goals, the theoretical underpinnings that represent these actions, as well as the implications of these actions on outcomes, schooling and society. As teacher educators we need to be careful how such issues and problems are presented to students. In essence, the questions we ask influence the types and extent of the student reflections. Primary considerations should be given to encourage reflections about oneself, one's practice, and the classroom, school and societal contexts in which they work (Zeichner & Liston, 1987).

Therefore, careful consideration should be given regarding what types of portfolio artifacts are required for inclusion and regarding emphasis on helping students recognize that different kinds of portfolio items yield different levels of reflectivity. The activities emphasized during student teaching and the corresponding seminars should be designed to encourage teaching as a problem-solving endeavor. Many teacher education programs are beginning to approach preservice education as a problem-centered approach (Casey & Howson, 1993) where teachers reflect on problems in order to create a solution. In addition, programs that emphasize reflectivity invoke an inquiry orientation (Copeland, et al., 1993; Zeichner & Liston, 1987). In doing so, teacher educators encourage independent decision making and reflectivity.

Limitations and Future Research

Beginning the construction of the portfolio during the student teaching experience did not give the students enough time to reflect on the learning that occurred during their entire teacher education program. Although various professors had portfolio assignments within their courses, the students needed more support for figuring how these fit with the portfolio process during student teaching. To encourage reflection, teacher educators need to include time for development and for review of portfolio artifacts throughout the teacher education program and at the beginning of the student teaching seminar. Furthermore, student teachers need to be given more than two one-hour lectures about portfolios before they proceed on their own. Modeling how to select and reflect on an artifact and then having students bring an artifact to the seminar might have increased student understanding of the task and their reflectivity. Within the portfolio construction process, the student teachers needed to discuss various aspects of portfolio, then write a reflection and attach it to an artifact. This process did not happen. As Pailliotet (1997) suggests, both students and faculty need to agree on the purposes and procedures of the portfolio and consistently discuss these throughout the teacher education program. Finally, because many of the curriculum and course projects were not included in the portfolio, it is possible that the student teachers may have viewed these products as really being owned by the professor for whom they were completed rather than their own creation. Defining and discussing ownership likewise did not occur while the students were developing their portfolios. In future research, interviews of the student teachers while they presented their portfolios would have lead to greater understanding of why they included certain artifacts and not others. In future research, student teachers could also be video taped as they present their portfolio to ascertain what and why they included particular artifacts.

In conclusion, the old idiom you can lead a horse to water but . . . provides us with a humbling conclusion. Reflection is characterized as a means of assuming a critical stance toward the educational status quo (Van Manen, 1977; Leland, Harste, & Youssef, 1997) and as a mechanism for liberation (Zeichner & Liston, 1987). The process cannot simply be solved by a single portfolio in the final semester of coursework. Student teacher ideologies are difficult to change (Zeichner & Liston, 1987; Korthagen, 1992). This study seems to indicate that helping student teachers view teaching as critical reflection is not a simple process. It is going to take a collaborative effort across teacher education programs as well as structured activities during portfolio development to support reflective practice.

References

Bullough, Jr., R. V. & Gitlin, A. D. (1994). Challenging teacher education as training: Four propositions. *Journal of Education for Teaching 20* (1), 67-81.

Black, A. & Ammon, P. (1992). A developmental-constructivist approach to teacher education. *Journal of Teacher Education, 43* (5), 323-335.

Casey, M. B. & Howson, P. H. (1993). Educating preservice students based on a problem-centered approach to teaching. *Journal of Teacher Education, 44*(5),361-369.

Christensen, L. & Walker, B. J. (1992). Researching one's own teaching in a reading education course. In N. Padak, T. Rasinski, & J. Logan (Eds.), *Literacy research and practice: Foundations for the year 2000*(pp. 57-63). Pittsburg, KS: College Reading Association.

Copeland, W. D., Birmingham, C., De La Cruz, E., & Lewin, B. (1993). The reflective practitioner in teaching: Toward a research agenda. *Teaching and Teacher Education, 9* (4), 347-359.

Florio-Ruane, S. & Lensmire, T. J. (1990). Transforming future teachers' ideas about writing instruction. *Journal of Curriculum Studies 22* 277-289.

Gore, J. & Zeichner, K. (1991). Action research and reflective teaching in preservice teacher education: A case study from the United States. *Teaching and Teacher Education, 7,* 119-136.

Guillaume, A. M. & Rudney, G. L. (1993). Student teachers' growth toward independence: An analysis of their changing concerns. *Teaching and Teacher Education, 9* (1), 65-80.

Hultgren, F. H. (1987). The student teacher as a person: Reflections on pedagogy and being. *Phenomenology and Pedagogy, 5* (1), 35-50.

Korthagen, F. A. J. (1992). Techniques for stimulating reflection in teacher education seminars. *Teaching and Teacher Education, 8* (3), 265-274.

Leland, C. H., Harste, J. C., & Youssef, O. (1997). Teacher education and critical literacy. In Kinzer, C. K., Hinchman, K. A. & Leu, D. J. (Eds). *Inquiries in literacy theory and practice* (pp. 385-396). Chicago, Ill: National Reading Conference.

Oropallo, K., & Gomez, S. (1996). Using reflective portfolios in preservice teacher education programs. In Sturtevant, E. G. & Linek, W. M. (Eds). *Growing literacy* (pp. 120-132). Harrisonburg, VA: College Reading Association.

Pultorak, E. G. (1993). Facilitating reflective thought in novice teachers. *Journal of Teacher Education 44* (4), 288-295.

Risko, V. J. (1995). Using videodisc-based cases to promote preservice teachers' problem solving and mental model building. In Linek, W. M. & Sturtevant, E. G. (Eds). *Generations of literacv* (pp. 173-187). Harrisonburg, VA: College Reading Association.

Schon, D. (1987). *Educating the reflective practitioner: Toward a new design for teaching and learning in the professions.* San Francisco: JosseyBass.

Tierney, R. J., Carter, M. A., & Desai, L. E. (1991). *Portfolio assessment in the reading-writing classroom.* Norwood, MA: Christopher Gordon.

Van Manen, M. (1977). Linking ways of knowing to ways of being practical. *Curriculum Inquiry 6* (3), 205-228.

Walker, B. J. & Ramseth, C. (1993). Reflective practice confronts the complexities of teaching reading. In Rasinski, T. & Padak, N. (Eds.) *Inquiries in literacy learning and instruction* (pp. 171-178). Pittsburg, KS: College Reading Association.

Wolf, K. (1991). The school teacher's portfolio: Issues in design, implementation, and evaluation. *Phi Delta Kappan 73* (2), 129-136.

Zeichner, K. M. & Liston, D. P. (1987). Teaching student teachers to reflect. *Harvard Educational Review 57* (1), 23- 48.

Appendix A. Portfolio Development

Major _____

We would like to review the types of artifacts you selected for your portfolio. Please respond to the following questions.

1. Write the type of artifacts you selected in the following categories. Use a one or two word description like lesson plans from clinic, observation from middle school, essay on legal issues, creative writing, etc.
   - Experiential-Based Items (lesson plans executed with students, classroom observation, tutoring lessons executed, etc.)
   - Curriculum-Based Projects Designed but not implemented (thematic unit, inetrgated science.math unit, etc.)
   - Formal Assessment (essay exams, objective exams, short answer exams, . . .)
   - Assigned Writing (research paper, position paper, abstract, etc.)
   - Excerpts from Textbooks
   - Class Handouts (professor, classmates, guest lecturer, . . .)
   - Personal Data (references, resume, etc.)
   - Out of Profession Items (artifacts such as songs, awards, etc.)
   - Other

2. Of the above categories, which category appears most often? Why do you think it does?

3. Which artifact is the most important in describing you as a teacher? Why?

IT TAKES AN INFORMED VILLAGE TO MAKE POSITIVE CHANGES

Sherry Kragler
Valerie Hall
Carolyn Walker

Ball State University

Madge Craig

University of North Texas

Betty Goerss

Indiana University East

Rosemarry Murry

State College-Buffalo

Abstract

Journalists, educators, and legislators engaged in both rhetoric and action during 1997. Several themes were present in rhetoric and legislative action regarding reading instruction, teacher effectiveness, and teaching practices. This article describes action taken at both the federal and state levels regarding these themes. Political action regarding special needs students has also been included. The IDEA legislation is still being considered. Finally, the article encourages individuals in the literacy education field to become politically active and lists World Wide Web addresses individuals can use to keep informed regarding these issues.

During 1997, an increased movement toward solving the "reading problems" and raising test scores of our children has occurred by various groups. Rhetoric describing the ills of whole language and the abilities of our nation's teachers increased as national legislators have moved toward legislation at the national and state levels to fix our seemingly sagging public schools.

All levels, from the elementary level to teacher education preparation programs, have been affected by this latest discussion. The purpose of this article is to outline some of the recent legislative issues that are part of the discussion on various aspects of education. The article ends with suggestions for all of us to become more active in any discussion that affects education. The issues are described according to three educational areas: special needs, K-12, and teacher education.

Special Needs

An area of growing importance in education is that of children with special needs. Recent figures show that 5.4 million children have disabilities with a growing number identified as learning disabled. The number of students identified as learning disabled has risen in the last ten years to 2.5 million. Because many of these children are in need of assistance in the area of literacy, the International Reading Association believes reading specialists should be included with the professionals providing services. Reading teachers should be aware of legislative issues related to disabilities.

Individuals with Disabilities Education Act

The most urgent issue currently is the discussion about revisions to the Individuals With Disabilities Education Act (IDEA). In the years since this act was implemented, education for children with disabilities has improved. Much has been accomplished through the IDEA. Over 1 million children are now educated in neighboring schools, saving $10,000 per child per year. Many individuals are learning and achieving at levels previously thought impossible. Since the implementation of this act, nine percent more children with disabilities graduated from high school between 1984 and 1992. Three times the number of young people with disabilities are enrolled in colleges or universities, and twice as many of today's twenty-year-olds with disabilities are working. Nearly half of all adults with disabilities have successfully completed course-work in colleges and universities. In addition to the educational advances for individuals with disabilities, new knowledge used to improve the lives of the disabled has resulted in technologies that have enriched all our lives. For example, the Braille machine was the forerunner of the fax machine.

Although the IDEA has brought about many improvements, the legislature is concentrating efforts on revising the act. The House and Senate have some differences in their proposals that will need to be resolved; both agree that a strong form of discipline needs to exist for the exclusion of seriously disruptive students. The form of discipline and the behaviors that require it have not yet been clearly defined. The House Bill proposes that schools be allowed to place disabled students who bring weapons or illegal drugs to school into an alternative education setting for up to 45 days. The Senate Bill proposes that schools be allowed to place a disabled student who causes serious bodily injury, carries a weapon, brings illegal drugs to schools, or engages in seriously disruptive behavior in an alternative education setting for up to 35 days.

In addition to appropriate discipline measures, a variety of other related issues are being discussed. First, a formula needs to be devised to determine funding. Next, the establishment of general academic goals for disabled students and a method of measuring student progress are issues to be resolved. Finally, the legislature is discussing the concern of overclassification of students into the learning disabled category.

Both the House and Senate propose several areas of improvement for the IDEA. These proposals include increasing parental involvement in the education of their children and ensuring regular education teachers are involved in planning and assessing children's progress. It is also proposed that the legislature support quality professional development for all personnel who are involved in educating children with disabilities. Finally, it has been determined to be important to include children with disabilities in classroom assessments, performance goals, and reports going to the public.

Early Interventions

This year has shown greater emphasis on early intervention to prevent later problems. Reading Recovery is growing in popularity along with newer programs. Early Recognition Intervention Network (ERIN) is a curriculum/assessment program for teachers, coordinators, and parents to assist young children with special needs in regular and special education settings. It is designed for children ages 3-7 with mild to severe disabilities in mainstream or special settings. It is appropriate for regular and special education teachers, program coordinators, and parents.

Summary of Special Needs

The decisions made about special needs students will affect all teachers. With inclusive classrooms in many areas of the country, classroom teachers will be dealing with discipline, academic goals, assessment, and classification of special needs students. Reading specialists should be included in providing services to special needs students.

K-12

Journalists, educators, and legislators engaged in both rhetoric and action during 1997. Several themes were present in rhetoric regarding reading instruction, teacher effectiveness, and teaching practices. These include: a grass roots and national media campaign against whole language, a dichotomized view of phonics and whole language, negative images of education and teaching presented by the media, and legislative discussions about the need for quality reading instruction and children's low reading levels.

Whole Language Versus Phonics

From talk radio to national publications, whole language has been criticized for not providing the structure needed to effectively teach children to read. Syndicated columnists such as Joan Beck and John Rosemand both write that phonics is the way for children to learn how to read. Represented as the opposite of phonics, whole language is routinely described in simplistic ways such as whole word identification and identification of words using context. In the October 27 *Newsweek* article, titled "How Johnny Should Read," author James Collins (1997) mentions influential individuals representing differing views of reading, describes a "bruising battle" between approaches, and describes a need for systematic and explicit phonics instruction.

Clinton's Initiatives

National figures including President Clinton and Bill Goodling have discussed reading and educational issues including national voluntary testing, America Reads, and the National Panel on Early Reading. Throughout 1997, discussions regarding the potential viability of such programs and funding for these programs occurred. Funding for President Clinton's National Voluntary Testing and America Reads, a literacy volunteer program, was passed. Some states have already signed up to participate in the voluntary testing.

In December 1997, Congress passed by a voice vote a bill to establish a National Panel on Early Reading Research and Effective Reading Instruction. This panel would target children at risk for reading failure. These children would be identified during the kindergarten and first grade years. The National Panel would also conduct an assessment of research and knowledge relevant to early reading development and establish a panel to review early reading research and effective reading instruction. The membership of the panel would include 15 individuals who are leaders in reading research and who have knowledge relevant to early reading. These leaders would represent academic institutions such as colleges of education. In addition, the panel would be charged with the dissemination of this information.

Standards

New education standards have been instituted in many states in an effort to make schools accountable. Ohio has determined that schools that do not meet the requirements must submit plans detailing how they will improve. Failure to meet standards or show improvement will lead to increases in state scrutiny or possible loss of local control. Michigan, Ohio, and Indiana have all put into place some type of proficiency test to evaluate students' performances. These states also have proficiency tests for high school students to pass before receiving an academic high school diploma. In New York, standards have been debated, drafted, accepted, and implemented. Some of these are currently facing revisions. New York State is one of the few states currently requiring state examinations at all levels to assess the competency of students and programs based on their standards. Students identified as eligible for special education will be required to take the same examinations as those in general education classes. In Texas, the goal of the Governor's reading initiative for literacy instruction continues to be, "all students reading on or above grade level by the end of third grade and continue to read on grade level or above throughout their schooling." Current moves to facilitate meeting this initiative include suggestions for literacy instruction and teacher certification.

Summary of K-12

One aspect that makes 1997 unique is the movement of directing schools and teachers toward specific teaching practices. While previous educational movements have focused on the need to improve education, national trends indicate that individuals and representative groups want a voice in the way reading is taught. Implicit in this trend is the belief that teachers and teacher educators are not performing satisfactorily and may not be capable of making appropriate decisions.

Teacher Education

In the area of teacher education, emphasis has been on standards-based programs. Many states are describing the types of behaviors, dispositions, and performances they expect from beginning as well as expert teachers. These standards are impacting teacher certification.

New standards for teacher education in Ohio are quickly being integrated into existing programs and became effective January 1, 1998. Licenses for teaching in Ohio will no longer be by grade level, but by ages. There will be an early childhood, middle childhood, and adolescent licensure. One change that directly affects reading is a requirement that all preservice elementary teachers must take a separate three-semester-hour course in the teaching of phonics for early childhood and middle childhood license.

Indiana created the Indiana Alliance for National Board Certification to promote national certification of teachers. They adopted standards for accreditation and have tied licensing and professional development to a performance-based assessment in teacher education. All universities and colleges with teacher preparation programs are offered the opportunity to develop their own plan for assessing their preservice teacher candidates.

In Michigan, preservice teachers must pass test(s) in their subject areas.

Some university programs are also requiring students to present a portfolio for completion of their programs. A state-wide committee looking at a pedagogy test based on entry level standards has been stalled in its efforts. There is a Professional Standards Commission for Teachers charged with investigating and recommending standards of professional practice to improve the quality of teaching in Michigan.

Kentucky has developed performance-based standards for preparation and certification of teachers which include a yearlong internship for new teachers. Their professional Standards Board is still working on new standards for teacher preparation. Ohio and Kentucky are listed among the states that have significantly improved the quality of classroom teachers in a report released in the fall of 1997 by the National Commission on Teaching and America's Future. This report gives Ohio and Kentucky five stars of a possible 12 in quality, third only to seven for Minnesota and six for North Carolina.

In Texas, the State Board of Educator Certification, made up of 15 members appointed by the Governor, is also examining reading certification. The framework of competencies for the proposed Pre-K-3 Specialist is based on NCTE, IRA, and TEA documents and *Putting Research to Work*. At this time, the framework is in draft form. In addition, the board is considering the number of credit hours required of teachers who will teach reading.

Stringent requirements in Teacher Education Programs are being strongly recommended by the New York State Education Department. The Board of Regents proposes that permanent certification be eliminated and be replaced by a five year re-evaluation cycle. Included in this new proposal is a suggestion that university personnel be required to mentor newly hired teachers for the initial years of service.

Summary of Teacher Education

There is a general movement to standards-based teacher education and certification. Preservice teacher preparation programs are realigning their curricula with each state's standards. Each university will be evaluating its programs to determine whether or not it facilitates the preservice teachers' professional development in the areas of: attitudes, knowledge, and teaching performances.

Conclusions

Generally, there has been increased movement at all levels for educational reform. Teacher education has been affected by the current disenchantment with the public schools. More testing and curriculum directives have been seen as additional solutions to fixing the test score issue. We need to find our voice as individuals and as group members. At recent national meetings, there have been discussions about the need for literacy educators to be involved in the political process. Therefore, teacher educators can become involved in several ways: reading about the issues, writing legislators, and writing for the public press.

Two new informative books are available to help educators to become informed in the special needs area. *Including Your Child*, published in April 1997, addresses parents who are raising a child with special needs. This book covers the first eight years of the child's life and gives information to answer some questions and guide parents in their search for the education and services that will best help their children succeed. A second book is *Education Reforms and Students at Risk: Findings and Recommendations*, published in October 1996. This book provides information that will help the development, implementation, maintenance, and replication of effective programs for students at risk.

Educators can stay informed about the federal level by becoming members of the various listservs available on the internet. For example, EDINFO listserv provides information regarding federal government education actions. Types of information on this listserv are Secretary Riley's priorities, actions by President Clinton, speeches by Riley and Clinton as well as budget information. To subscribe send message to listproc@inet.ed.gov. Then write SUBSCRIBE EDINFO YOURFIRSTNAME YOURLASTNAME in the message. See references for other pertinent listserv addresses.

Educators need to be regularly contacting their legislators at both the state and national levels about current issues, especially those that will impact teacher education and teaching practices. Legislators do count the amount of mail they receive. Each contact represents many constituents. One phone call may represent 100 constituents, so it is important to write letters or call with your opinions. Maintaining contact with chairpeople of committees that influence literacy legislation is also important. When contacting your legislators, be sure to state your concern and suggest an alternative. Be polite but to the point, and include an example if possible.

Educators need to respond to the public press at both the national level and local levels. There are numerous columnists without backgrounds in literacy education writing about how to teach reading in our public schools. Educators need to write to the papers and to the public media to clarify issues. Well-informed letters will get printed.

References

Beck, J. (1997, October 23) . Phonics program proven to be easiest way to teach reading. *Chicago Tribune, 1,* 27.

Berliner, D., & Cassanova, U. (1993). *Putting research to work in your school.* New York: Scholastic.

Collins, J. (1997, October 27) . How Johnny should read. *Time, 150,* 78.

Gruskin, S. (1997). *Including your child.* Washington, DC: U.S. Department of Education.

National Commission on Teaching and America's Future (1997). *What matters most: Teaching for America's future.* (Research Report No. 395931.) New York.

Rossi, R. (1997). *Education reforms and students at risk: Findings and recommendations.* Washington, DC: U.S. Department of Education.

Resources

National Assessment Governing Board (Online). Available: http://www.nagb.org/

National Institutue for Literacy (Online). Available: http://novel.nifl.gov/

The Phi Delta Kappan Washington Newsletter. (Online). Available: http://www/pdkintl.org

The U. S. Department of Education. (Online). Available: http://www.ed.gov/EdRes/index.html

Voluntary National Tests (Online). Available: http://www.ed.gov/nationaltests/